the
unfinished
system of
nonknowledge

the

unfinished

system of

nonknowledge

Georges Bataille

Edited and
with an Introduction
by Stuart Kendall

Translated by
Michelle Kendall
and Stuart Kendall

University of Minnesota Press

Minneapolis — London

The University of Minnesota Press gratefully acknowledges financial assistance provided by the French Ministry of Culture for the translation of this book.

This translation presents selections from Georges Bataille's Œuvres complètes, copyright Éditions Gallimard, 1973–88 (12 volumes).

English translation and introduction copyright 2001 by the Regents of the University of Minnesota

Published by the University of Minnesota Press
111 Third Avenue South, Suite 290
Minneapolis, MN 55401-2520
http://www.upress.umn.edu

Printed in the United States of America on acid-free paper

Library of Congress Cataloging-in-Publication Data

Bataille, Georges, 1897–1962.
   [Works. 2001]
   The unfinished system of nonknowledge / Georges Bataille ; edited and with an introduction by Stuart Kendall ; translated by Michelle Kendall and Stuart Kendall.
     p.   cm.
   Includes bibliographical references and index.
   ISBN 0-8166-3504-8 (HC/J : alk. paper)
   1. Philosophy.   I. Kendall, Stuart.   II. Title.
   B2430 .B33952 2001
   848'.91209—dc21

2001000711

11 10 09 08 07 06 05 04 03 02 01   10 9 8 7 6 5 4 3 2 1

The foundation of one's thought is the thought of another; thought is like a brick cemented in a wall. It is the simulacrum of thought if, in his looking back on himself, the being who thinks sees a free brick and not the price this semblance of freedom cost him: he doesn't see the waste ground and the heaps of detritus to which a sensitive vanity consigns him with his brick.

The work of the mason, who assembles, is the work that matters. Thus the adjoining bricks, in a book, should not be less visible than the new brick, which is the book. What is offered the reader, in fact, cannot be an element, but must be an ensemble in which it is inserted: it is the whole human assemblage and edifice, which must be, not just a pile of scraps, but rather a self-consciousness.

In a sense, the unlimited assemblage is the impossible. It takes courage and stubbornness not to go slack. Everything invites one to drop the substance for the shadow, to forsake the open and impersonal movement of thought for the isolated opinion. Of course the isolated opinion is also the shortest means of revealing what the assemblage essentially is—the impossible. But it has this deep meaning only if it is not conscious of the fact.

This powerlessness defines an apex of possibility, or at least, awareness of the impossibility opens consciousness to all that is possible for it to think. In this gathering place, where violence is rife, at the boundary of that which escapes cohesion, he who realizes cohesion realizes that there is no longer any room for him.

—Georges Bataille, *Theory of Religion*

Contents

A Note on the Translation

Michelle Kendall and Stuart Kendall

This book presents complete essays, poetic aphorisms, and polished lectures. But it also includes unfinished lecture notes, transcripts of discussions, notes for essays and aphorisms, and texts, like *Method of Meditation*, that one hesitates to classify, that function by means of various discursive genres assembled in such a way as to afford a particular reading experience. Bataille's writing can be, by turns and by design, philosophically rigorous and poetically evocative. The task of the translator finds its challenge and its limit in a certain fidelity to this heterogeneity. Accepting this challenge, we have attempted to remain faithful to both the philosophical and the poetic registers of Bataille's text. Such an affirmation carries a caveat to the reader: these texts make unique demands; they are not of a piece, either stylistically or generically. Further, we have not attempted to ease the shifts and ruptures between and within these writings by means of editorial incursion or apparatus. Our endnotes have been kept to a minimum, our comments confined to the editor's introduction.

The occasional inconsistency of Gallimard editorial practice across Bataille's *Œuvres complètes* in regard to the presentation and annotation of manuscript materials should be noted. Many of our selections present materials, typically lectures and "notebooks," that Bataille himself did not ready for publication. For the lectures, we have followed the Gallimard presentation explicitly, though here as throughout the volume we have omitted the selections they present in their editor's notes as alternative readings of various passages. In the case of the "notebooks" however, we have regularized the presentation of these materials in order to maintain stylistic consistency throughout. Gallimard editorial notes have been incorporated into our endnotes with remarks as to their authorship.

A number of our selections have been previously translated. Annette Michelson's translations of "The Consequences of Nonknowledge," "Nonknowledge and Rebellion," and "Nonknowledge, Laughter, and Tears" appeared in *October* 36 (1986); "Initial Postulate" is included in Georges Bataille, *The Absence of Myth: Writings on Surrealism,* edited and translated by Michael Richardson (London: Verso, 1994); and "The Absence of God," "Nonknowledge," and "Beyond Seriousness" are included in *Georges Bataille: Essential Writings,* edited and translated by Michael Richardson (London: Sage Publications, 1998). Annette Michelson's translations were unavailable to us while we were preparing our versions. Although Mr. Richardson's versions of these texts were occasionally instructive, the translations in this volume are entirely new and our own.

Brackets within the text indicate omissions [. . .] and speculation [*word?*] on the part of the Gallimard editors or French words [*mots*] provided for clarification by us.

We would like to thank Robert Harvey for his encouragement and assistance in regard to this project. This translation is dedicated to our grandparents.

Editor's Introduction: Unlimited Assemblage

Stuart Kendall

I am not a philosopher, but a *saint,* maybe a madman.

—Georges Bataille, *Method of Meditation,* note 6

The day I began writing *Guilty,* September 5, 1939, I abandoned an intention that, even abandoned, set the ensemble of writings that I assembled apart. Before beginning to write in this way, the project that I had formed (if you will: that I was unable to reject) was the following: I believed myself drawn to found a religion, at least in a paradoxical way.

—Georges Bataille, *Œuvres complètes,* 6:373

Each book is also the sum of the misunderstandings it occasions.

—Georges Bataille, *On Nietzsche,* 184

Georges Bataille (1897–1962) published a second edition of *Inner Experience* in 1954. A paratextual note designated this edition as the first of five volumes to be collectively recognized under the title *La Somme athéologique.* The note listed these five volumes as: *Inner Experience, Guilty, On Nietzsche, Le Pur Bonheur* [Pure happiness], and *Le Système inachevé du non-savoir (The Unfinished System of Nonknowledge).*[1] The first three had appeared in Gallimard's N.R.F. series during the war, in 1943, 1944, and 1945, respectively; the final two were listed as "à paraître" (to appear).

In addition to the reedition of *Inner Experience,* this first volume of *La Somme athéologique* also included *Method of Meditation,* a text that had originally appeared as a small book in 1947, and a new afterword, "Post-Scriptum 1953."[2] What, if any, additional materials Bataille planned to include in the other reedited volumes as they appeared was not indicated, nor were the contents of the two final volumes suggested in his 1954 paratextual note. Four years later, in 1958,

Bataille published a group of short aphoristic texts on various topics in the international literary review *Botteghe oscure* under the title "Pure Happiness,"[3] perhaps anticipating the form and content of the planned volume. By the time the second edition of *Guilty* was published in 1961,[4] however, a paratextual note limited *La Somme athéologique* to the three volumes that had previously appeared. *Le Pur Bonheur* and *Le Système inachevé du non-savoir* had apparently been abandoned.

Bataille's death, of cerebral artereosclerosis on the morning of July 8, 1962, precluded the anticipated reedition of *On Nietzsche,*[5] but it has not prevented his readers from associating *Inner Experience, Guilty,* and *On Nietzsche* together with his project for an atheological summa. Yet questions remain. What might Bataille have included in the reedition of *On Nietzsche?* And, more important, how might the other volumes in the series have been constructed? Outside of the cited paratext, Bataille described his project in numerous editorial letters, notes, drafts, and outlines, all of which suggest possible variations on the contents of the anticipated volumes.[6] *La Somme athéologique,* then, exists largely as an editor's dream, a phantasm in paratext, a project in search of a reader.

Although *La Somme athéologique* remained unfinished at Bataille's death, portions of the anticipated volumes already existed in fragmentary form as articles, lectures, or folders of notes. The present volume represents an attempt to bring together in one place the majority of those writings that Bataille associated, whether thematically, stylistically, or editorially, with his project for an atheological summa.[7] *The Unfinished System of Nonknowledge* collects these articles, lectures, and notes, more or less chronologically, around the shifting outlines of Bataille's various plans for *La Somme athéologique.*

Denis Hollier reminds us in *Against Architecture* that "incompletion in Bataille's texts must always be considered as one of the constitutive gestures of his writing, never as mere accident."[8] The present collection represents an elaboration of this notion. It is not so much a book as the remains of one. It is a study in incompletion. It is a labyrinth and an invitation, a Baedeker to the ruins of a *Somme* that does not exist, a blue guide to an editorial phantasm.

Inner Experience was written as a hole into which the reader might fall without hope of escape; the other texts of *La Somme* deepened that hole. This introduction aspires to be a provisional, even fragmentary, map of this space.

Bataille grew up in and around Reims, amid the chalk hills of Champagne. His childhood was scarred by his blind father's syphilitic paralysis and mounting dementia, as well as his mother's nervous disorders. (In the late 1950s, his brother Martial would not so privately dispute Bataille's memories of their father's health and the familial scene.)[9] A poor student early on, Bataille quit school in 1913, only to return the following year, completing his first *baccalauréat* while a newfound fervent Catholicism deepened within him. He contemplated becoming a monk, but his faith vacillated as Reims came under German attack. The cathedral was bombed, burned, its windows blasted out. Bataille's father died alone in the city under siege, having been abandoned to the approaching German army by his family. Called up for military service in January 1916, Bataille never saw the front: he spent a year in a military hospital, a lifetime of pulmonary crisis having begun with tuberculosis contracted in a military boot camp. Discharged as the war came to a close, he returned to Reims and to his religious faith. He enrolled in a seminary program for a year but abandoned it in favor of a scholarly vocation. He studied as a medievalist librarian at L'École des Chartes from 1918 to 1922, and for a year, 1923, at L'École des Hautes Études Hispaniques in Madrid. While conducting research in London in 1920, a chance meeting with the philosopher Henri Bergson at a dinner party would prove decisive: though Bataille linked philosophy to the meaning of his life, the limits imposed by the academic life and attitude seemed worse than stifling. A rift had already begun to split Bataille's own life in two: the responsible scholar, librarian, and archivist found himself working in the Bibliothèque Nationale by day, while the *débauché* spent his evenings in Parisian brothels and in the studios of the artistic avant-garde. Nietzsche's hammer shattered Bataille's Catholicism in 1923.[10] Alongside Nietzsche, Bataille read widely: Proust and Dostoevsky, Freud and Frazier's *The Golden Bough.* Through an anthropologist friend, Alfred Métraux, he became interested in Marcel Mauss's notions of sacrifice and the gift.[11] Yet it was his reading of Nietzsche that had the deepest impact, as we will see. In 1923, Bataille also became acquainted with the Russian émigré philosopher Lev Shestov, who guided his readings in the history of philosophy, notably Plato, and colored Bataille's reading of Nietzsche with shades of Pascal. Bataille cotranslated Shestov's *The Idea of the Good in Tolstoy and Nietzsche* in 1924,[12] but their friendship waned as Bataille found himself, like the rest of his generation, drawn toward Marxism.

Through such friends as Michel Leiris and André Masson, Bataille also found himself on the fringes of the Surrealist group soon after the publication of its first manifesto in October 1924. A mutual animosity, personal and intellectual, between Bataille and André Breton, however, kept Bataille out of the group and led Breton to structure much of the *Second Surrealist Manifesto* (1929) around an attack on Bataille. He saw Bataille as an "excremental philosopher,"[13] and suggested that he was in fact an obsessive who, while fascinated by base, formless matter, by the heterogeneous in all its guises, nonetheless attempted to reason, to formulate ideas around this obsession. Bataille's writing and thought at this point were limited to a small pseudonymous publication of *The Story of the Eye* in 1928 and a number of articles, some scholarly writings on ancient coins published in *Aréthuse* in 1926 and 1927, and some articles of an entirely different kind published in the review *Documents* during its first year, 1929. These latter were much more significant, much more radical, and much more disturbing to Breton. *Documents* presented itself as a kind of cultural review of the arts and of ethnographic concerns. Bataille was a coeditor of the illustrated review and took responsibility for commissioning photographs and articles from dissident Surrealists such as Robert Desnos and Georges Limbour. The contents ranged from the ethnographic to the avant-garde by way of mass culture and the slaughterhouse. Bataille's articles were investigations into the dialectic of forms and formlessness, investigations into the nature of images and monstrosity: "The Big Toe," "Formless," "The Language of Flowers," "The Deviations of Nature." To Breton, Bataille seemed to be attempting some kind of intellectual coup d'état, cultivating an alternative group of dissident Surrealists around a notion of base materialism. But no such group existed and *Documents* folded after its second year, having alienated its financial backers.

Over the next ten years Bataille would lay the foundations for his thought in articles, reviews, and lectures, published and delivered in connection with various artistic, intellectual, and revolutionary causes.[14] Between 1931 and 1934, his initial faith in political activism led to his participation in Boris Souvarine's Democratic Communist Circle, and his publishing of such articles as "The Notion of Expenditure," "The Psychological Structure of Fascism," and, with Raymond Queneau, "Critique of the Foundations of the Hegelian Dialectic" in *La Critique sociale,* the house journal of the group. But the group, Bataille's first marriage, and his friendship with Souvarine all fell apart when Bataille began an intense love affair with Souvarine's girlfriend and collaborator, Colette Peignot, in 1934. Before the dissolution of the Democratic Communist Circle, Bataille had intended to write a book on fascism in France. The following May, he recast his social and political analysis as a novel, *Blue of Noon*, that would go unpublished for twenty-two years.[15] Bataille's turn to fiction at this moment was not without precedent in his work. He had written pornographic fictions, *W.C.* and *The Story of the Eye*, during the late 1920s, but he had also written, and would continue writing, a number of unclassifiable speculative texts, generically located somewhere between philosophical anthropology, prose poetry, and myth, texts such as "The Solar Anus," "The Jesuve," "The Pineal Eye," and "Sacrifices."[16] For Bataille, affirming the death of God meant affirming the absence of the sacred in modern society, affirming the absence of a totalizing myth of transcendence. Texts such as these in many ways represented an attempt to forge such a myth.

In 1935, Bataille (and such friends as Pierre Klossowski and Georges Ambrosino), the principal members of the Surrealist group (Breton, Éluard, Péret), and a few others (among them the Sade scholar Maurice Heine) attempted to infuse political agitation with a revolutionary violence capable of creating new myths in a group named Contre-Attaque. But the group was short-lived. Typically, questions of leadership (Breton or Bataille?) plagued its meetings and initiatives. Worse, the Surrealists considered Bataille's vision of revolutionary conflagration as fascist in its own right. Bataille, for his part, already understood that fascism appealed to the stabilizing power of a strong leader, a leader capable of forcing the exclusion of heterogeneous social and even material elements: in short, that hierarchy and leadership were themselves the problem.[17] His old quarrel with Breton had merely resurfaced in another form. His next initiative would foreground these problems of hierarchy and leadership in negative relief. With André Masson, Bataille elaborated a vision of virulent, contagious headlessness inspired by Masson's drawing of the mythological figure Acephallus in the spring of 1936. Five issues of the journal *Acéphale: Religion-Sociologie-Philosophie* would appear between 1936 and 1939.[18] A secret society by the same name was inaugurated in January 1937 by Bataille and Peignot, Klossowski, Patrick and Isabelle Waldberg, Ambrosino, and others. Meetings would be held in a forest at night beside a tree that had been struck by lightning. The goals of the group were religious rather than political. Its methods were to be rigorously conceived ritual actions culminating in the slaughter of a human being. In tandem with this secret society, Bataille cofounded the Collège de Sociologie in March 1937 with Roger Caillois, Michel Leiris, and Klossowski, among others. If the agenda of Acéphale consisted in the enactment of rituals intended to found a new myth, the Collège de

Sociologie represented an investigation of the social structures based on such myths, specifically, an investigation into the sociology of the sacred, into the "problems of power, of the sacred, and of myths," as Caillois would write in "For a College of Sociology: Introduction" in 1938.[19] Bataille, Caillois, Leiris, Alexandre Kojève, Klossowski, Denis de Rougement, René Gustalla, Anatole Lewitzky, Hans Mayer, Jean Paulhan, and Georges Duthuit in turn delivered biweekly lectures through the winter and spring of 1937–38 and 1938–39. Then, in September of that final year, everything collapsed. Caillois went to Argentina, Klossowski became a Benedictine, and Hitler made plans to be in Paris by the following May.

Three years later, in *Inner Experience,* Bataille would write: "The war put an end to my 'activity' and my life became all the less separated from the object of its search" (92). His thought and writing in the 1930s had been associated with an effort to change the world around him, to create a contagious myth that would overwhelm an already turbulent world. And yet a rift had perhaps always been apparent in his work, a rift between the theoretical and the experiential, a rift perhaps most apparent in the split between his lectures at the Collège de Sociologie and his participation in the secret society Acéphale. Significantly, both of these initiatives, like his previous forays into explicitly political activism, had come to nothing, had been failures even before the war forced their dissolution. But these were not the only initiatives Bataille undertook in those years.

A third way came into view in yet another project begun in 1938. With the help of a friend, Bataille had become an initiate in the practice of yoga. Whereas Acéphale endeavored to provoke ecstasy via rituals enacted in the world, the practice of yoga redirected this search in keeping with the paradox: the way in is the way out. For Bataille, yoga followed this *other* way, but it was not without its flaws.[20] The end of "activity" meant the beginning of inner experience, the end of Bataille's search for a new language of myth, and the beginning of his war on the myth of language.

Guilty begins with a Hegelian overture, consciousness measuring its historical moment: "The date I start (September 5, 1939) is no coincidence."[21] The battle of Jena provided Hegel with his world-historical moment, Hitler's total war offered Bataille his. That Bataille should begin a notebook at such a moment was not without other precedents as well. He had kept a diary during France's general strike of February 1934, giving it the title "Les Présages" (The omens).[22] Yet if *Guilty* is a diary at all, it is a diary of a very peculiar kind (109). Indeed, the autobiographical elements in Bataille's writing represent only one element in a complex compositional strategy, designed to dramatize the plight of consciousness grappling with the objects of the immanent world and the ensuing inevitable failure. The drama of Bataille's writing, like Nietzsche's, owes much to the conflicts of tragic stagecraft.

In June 1939, Bataille wrote and published the fifth and final volume of *Acéphale*. At once memorializing the fiftieth anniversary of Nietzsche's descent into madness and bracing for the advent of war, Bataille seeded the storm with a tonic recognition of conflict as the condition of all life and proposed a mystical practice of joy before death designed to turn the night of conflict into an ecstatic sun through the practice of meditation. The major text of *Acéphale 5*, "The Practice of Joy before Death," begins its own ending with Bataille's "Heraclitean Meditation": "I MYSELF AM WAR."[23] Although the first few notebooks of *Guilty* attempt to maintain something of this relationship—a reflection of war within *as* war without—an important caveat enters the fray: "No one relates to the war madness, I'm the only one who can do this. Others don't love life with such anguished drunkenness: in the shadow of bad dreams, they don't recognize *themselves*" (12). The war is real and outside of him. *Guilty* offers us his negotiation of this split between his own particular solitude and the world-historical meaning of the undisputedly major events of the day. The problem for Bataille is the problem of isolation—our isolation from the world and the isolation of events within the world. Isolated incidents—like a train pulling into the Gare Saint-Lazare (30)—could have meaning only if the world were conceived as a meaningful and completed totality. But, for the isolated consciousness, the world is incomplete, because objective reality is in constant flux, because objective reality consists of "fragments that shift and change" (ibid.). Chaos is the condition of his world, his reality, his consciousness, and his book (28) because his attempts to identify the meaning of this war-torn reality consistently, constantly fail him. This failing opens the wound through which communication becomes possible.

Bataille began writing the first extended draft of what was to become *The Accursed Share* alongside and in between notebooks for *Guilty* in 1939.[24] And yet *Guilty* explores the notion of general economy in its own way, as a field of experience, and ecstasy. Bataille writes,

"On the same level you find *the ridiculous universe, a naked woman, and torture*" (31; translation modified). And we see in embryo the separate volumes of Bataille's trilogy on general economy, *The Accursed Share*, vol. 1, *Consumption*; vol. 2, *Eroticism*; vol. 3, *Sovereignty*. Although Bataille evokes the problem of genres in relation to *The Accursed Share*, fearing for the fate of his project of eighteen years— because it addresses a previously "unframed" problem from a perspective "outside the separate disciplines"[25]—the text itself betrays little by way of radical textual heterogeneity. Rather, *The Accursed Share* attempts to present a coherent theoretical perspective on the movement of energy within the world. Bataille recognized the absurdity of attempting to achieve a totalized view of a movement in which he was caught up: "The ebullition I consider, which animates the globe, is also *my ebullition*" (10). And in a footnote, he admitted: "It will be said that only a madman could perceive such things [. . .]. I am that madman" (197). But he qualifies his use of these terms very carefully: consciousness will either continue in its quest for total identification with the whole of the universe or it will recognize its limitations, and, persisting in quest of an impossible *self-consciousness*, its own madness. Yet *The Accursed Share* does represent a reasoned theoretical perspective, presumably the furthest thing from madness.

The texts of *La Somme athéologique*, on the other hand, offer something altogether different. In the preface to *On Nietzsche*, Bataille admits "Motivating this writing—as I see it—is fear of going crazy."[26] The stakes are the same, but *La Somme* stages the drama of self-consciousness as a tale of unsatisfied desire. "In the helter-skelter of this book, I didn't develop my views as theory" (xxiv). In place of a coherent theoretical position, this writing marks the outline of a failed recognition; it presents the movement of a thought as that thought is lost to itself.

The Last Gasp: September 1939 brought the phony war. Spring 1940 brought the war itself and a mass exodus of French citizens seeking the relative safety of the south as the Germans moved in and occupied the City of Light. The second section of *Guilty* chronicles these misfortunes of the present time: the disorder and oppression of war threatening the faithful French with the gravity of saints' lives (53). By autumn, the country had settled under the weight of defeat. Bataille had returned from Clermont-Ferrand, after the dust had cleared, returned to his job at the Bibliothèque Nationale and to his life with his companion of these years, Denise Rollin. But 1941 would be another year of changes.

A friend of several years, Pierre Prévost, through his association with a number of French intellectuals who met under the name Jeune France, introduced Bataille to Maurice Blanchot. Their profound understanding and agreement was such that this meeting and friendship would change everything and nothing, for both of them. Blanchot was about to publish his first novel, *Thomas the Obscure,* with a second novel, *Aminadab,* appearing the following year.[27] Bataille would incorporate passages from each of these novels into both *Inner Experience* and *Guilty,* as though Blanchot's fictions were meant to serve some evidentiary function.

Bataille's writing had begun to change. Although he was interested enough in what he had been writing to have published selections from his notebooks for *Guilty* pseudonymously under the title "L'Amitié" in the Belgian journal *Mesures,*[28] he set these notebooks and those for *La Limite de l'utile* aside. He wrote *Madame Edwarda,* in September and October of 1941, and began the central panel of *Inner Experience,* "Le Supplice," immediately thereafter. Later, Bataille would explicitly associate *Inner Experience* and *Madame Edwarda,* saying, "they are very closely linked and one cannot understand one without the other" (*Inner Experience,* 168). These two texts stage and record the shattering and self-loss that constitute inner experience. Significantly, inner experience is also a communicable experience. In the preface to *Inner Experience,* Bataille writes: "Such an experience is not ineffable, while I communicate it to those who are unaware of it: its tradition is difficult (its written form is barely an introduction to its oral form); it demands preparatory anguish and desire from the other" (ibid., xxxii; translation modified).

This reference to the oral form of his thought was no mere suggestion. Much of the thought behind *Inner Experience* had been developed, as he notes in that text, in conversation with Blanchot. And not only Blanchot. As his writing progressed, Bataille began assembling groups of friends on an irregular, more or less bimonthy basis at Denise Rollin's apartment, or in the back room of a restaurant, among other places, to meet and discuss his writing and ideas. There seem to have been two such groups,[29] the first including Raymond Queneau, Michel Leiris, and Michel Fardoulis-Lagrange, the second members of Jeune France such as Pierre Prévost, Xavier de Lignac, and Louis Ollivier. Blanchot participated in both groups. By the spring of 1942,[30]

Bataille was no longer satisfied with the "chance" nature of these encounters: in a lecture written for this purpose, he proposed that the assembled members form a Collège d'Études socratiques dedicated to the exploration of what Bataille was then calling "negative inner experience." According to Maurice Blanchot, writing forty years later, "The project of the 'Socratic College' could only fail and was projected only as the last gasp of a communitarian experience incapable of realizing itself."[31]

Like the Collège de Sociologie, the proposed Collège d'Études socratiques would hold regularly scheduled meetings, focused on predetermined themes, specifically tied to "propositions" concerning negative inner experience. Like the secret society Acéphale, the Collège would not advertise itself, it would produce no publications,[32] and it would be dedicated not only to communicating negative inner experience but to experiencing it. This Collège would meet as did philosophical courses at the Sorbonne, but it would not associate itself with the philosophical tradition. In Bataille's view, the philosophical tradition was dead (and "Aren't those who fight for the dead already dead themselves?" ["Socratic College"]), its terms and projects had been exhausted, corrupted by the liberal world order: philosophy could no longer change the world, could no longer have any consequences in everyday life. And philosophy was not alone: modern poetry, and indeed all of the arts, had fallen into a similar state of comfortable inconsequence. The lyrical phrases of contemporary poetry were merely subjective effusion, poetic "messiness," a vehicle for the unconscious, not for consciousness.

Bataille had something quite different in mind. He intended a Nietzschean "revision of values and *of behaviors connected to values*." The modern world had become obsolete, valueless. The objects and experiences offered by this liberal world had become empty. Inner experience offered a way out, a means of creating value in everyday life. Smoking, he said by way of example, was an elegant means of achieving the same ends that had previously been sought by the sacrifice of animals. It was a way of opening oneself to a realm of values beyond the here and now, an absurd act, a way to rip the world apart, but without the heaviness, the blood, and the brutality of ritual slaughter. But smoking, and many other daily activities, though linked to this quest for the beyond, were distant from their own ends because they were unconsciously motivated and pursued. For Bataille, the revolution of everyday life would have to be a revolution in consciousness (his antipathy to the Surrealist project on this point never wavered).

But what of the name for this Collège d'Études socratiques: Socrates, the great opponent of Dionysus, the typical nonmystic, associated with a Nietzschean project, how now? The irony was no doubt appealing, but not only that. True, the Socratic maxims would be turned on their heads: "know thyself" becomes a quest for inner experience, an inner experience of self-dissolution, while the irony of Socrates' famous admission of ignorance is ironically reversed in Bataille's praise of nonknowledge. But beyond this turn, Bataille's appropriation of the great ironist was perhaps motivated by a Nietzschean reading of the Socratic will to know. In Socrates, the creative impulse aligns itself with the critical consciousness at the expense of baser creative forces, and a monster is born *per defectum*.[33] Bataille's love for deviations of nature accepts this will to know as a creative daemon, but, in his case, a daemon against itself. Whereas Socrates used his critical consciousness in a massive rejection of the objective world, inner experience deploys consciousness against itself in order to commune with this universe, in an ecstatic affirmation of appearances.

In an attempt to understand inner experience, to bring it within the realm of consciousness, to make it possible, propositions were to be advanced, and Bataille and Blanchot had already begun the process.[34] Their initial proposals were three: they held to the rejection of all hope for salvation, indeed all hope of any kind, the acceptance of experience itself as the only value and authority, and the recognition that experience meant self-expiation, as experience occurs only in the context of self-contestation. Although these propositions represented little more than a beginning, Bataille would later include them in *Inner Experience*.[35] He recognized that they would need to be explored, tested, verified by actual experience, by experiences that could be shared by the group. Further research would follow into various methods of experience and forms of consequential language. He foresaw that these propositions would eventually be shattered, denied, reordered. Their rejection would follow not from their failure to adequately correspond to the world in some positivist, mimetic sense, but from their failure to produce consequences, new experiences. As Bataille wrote in *On Nietzsche*: "Sentences will be confined to museums if the emptiness in writing persists" (7).

Bataille encountered a model of consequential language in Nietzsche, whose Zarathustra enjoins us to "write with blood."[36] Nietzsche specifies, "To understand one another, it is not enough that one use the same words; one also has to use the same words for the same species of inner experiences; in the end one has to have one's experiences in *common.*"[37] For Bataille, Nietzsche's inner experience sprang from his sickness, from the sickness that required Nietzsche to resign his professorship at Basel in 1879, the sickness that ended in a silent room in Weimar, after taking a decisive turn in Turin. That Nietzsche should turn away from Schopenhauer's pessimistic thought at just that moment in his own life when pessimism was most justified staggered Bataille, who found solace and inspiration in Nietzsche's affirmative leap—and not idly so, as Bataille himself had been forced to quit his job at the Bibliothèque Nationale in April 1942, tuberculosis having again bloodied his breath after eight years of health. This is not to claim that Nietzsche's company comforted Bataille with thoughts of salvation. Quite the opposite.

Reading Nietzsche in 1923 had delivered Bataille from the deep religious crisis of his late adolescence and early adulthood, and Bataille had repaid his debt by defending Nietzsche against fascist misinterpretations of his thought throughout the late 1930s. Many of the texts published in the journal *Acéphale* had been dedicated to this project, not only on Nietzsche's behalf, but against the fascists. Indeed, Bataille's unending defense of Nietzsche from totalitarianist readings would prove the cornerstone of his own political thought, both against fascism and against Stalinist communism after the war.[38] *On Nietzsche,* written from February through August of 1944, can be read as an act of war. Bataille wrote the book in honor of Nietzsche's centenary (October 15, 1944), "counting on the German retreat to make publication possible" (*On Nietzsche,* xxiv). Of course, writing on Nietzsche under such conditions was also yet another way of pleading guilty.

In November 1942, just as the tide of the war was finally turning against the Germans, at Stalingrad and El Alamein, Bataille published "Nietzsche's Laughter" in the Belgian review *Exercice de silence.* The ironic title of the review must have pleased him. As he wrote in *Guilty*: "I can't abide sentences. . . . Everything I've asserted, convictions I've expressed, it's all ridiculous and dead. I'm only silence, and the universe is silence. [. . .] Deep complicity can't be expressed in words" (40). "Silence, only silence answers the condition of my laceration!" (52). And laceration proves the precondition for communication: "what's required [for communication] is the overlapping of two lacerations, mine, yours" (30). "Nietzsche's Laughter" offers a glimpse of this overlapping, an overlapping that becomes only more complete in *Inner Experience* and *On Nietzsche,* as Bataille rewrites Nietzsche's inner experience with his own bodily suffering. "I imagine myself ar-

riving at the shore of [Lake Silvaplana] and, at imagining it, I weep"
(*Inner Experience*, 154). Nietzsche's experience of the Eternal Return
is Bataille's experience. This suffering fulfills no Christian cleansing, no
purification of the soul on its spiritual ascent. Nietzsche's teaching
promises only the radical dissolution of the spirit, a leap beyond the
subjective, but equally beyond the objective, the universal—the subjective and the universal being but two faces of the same delusion, the
same illusion of totality. This is the meaning of the death of God.

Communication with Nietzsche means communion with the impossible, with the work of death in the world. "Nietzsche's Laughter" begins with an affirmation: "The possible and the impossible are both in
the world." The possible refers to the sphere of organic life, of materi-
ality, of continuity, of the real, while the impossible offers a share of
the world of death and destruction, of discontinuity. We imagine our
place within the possible world, identifying ourselves with its fragmentary appearances that we transform through the delusion of philosophy by thoughtfully conceiving a meaningful association of these fragments, an imaginary totality that we can understand. Our notion of
God guarantees the stability of this misbegotten conception. But we
are creatures of the night, of the impossible, our meaning cannot be
subordinate to the possible world. Bataille writes: "man's limit isn't
God, isn't the possible, it is the impossible, the absence of God." And
the absence of god means the absence of man, anthropomorphism
riped to pieces, (*Guilty*, 25). "Salvation," as he says, "is an intruder in
the realm of the impossible," (ibid.). Over and over again in these
pages, Bataille will efface himself behind Nietzsche's language, returning to the same quotation: "To see tragic characters founder and *to be
able to laugh*, despite the profound understanding, emotion and sympathy that we feel: this is divine."[39] Nietzsche's laughter is laughter occasioned by the going under, the foundering that is death. Recognizing
the changes and flux of objective reality means recognizing our place in
the economy of the impossible, and it means recognizing the impossible
work of death.

Within the economy of the impossible, writing, rewriting, even quotation, must be recognized as the opening of a fresh wound, as a laceration, a cut into always unstable discursive forms. Christianity, for
Bataille, is essentially a discourse, a crystallization of language (*Guilty*,
134) in a stable form of speech. But, for Bataille as for Nietzsche, language is unstable, meaning is manifold, even "God" is only a place-
holder, a word destined to be swept away with time. Recognizing the
death of God means recognizing discursive heterogeneity, the infinite

play of linguistic forms. That Bataille developed and deployed a fairly complex system of technical terminology (possible, impossible, non-knowledge, sovereign, etc.) throughout his career, though superficially a betrayal of this notion, should be read as symptomatic of his search for consequential language. Terms are adopted, refined, and abandoned based on their ability to produce inner experience. His reading of Nietzsche occasioned this search within him and his writing occasions it within us. "My life with Nietzsche as a companion is a community. My book is this community" (*On Nietzsche*, 9).

Bataille finished *Inner Experience* at Marcel Moré's mother's house in Boussy-le-Château in August 1942. Raymond Queneau broke a silence that had developed between him and his old collaborator by accepting the manuscript for Gallimard that fall. Queneau would serve as editor for the book, which appeared the following year, as did Sartre's *Being and Nothingness* and Camus's *The Myth of Sisyphus*. Some Parisian literary elites would reproach Bataille, as they did Sartre and Camus, for publishing during the German occupation; others would attack him for publishing the book that he published.

Inner Experience is an anthology of sorts: Part III in particular brings together writings from across a fifteen-year period, textual glimmers of the torture to come, now connected with bracketed reflective autobiographical and interpretive additions. Alongside passages of more or less standard, expository prose, the book deploys poetry, lengthy quotations from Nietzsche and Proust, and, most remarkably perhaps, aphoristic shards of text, texts from which continuity has, in many cases, been edited out. Bataille challenges our efforts to read the text as a whole, as a book, by foregrounding the editing process: he signals abrupt shifts in discursive continuity with fonts and brackets, with the "aphoristic" spacing of even occasionally narrative prose. The aphorism, for Bataille, is a mode of writing defined by isolation as a function of rupture. Ultimately, *Inner Experience* presents a theory of discourse, and of discursive knowledge, in the form of a poetics of ecstasy.

In his preface to *Inner Experience*, Bataille distinguishes between project-oriented writing and necessary writing: "The only parts of this book written out of necessity—in accordance with my life—are the second, *Torture*, and the last [the poetry]. I wrote the others with the laudable concern of writing a book" (xxxi; translation modified). He returns to this same distinction again and again, always admitting the inevitability of project-oriented thought, of system building, yet always valorizing another necessity. "Project is the prison from which I wish to escape (project, discursive experience): I formed the project to escape from the project!" (59). The project, then, "the laudable concern of writing a book," is set in motion against itself. The book, written against itself, sets out to describe an experience (torture), an experience that eludes all attempts at its designation. Like the tragic hero, the project is doomed from the beginning. This demonstration of the failure of all designation is the central movement and paradox of Bataille's oeuvre. It is the key to his understanding of transgression and to his theory of communication. And it is the most often misunderstood element of his work. It is not surprising that the failure to understand this paradox should have corrupted many early readings of Bataille's work. And, not surprisingly, *Inner Experience*—this book written against itself, this book ruined from within—would find no shortage of critics.

From Vézelay, in May 1943, Bataille wrote to his friend Jean Bruno: "I saw a Surrealist pamphlet that took me violently to task after the publication of my book: it calls me a priest, a canon . . . ! Without interest except comical."[40] "*Nom de Dieu*" was published by a group of Belgian Surrealists associated with the review *Messages*. Of the twenty or so people who signed the tract, René Magritte, Maurice Blanchard, and Noël Arnaud are among the few that might be remembered today. While André Breton and the other principal members of the Surrealist group were sitting out the war in New York, a number of other groups struggled to claim their mantle. "*Nom de Dieu*" repeated Breton's fears from the *Second Surrealist Manifesto,* that Bataille was attempting to establish his own thought as an alternative to the Surrealist position, but they inverted Breton's charges against him. Breton had labeled Bataille an obsessive and an "excremental philosopher." The authors of "*Nom de Dieu*" took him for an idealist.[41] Failing to understand the paradox of Bataille's thought, these Surrealists of the second or third rank mistook his use of the name of God in *Inner Experience* for idealism.

Bataille was pleased that Gabriel Marcel's 1944 review of *Inner Experience,* "The Refusal of Salvation,"[42] located his work within a tradition of mystical thought like that of Saint John of the Cross, but was troubled by Marcel's assertion that his "refusal of salvation" was the product of self-complacency, of nonchalance, rather than a deliberate and logical necessity born of rigor. Bataille simmered his response to Marcel in notes and drafts over the next eight years, without ever responding directly to Marcel's misapprehension of his thought.[43]

Marcel's primary criticism focused on Bataille's project against itself: "To condemn the formation of a project is simply to condemn man; and, be it understood, this is exactly the proposal, the *project* of Mr. Bataille" ("The Refusal of Salvation," 189). As Bataille himself says, his thought is "anthropomorphism ripped to pieces" (*Guilty*, 25). To Marcel, this is merely deliberate nihilism—virulent yes, but ultimately complacent, and corrupted by its own complacency ("The Refusal of Salvation," 198). Should Bataille go to the end of this project, Marcel believes, there he would find love, grace, deliverance, salvation—salvation, that interloper in the realm of the impossible, in Bataille's terms. In a final inversion of Bataille's work, Marcel, seeking to refute Bataille's antisystematic thought (*sic*), attempts to unveil the dogmatism behind Bataille's "renunciation of all hope": isn't this only dogma in reverse? he asks. For Marcel, the propositions on inner experience advanced by "Mr. Bataille and his friends" (read Blanchot) represent "a deliberately chosen attitude towards reality" (199), and little more than a repetition of Nietzsche at that. And while Nietzsche still stands as an "exemplary character"—because Nietzsche "went through with his adventure to the very depths, to madness and death" (ibid.)—Bataille stands in as nothing more than an imposter, a parvenu pretending to the Nietzschean corpus of illness and affirmation.

In an appropriately tragic mistake, this accusation is doubly disingenuous. Unable to recognize the Nietzschean mask on Nietzsche himself, Marcel fails to recognize its form and function in the dramatic turns of Bataille's text, wherein experience is *staged*. Mistaking the disorder of the text for a lack of systematic rigor, Marcel fails to recognize the systematic nature of Bataille's writing, of Bataille's own recognition of experience only in contestation, wherein the antiproject *is* the project, a project against itself. The tragic dramaturge, giving form to his player's mask with a hammer, or tuning fork, shatters it. And perhaps worse, most tragically, what was behind the mask after all? During the "Discussion on Sin," Louis Massignon says: "I was very struck by Mr. Bataille's simple, directly confessional tone." Arthur Adamov similarly notes: "What shocks me most in this discussion is Bataille's tone of voice: it seems absolutely authentic to me." Nonetheless, for Marcel, Bataille is the great pretender, who "misuses the word torture in a tiresome way."[44] The tragedy of this torture is revealed to be a case of mistaken identity, a comedy, something laughable.

Bataille, for one, recognized the proximity of seriousness and comedy in his work. He began his response to the extended review of *Inner Experience* that Jean-Paul Sartre published in *Cahiers du Sud*[45] in 1943 with an acknowledgment that "the disconcerting element in my writing style lies in the fact that its seriousness is not what it seems. The seriousness isn't intentionally deceptive, but what could keep extreme seriousness from turning into laughter?" (*On Nietzsche*, 179). Bataille would return to these terms in his essay "Beyond Seriousness," wherein seriousness is an explicitly Hegelian category, a category that Bataille associates with the possible—the realm in which *what happens* happens, in the terms of that essay—a category whose burdens Bataille attempts to escape.

For Sartre, seriousness refers to the spirit that finds human meaning and value outside of the individual, given in the facticity of the world. Sartre found his escape route through his faith in individual self-determination, through his faith in the capacity of consciousness to separate itself from its world through negation, through the upsurge of self-consciousness, or being-for-itself.[46] For Sartre, individuals are capable of willing their own values, of projecting their own values or cares in the world. The human being finds his or her meaning and passion in this projection. To fail to accept this responsibility for oneself is to fall into what Sartre calls bad faith. And for Sartre, this is precisely Bataille's failing.[47] Bataille, for his part, quickly agreed: "Sartre . . . aptly describes the workings of my mind, underscoring the foolishness of its workings better from the outside than I could from the inside (I was moved)" (*On Nietzsche*, 180). But Bataille's writing is rarely so simple, so direct, so self-effacing. Such moments typically evidence an element of parody, and this is no exception. Further proof that Sartre's review struck a cord with Bataille can be read in his reviews of Sartre's books on Baudelaire and Genet,[48] and in his notes and drafts over the next twenty years. Sartre, as Bataille says, "took my sovereign laughter for a sickly smile" ("Aphorisms for the 'System'"). Failing to accept the tragedy of Bataille's thought, Sartre came to represent the responsible philosopher within that thought.

During the "Discussion on Sin," Sartre took Bataille to task on similar grounds. He said: "Significantly, you have said, 'when I speak': and you skillfully made the fault fall on language. But there is, on the one hand, the presentation that you're making, and, on the other hand, your concrete research. It is this research alone that interests me. If the language is distorting, then you are at fault. We are at fault when listening to you." Language, for Sartre, is an extension of will and will is a force of conscious subjective desire. For Bataille, things are not so simple. In *Guilty* he writes: "Language is an organ of the will (action comes from it), and expressing myself is a function of the will, which continues on this path till the end. What would it mean to speak of relinquishing will in an act of speech if not—romanticism, lies, unconsciousness, and poetic messiness?" (111). But the end of will is the annihilation of will, an answer to the call for the Superman, Nietzsche's going under. Although Bataille's challenge to the renunciation of will as an appeal to "romanticism, lies, unconsciousness, and poetic messiness" is a precise claim against Surrealist poetics, his will to pass beyond the limits of will represents a poetics of its own. In his "Response to Jean-Paul Sartre (Defense of *Inner Experience*)," he writes: "What I tried to describe in *Inner Experience* is a movement that as it loses any possibility of coming to a halt, falls easily under the attack of a criticism that thinks it can effect a halt from outside, since this criticism isn't itself *caught* in that movement. My giddy fall and the *difference* it introduces into the mind can be grasped only by those experiencing it for themselves" (*On Nietzsche,* 183). For Sartre, language is a tool of the will, whereas for Bataille, both language and the will fall prey to a movement that neither fully control. Bataille acknowledged the accuracy of Sartre's description of his work, but preempted his criticism with the parenthetical statement: "I was moved" (ibid., 180).

Bataille answered his critics more directly as well. His faith in dialogue, evidenced throughout the 1930s and in his project for a Collège d'Études socratiques in the early 1940s, offered means to the development of his thought. Sometime during the late fall of 1943, Bataille approached Marcel Moré about hosting a dialogue between him and his critics at Moré's home. This was by no means the first such meeting to have been held there. During the first year of the war, Moré hosted biweekly discussions organized around various topics and attended, according to Bataille,[49] by a rather diverse group of French intellectuals, some of whom, such as Klossowski, had participated in the Collège de Sociologie, some of whom were associated with the review *Volontés,* and others, such as Paul-Louis Landsberg, with *Esprit.* Alexandre

Koyré, Jean Wahl, and Jules Monnerot were, like Bataille, occasional participants in these early meetings.[50] The discussion was scheduled for the afternoon of March 5, 1944, and, as *Guilty* had gone to press a few months earlier, Bataille would present an early version of the "Summit and Decline" chapter from his next book, *On Nietzsche,* as a lecture that would serve as the basis for the conversation. Jean Daniélou, a Jesuit and future cardinal, with whom Bataille had been discussing his ideas regularly since the spring of 1942, would present a prepared response to Bataille's lecture, before the philosopher Maurice de Gandillac led the discussion. The topic for the day would be "sin."

Despite the rationing enforced by the German occupation, Moré arranged a buffet lunch, and the guests took their places.[51] The list of attendees is incomplete but impressive. Three fairly distinct but overlapping groups stand out: those associated with Bataille, people like Maurice Blanchot, Pierre Klossowski, Jean Paulhan, Jean Bruno, Pierre Prévost, Michel Leiris, and, less closely, Jean Lescure and Couturier; second, the philosophers and/or existentialists: Sartre, Simone de Beauvoir, Camus, Merleau-Ponty, Jean Hyppolite, and Maurice de Gandillac; and third, the believers, including Catholics, the priests Jean Daniélou, Henri Dubarle, Augustin Maydieu, Moré, the religious philosopher Gabriel Marcel, and the Protestant Pierre Burgelin.

Bataille's lecture offered a philosophically grounded theory of communication founded on the willful sacrifice of being. He proposed a reading of the crucifixion as the "summit of evil": the death of God as the highest evil for humanity and for God, both of whom determine moral norms based on utility, servility, and the continuity of values. Communication, however, occurs only in the laceration of beings, in the sacrifice of values. Bataille proposed a notion of experience founded on the search for values beyond the limited means of the servile domain. Such values would necessarily be founded on the violation of servile norms and would therefore qualify as "sins." The highest evil (the violation of values), then, becomes coincident with the highest good (communication and the creation of value). Bataille proposed an ethics based on a Nietzschean immorality or hypermorality, which he discussed in terms of "summit" and "decline," again in keeping with his Nietzschean quest for moral heights. For Bataille, a morality of "decline" is a morality that recognizes servile or utilitarian values, whereas a "summit morality" goes in search of experience and communication through the violation of values, which is to say, through sin. Not surprisingly, Bataille's listeners were divided in their responses. The

Christians among them were primarily interested in the willfulness of Bataille's search; the philosophers, particularly Hyppolite and Sartre, were concerned with the reading of Hegel on which Bataille was basing his descriptions of communication and experience.

Father Daniélou, for his part, spoke directly to Bataille's alleged mysticism, charging that Bataille was incapable of conceiving of spiritual comfort, of comfort found beyond individual self-satisfaction, through the recognition of the Christian God. For Daniélou, and precisely for this reason, Bataille's "taste for nothingness" did not go far enough: it stopped short of mystical fusion with the divine. But Bataille had already answered this criticism: to speak of comfort is to speak of decline, whereas he was interested in experiencing ever higher summits of communication. For Daniélou and for Bataille, self-laceration reveals the sacred, but for Daniélou, and for the Christian mystic, this moment of rupture is healed through God's grace. The doctrines of salvation and of the resurrection of the body offer the Christian mystic access to a limitless sphere beyond the immanent realm, beyond the limits of biological individualism. Far from eternal, for Bataille, this realm is impossible. Yet this was not the primary difference of opinion between Bataille and the Christians. For the Christian, God offers his grace as a means of access to eternal salvation. For Bataille, the search for communication is willfully undertaken by the individual. Louis Massignon articulated this distinction succinctly: "You conceived of ecstasy as something that was sought after. But ecstasy is not sought after" ("Discussion on Sin"). Grace is God's gift to the faithful, not the mere product of some profane method of meditation. The mystical *mysterium* can only be given by God. Bataille might mention the writings of Christian mystics or the techniques of ecstasy developed by shamans and yogis in manuals of meditation, but the Christian argument maintains that whereas physical ecstasy may indeed be provoked in the body, mystical ecstasy occurs only within the soul, and remains an encounter of a subject before God. For Bataille, the moment the mystic designates this experience with the name God, the encounter has changed, its value has gone into stagnation, it has gone into decline. For Bataille, inner experience means sovereign experience, not subjective experience; it means experiencing the world not in relation to God, but from the position of God.[52]

Bataille cannot be considered a mystic because his thought and experience fail to hypostasize a limitless salvation behind the stable signifier of a supreme deity. For Bataille, experience occurs only in self-contestation and there is nothing beyond the self. His method leads nowhere (*On Nietzsche,* 184).

This was not the only argument against Bataille's work or the method he advanced during the "Discussion on Sin." Hyppolite and Sartre in particular questioned Bataille's reading of Hegel. It should be remembered that Hegel had only recently been rediscovered in France. Jean Wahl's *Le Malheur de la conscience dans la philosophie de Hegel* (Paris: Rieder, 1928) effectively began the revival, which continued in the work of Alexandre Koyré and Emmanuel Levinas. Henri Lefebvre's translation (with Norman Gutermann) of Lenin's *Notebooks on Hegel's Dialectic* (1935) and his own *Dialectical Materialism* (1936) effectively set the stage for a Marxist reading of Hegel in France. Jean Hyppolite's translation of the *Phenomenology of Spirit* appeared in two volumes in 1939 and 1941, and his *Genesis and Structure of Hegel's Phenomenology of Spirit* in 1946. Alexandre Kojève's spring lecture course, an oral translation and commentary of Hegel's *Phenomenology,* at the École des Hautes Études, was attended more or less regularly from 1934 to 1939 by Raymond Aron, André Breton, Roger Caillois, Pierre Klossowski, Jacques Lacan, Merleau-Ponty, Raymond Queneau, and Bataille. After the war, Queneau assembled transcripts of the lectures and a few published articles by Kojève into a book. With the publication of this *Introduction to the Reading of Hegel* in 1947, this early era in French Hegelian thought had effectively come full circle.[53]

Despite Queneau's testimony that Bataille occasionally nodded off mid-session,[54] the influence of Kojève's reading of Hegel on Bataille's thought can hardly be overestimated. Bataille lived with Hegel's thought as with the inevitability of law: the law he would be guilty of breaking, but that he could never escape. He wrote: "I think of my life—or better yet, its abortive condition, the open wound that my life is—as itself constituting a refutation of Hegel's closed system" (*Guilty,* 124). Yet the closure of that system could not be logically refuted, nor could it be refuted once and for all.

Here again we return to the central paradox of his work: the project against itself, the action of a consciousness that, failing to attain knowledge, attains a sovereign silence. Yet the project written against itself remains a project, the system against systems is not antisystematic. Bataille's thought is, in fact, systematic, it uses systems, depends on discourses always plural, to achieve its own ends, which is to say, to reach the end of systematic thought. Bataille needs Hegel—the ultimate philosophical system builder—as a means to his own ends. "The will" he says, in an appropriately Nietzschean fashion, "affirms itself in contradiction"("The Consequences of Nonknowledge").[55] So *Inner Experience* sets out to mimic the Hegelian system, to mimic the Hegelian project of consciousness in search of absolute knowledge, ultimately to think the moment when absolute knowledge recognizes itself as an empty tautology, as absolute nonknowledge (*Inner Experience,* 108). "My efforts recommence and undo Hegel's *Phenomenology.* Hegel's construction is a philosophy of work, of 'project'. The Hegelian man— Being and God—is accomplished, is completed in the adequation of project" (ibid., 80). Bataille's construction mimics or parodies this philosophy of work, of "project," toward an experience of incompleteness, of play, and of uselessness. Negation, in Hegel's thought, as Hyppolite and Sartre make clear during the "Discussion on Sin," is always recuperated in a moment following: negation becomes the negation of negation through the course of history. For Hegel, there can be no true loss. Negativity performs a necessary function within the realm of possibility and therefore can, and indeed must, be regarded as useful. For Bataille, however, negativity cannot always be recuperated within possibility. Bataille recognizes an "unemployed negativity," a negativity without function, without designation, without content. He recognizes this negativity as the substance of his own life in its isolation and insignificance. Hegel, then, remains the philosopher of work, of utility, of project, while Bataille recognizes himself as outside this system, as unemployable. Thus Bataille's method ultimately consists in a tragic doubling of Hegelian thought. For the eternal circularity of absolute knowledge encountered at the end of history, Bataille substitutes a single Nietzschean moment: the tragic recognition of absolute nonknowledge; for the completed philosophical system of the ultimate system builder, the unfinished system of nonknowledge; for the completion of the servile Hegelian mind, the shattering of the sovereign Nietzschean body.[56]

In May 1945, Bataille returned to Vézelay, where he would live until 1949, when his ever-deepening financial troubles forced him to take a position as the director of a municipal library in Carpentras. Over these four years, he visited Paris regularly, both in his capacity as editor for *Critique,* after 1946, and to see friends, new and old: Alberto Giacometti, Henri Michaux, and Maurice Merleau-Ponty among the new, Leiris, Ambrosino, and others among the old. In the meantime, he tried to write his way out of financial disaster. Toward this goal, his letters to Queneau, in the latter's capacity as editor at Gallimard, boast a number of projected volumes that would never come to light, and several others that would come to light only in a substantially modified form.

Already in December 1946, Bataille was anticipating the publication of new editions of *Inner Experience* and *Method of Meditation,* the latter of which had not yet even appeared in book form.[57] He seems to have been motivated at least in part by financial concerns: he mentions the projected reeditions while asking for an advance on his anticipated royalties. But we should take this with a caveat. In a notebook for *Method of Meditation* and *The Accursed Share* from 1945, Bataille had already contemplated reediting these volumes into a single multivolume work to be published under the collective title *Par-delà la poésie.* This four-volume series would include *Inner Experience, On Nietzsche,* and *La Haine de la poésie*—the then anticipated version of which would have been followed by *Method of Meditation*—with *Guilty, Alleluia,* and "Histoire de Rats" appearing in a revised edition at a later date. *La Haine de la poésie* itself did not appear until 1947; the same year, *Method of Meditation* first appeared in book form.[58] The fictions brought together as *La Haine de la poésie*—if fiction is the right word: he himself says, "the hatred of poetry is the hatred of a designation" (*Œuvres complètes,* 5:459)—were written after *Inner Experience,* but in tandem with *Guilty, On Nietzsche, Method of Meditation,* and *Alleluia,* so they are at least chronologically related to the series. The phrase "par-delà la poésie" had been printed on the band wrapping the first edition of *Inner Experience* in 1943, and, as a general title for these works, seems to have anticipated *La Somme athéologique* in Bataille's thinking by four years. The project would be shelved for the time being, to be reinvigorated in 1949 as the fiftieth anniversary of Nietzsche's death approached.

In the meantime, Bataille continued working on his projected treatise on general economy, *The Accursed Share,* as well as considering the expansion of a number of review articles initially published in *Critique* and lectures delivered in various postwar forums into full-length works. Two such projects included *Maurice Blanchot et l'existentialisme* and *Philosophie et religion surréalistes,* both of which were announced as "in preparation" in a letter to Gallimard from December 29, 1948 (*Choix de Lettres,* 392), though neither seems to have gotten off the ground. *The Accursed Share,* however, did.

The Accursed Share: An Essay on General Economy; vol. 1,

Consumption was written between 1945 and 1948, from previous drafts and articles written for *Critique,* and published in 1949. From the beginning, Bataille saw this work as part of a larger whole, as only the first volume in a series of volumes on the problem of general economy.[59] In a paratextual note, Bataille announced the second volume under the title *La Part maudite, II: De L'Angoisse sexuelle au malheur d'Hiroshima* (The accursed share, II: From sexual anguish to the misfortune of Hiroshima).[60] During the late 1940s and early 1950s, outlines and drafts for this anticipated second volume evolved from a consideration of sexual anxiety and mass death through various considerations of the life and work of the Marquis de Sade into the volume that Bataille published under the title *Erotism* in 1957.[61] The 1954 re-edition of *Inner Experience* announced the third volume of the trilogy under the title *Sovereignty,* and this volume too seems have enjoyed a complex gestation. In the late 1940s, Bataille planned to write a book titled *Albert Camus, la Morale et la Politique* (Albert Camus: morality and politics), which, in addition to his discussion of Camus,[62] would have included materials on the Marquis de Sade and Nietzsche, all in relation to the problem of a Nietzschean hypermorality. By 1950, this volume had become a collection of literary essays on Sade, Camus, Baudelaire, Michelet, and others, still couched in the terms of a moral debate.[63] This volume, an obvious precursor to Bataille's *Literature and Evil* (Gallimard, 1957), would be listed as volume 4 in the outline Bataille drafted for *La Somme athéologique* in 1950. Perhaps for this reason, *La Sainteté du mal* (The sanctity of evil), as this volume was called, was replaced with a long-projected volume, *Nietzsche et le communisme* (1950),[64] or later, *Nietzsche et le communisme ou la souveraineté* (1953), before finally becoming *Sovereignty* (1953–54). Both of these volumes opposed a Nietzschean hypermorality to the communist exigency: Nietzsche contra politics.[65]

Although Bataille wrote the primary texts of *La Somme* under wartime conditions, and anticipated collecting them under a general title (*Par-delà la poésie*) as early as 1945, *La Somme athéologique* did not begin to take shape until the fall of 1949 when he mentioned it to Raymond Queneau. As a title, *La Somme athéologique* mimics the *Summa theologica* of Thomas Aquinas, reasserting the importance of Bataille's training as a medievalist librarian and both the positive and negative influence of scholasticism on his thought. Already in "Socratic College" Bataille had appealed to the scholastic model in his attempt to formulate systematic "propositions" on negative inner experience. His project for *La Somme athéologique* only reinforced that reference: the system would be wrought against itself but it would be a system nonetheless. During the spring of 1950, Bataille discussed his proposal at length in a letter to Queneau.

By 1950, Bataille was miserable. Moving to Carpentras the previous year made trips to Paris more difficult. *Critique* had lost its publisher in September 1949: it would not reappear for more than a year, when Éditions de Minuit took over sponsorship of the journal. *The Accursed Share*, Bataille's first book in two years (and an "unexpected" one at that) had appeared in 1949, and despite Bataille's later claims that it had reached its intended readers, it sat on its publisher's shelves, unsold. At fifty-two, Bataille had finished *L'Abbé C.*, the first novel he would publish under his own name, during the fall of 1949. It would appear, not without controversy, over the summer of 1950. Bataille spent time at the bullfights with René Char and Picasso, among other friends, and, occasioned by the approaching fiftieth anniversary of Nietzsche's death, drafted his first outline for *La Somme,* presenting it to Queneau in a letter dated March 29, 1950.

This first sketch anticipated four volumes: *Inner Experience, Le Monde nietzschéen d'Hiroshima* (The Nietzschean world of Hiroshima), *L'Amitié* (Friendship), and *La Sainteté du mal* (The sanctity of evil). The volume including *Inner Experience* would serve as an introduction to *La Somme* as a whole and would include a second edition of *Inner Experience* as well as a second edition of *Method of Meditation* and several *Études d'athéologie* (Studies in atheology), "on existentialism, on poetry, on eroticism, and so on."[66] *Le Monde nietzschéen d'Hiroshima* would include a second edition of *On Nietzsche* and a second edition of *Mémorandum* (Bataille's selection from and arrangement of Nietzsche's writings).[67] *L'Amitié,* reasserting Bataille's original title for *Guilty,* would include a second edition of that text, a second edition of *Alleluia,* and *Histoire d'une société secrète,*[68] which he had not yet written. An outline for *Le Sainteté du mal* anticipated a volume similar to Bataille's 1957 collection of essays *Literature and Evil* (Gallimard).

Another outline, included on the back of his letter, differed significantly from the plan discussed in the body of the letter. This outline projected three volumes, not four, grouping *La Sainteté du mal* with the materials on Nietzsche (*On Nietzsche, Mémorandum*) together as a single volume, and changing the title from *Le Monde nietzschéen d'Hiroshima* to *La Mort de Nietzsche*. The order of the volumes within *La Somme* was also changed by relocating *L'Amitié* (the volume collecting *Guilty*, *Alleluia*, and *Histoire d'une société secrète*) as the second panel in the trilogy, in keeping with the original order of publication. The first volume would still collect *Inner Experience, Method of Meditation*, and the *Études d'athéologie*, but it would also include an introduction on *L'Athéologie*, and pass under the general title *Le Moment souverain*. But these were just plans, anticipations. It would be four years before this series of reeditions would begin. By then Bataille would have projected two additional volumes toward the completion of the series—*Le Pur Bonheur* and *Le Système inachevé du non-savoir*—and projected, then effaced, a third volume, *Mourir de rire, et rire de mourir* (To Die Laughing, and To Laugh Dying).

Mourir de rire, et rire de mourir was to have consisted of a series of texts based on the lectures that Bataille had given at the Collège Philosophique over the past several years. Jean Wahl founded the lecture series that constituted the Collège Philosophique in 1947 as a place for philosophical discussion on the fringes of the university system. The Collège was not the only such organized lecture series in postwar Paris: Club Maintenant, where Sartre delivered his "Existentialism Is a Humanism" speech in 1946, had been meeting since 1945. Bataille would lecture in both forums during these years, but it seems that he regarded the lectures he delivered at the Collège Philosophique as constituting something of a piece. He delivered seven lectures at the Collège over the six years from 1947 to 1953. Beginning on May 12, 1947, with "Le Mal dans le Platonisme et dans le Sadisme" (Evil in Platonism and Sadism), his lectures included "Schéma d'une Histoire des religions" (Outline of a history of religions) (February 26, 1948), "Philosophie de la dépense" (Philosophy of expenditure) (February 24, 1949), "Consequences of Nonknowledge" (January 12, 1951), "The Teaching of Death" (May 8 and 9, 1952), "Nonknowledge and Rebellion" (November 24, 1952), "Nonknowledge, Laughter, and Tears" (February 9, 1953). From March to May 1948, Bataille rewrote the second of these—"Schéma d'une Histoire des religions"—into book form as *Theory of Religion*. This book was announced as forthcoming by Éditions "Au Masque d'Or" in December of 1948, but Bataille was not ready to publish the text at that time. This is not to say, however, that he abandoned it. By 1952 he was including it in notes and drafts for *La Somme*. As for the other lectures, Bataille recognized "Consequences of Nonknowledge," "The Teaching of Death," "Nonknowledge and Rebellion," and "Nonknowledge, Laughter, and Tears" as a "coherent series of lectures" (*Œuvres complètes* 6:362), eventually publishing them in *Tel Quel* (10 [summer 1962]) under the title "Lectures on Nonknowledge." Within *La Somme*, *Theory of Religion* and the "Lectures on Nonknowledge" were to have been published together as a volume titled *Mourir de rire, et rire de mourir*. Together, these texts constitute "a general work on the effects of nonknowledge" (ibid.).

As he indicates at the beginning of "Post-Scriptum 1953," his belated introduction to *Inner Experience*, Bataille was not entirely satisfied with *Inner Experience*: "I hate its slowness and obscurity," he wrote ("Post-Scriptum 1953"). For this reason, we are not surprised when we read, among the notes Bataille gathered around the notion of atheology in 1952 or 1953: "The lectures from the Collège Philosophique. My articles. This is the mature—or nearly—oeuvre that I offer the critics" ("Aphorisms for the 'System'"). The lectures were to have appeared as *Mourir de rire, et rire de mourir*, but what of "my articles"?

The articles that Bataille published during these years fall into two general categories: they are either reviews or speculative essays. They can generally be distinguished as such according their place of publication. Articles published in *Critique* were, in keeping with the format of that journal, primarily intended as reviews. If Bataille wanted to publish theoretical or literary pieces that were not reviews, he would have to publish them elsewhere. There was no shortage of options, and Bataille published widely, but he contributed regulary to *Botteghe oscure, Troisième convoi, Deucalion,* and *La Nouvelle N.R.F.*, once it resumed publication.[69] Bataille had close personal ties to each of these journals: René Char was associated with the Rome-based international literary review *Botteghe oscure*, Michel Fardoulis-Lagrange edited the Surrealist journal *Troisième convoi*, Jean Wahl edited *Deucalion*, and Jean Paulhan edited *La Nouvelle N.R.F.* Without pushing this idea too far, one can say that Bataille wrote the various volumes of *The Accursed Share* around the reviews he published in *Critique*, while he used these alternative venues—*Botteghe oscure* in particular—to advance his project for an atheological summa. The operative distinction here is generic: while the articles collected in the volumes of *The Accursed Share* present a coherent theoretical perspective, the essays, aphorisms and lectures of *La Somme athéologique* stage the demise of discursive thought.[70]

Atheology: The "system" that emerges from these articles, notes, and lectures should be understood as an atheology.[71] Bataille defined atheology as "the science of the death or destruction of God (the science of the thing being destroyed inasmuch as it is a thing)" ("Aphorisms for the 'System'"). Atheology is not an objective science but a science of immediacy. The objectivity of science is present in Bataille's Cartesian concern for clear and distinct knowledge of the world, but Bataille nonetheless maintains a deep ambivalence in regard to science throughout, claiming his project is "not precisely a science, but what I might call a study of sovereign moments" ("The Teaching of Death"). The objectivity of science separates human beings from their world, whereas Bataille is interested in establishing an impossible ecstatic connection with the world. His project follows in the footsteps of science and philosophy inasmuch as his method appeals to consciousness grappling with its world. But his project exceeds science and philosophy inasmuch as Bataille admits that consciousness inevitably fails to grasp the totality of its world and experience. Science and philosophy endeavor to formulate useful knowledge about the world, to develop and improve our human consciousness of our world. Bataille, on the other hand, is interested in another kind of consciousness altogether: "the consciousness of nonknowledge, a consciousness of the absence of consciousness" ("Nonknowledge and Rebellion"). And yet, as in the Hegelian model, such a consciousness, or absence of consciousness, is swept away by the relentless movement of time, thrown into experience once again. *La Somme* reveals a movement, the operation of a mobile thought, a search for lost immediacy, the immediacy of the animal who is lost in the world, like water in water. As Bataille says of his project: "This search is the same thing as religion, not as philosophy, but it is the ambition of this search, to simultaneously suppress religion and philosophy" ("Notebook for 'Pure Happiness'"). Atheological thought is a search for the death of objectivity—a science against science, a philosophy against knowledge—and the death of God. Atheology seeks the presence of the impossible, the place of God.

Atheology is a search for immanence. The goal of atheology is to "create . . . the experience of the instant" ("The Teaching of Death"). Inner experience cannot be subordinate to future concerns: it is to be found only in the moment. Atheology depends on an understanding of the animality of man, of the lost animality of man, an understanding of the relationship between consciousness and the body. In inner experience, consciousness becomes consciousness of nothing: knowledge becomes nonknowledge. And Bataille admits: "I don't think it is possible to talk seriously about nonknowledge independent of its effects" ("Nonknowledge, Laughter, and Tears"). And what are its effects? Delirium; ecstasy; poetic, sexual, sacred effusions; the absence of consciousness; the debauchery of thought; the death of thought. "The death of thought is the voluptuous orgy that prepares death, the festival held in the house of death" ("Nonknowledge"). Atheology is a theology of delirium, a study in effects and affects, a scream at the threshold of madness.

Atheology implies a general economy of forces: bodily, psychic, solar, molecular. Bataille admits that if he is "doing philosophical work, [his] is a philosophy of laughter . . . a philosophy founded on the experience of laughter" ("Nonknowledge, Laughter, and Tears"). But this laughter is the laughter that shatters all hierarchies, all distinctions. Laughter, finally, like tears, like art, like poetry, like meditation, like eroticism, like religious ecstasy, is one among many effusions, one among many deliriums, one among many means to the impossible. Atheology admits no priorities save the priority of experience alone. And for this Atheology requires discipline, method, techniques like the techniques of yoga, methods of meditation. But methods are not formulas. Religions are closed systems, stable systems, guarantees. Atheology is the eradication of such guarantees. But it is not the will to unconsciousness, as in Surrealism. Bataille is a Surrealist to the extent that he subscribes to the Surrealist endorsement of chance and revolt, but Bataille's great quarrel with Surrealism consists in the willfulness of his search. "I situate my efforts beyond but alongside Surrealism," he maintains ("Method of Meditation").

Atheology, finally, concerns itself with the incarnation of revolt. Atheology is the study of sovereignty, which opposes the spirit of revolt to the spirit of submission. "The rebel wants to suppress the master, chase him from the world—but at the same time he conducts himself like a master since he defies death" ("Nonknowledge and Rebellion"). The rebel defies death not by turning his or her back to it but by laughing in the face of it, by practicing joy before death. "Taking death and suffering seriously is the servility of thought" ("Post-Scriptum 1953"). The master defies death through knowledge, through the will to self-preservation: the rebel defies death in death itself, through the will to chance. The sovereign does not attempt to recuperate death into a positivity, necessary evil. Bataille insists: "I approve of neither exploitation nor murder" (ibid.). Yet the sovereign admits the inevitability of death and loss as the truth of life, the inevitability of isolation as the truth of individual experience. Communication can only commute silence. Immanence cannot be shared. In the end, our death is not even our own. The atheological community is "the community of those who have no community," (*Œuvres complètes*, 5:483).

In the paratextual outline of *La Somme* in the 1954 reedition of *Inner Experience*, *Mourir de rire, et rire de mourir* was superseded by *Le Système inachevé du non-savoir* as the fifth and final volume in the series. In a note from 1959, Bataille described *Le Système inachevé du non-savoir* not as a volume collecting *Theory of Religion* and the "Lectures on Nonknowledge" but as a volume collecting "the remainder of my aphorisms," (*Œuvres complètes*, 6:364). *Mourir de rire, et rire de mourir* had been effaced in name and content. But this was not the only new volume anticipated in the 1954 reedition of *Inner Experience*. Like *Le Système inachevé du non-savoir*, *Le Pur Bonheur* never appeared. Bataille does not seem to have even drafted an outline for *Le Pur Bonheur, ou la part du jeu* until 1958. The title takes up the themes of laughter and seriousness once again, while the subtitle recalls that of *On Nietzsche: The Will to Chance*. The outlined volume would have contained "Initial Postulate" or another text by this title as an introduction, "Hegel, Death, and Sacrifice," "L'Homme et l'histoire" (Man and history),[72] "Sommes-nous là pour jouer?" (Are we here to play?),[73] "Beyond Seriousness," "The Sovereign," and "Nonknowledge." The article published under the title "Pure Happiness" in 1958 was not included in Bataille's outline, and need not necessarily have been included in the final volume.[74] "The Congested Planet," Bataille's contribution to the issue of *La Ciguë* that was published in his honor, takes up themes and actual language that can be found among Bataille's notes for *Le Pur Bonheur*, and is therefore at least formally related to this project.[75] According to a note from 1958–59, *Le Pur Bonheur* was to have been prefaced by Alexandre Kojève's "Préface à l'œuvre de Georges Bataille" from 1950.[76]

In "Post-Scriptum 1953," Bataille wrote: "If one had to grant me a place in the history of thought, I believe it would be that of having discerned the effects, in our human life, of the 'disappearance of the discursive real,' and of having drawn a senseless light from the description of these effects." Atheology is a study of the effects of nonknowledge. If knowledge is always mimetic, always the equation of some subjective thought model to the objective world, nonknowledge effects the eradication of that consciousness and that model. As Bataille says in *The Impossible,* "realism gives me the impression of a mistake."[77] At the antipodes to realism, Bataille's writing in *La Somme* pushes language to its silent end. The philosophical theory of correspondences founding the discursive real fails, in the end, to cohere: correspondences no longer correspond to anything but silence.

But silence does not last: "discourse endures, whereas transgression is in the instant" ("Notebook for 'Pure Happiness'"). On one hand, writing can never be anything but a betrayal of silence: "Writing, thinking are never the opposite of work" ("Pure Happiness"). On the other, "description, from the point of view of discursive knowledge, is imperfect, if through the description, at the desired moment, thought does not open onto the very point wherein totality, the annihilation of this description, is revealed" ("Nonknowledge"). Bataille writes toward the ruin of language, in search of words that slip from their meanings, that slide into the night. Bataille admits that although "language only designates things, . . . the negation of language opens up to the absence of a limit of *what is,* which is *nothing*" ("Pure Happiness"). Such language is poetry: "Pure happiness is . . . the negation of language. This is, in the most *senseless sense,* poetry. Language, stubborn in refusal, is poetry, turns back on itself (against itself): this is the analogue of a suicide" (ibid.). Beginning with the suicide of language, his famous holocaust of words, Bataille effects the annihilation of consciousness, the death of thought, a prelude to the final shattering. On the one hand, thought, consciousness, discourse, knowledge and, on the other, transgression, impossibility, inner experience, nonknowledge, silence.

Bataille's greatest contribution to twentieth-century letters consists in his development and deployment of this writing against itself. Bataille uses language (and the discourses of theology, philosophy, and literature) against themselves to return us to ourselves, endlessly. This writing is not antisystematic, not disorganized, but organized on a different order, an order against itself, an unworking, an incompletion. In *Guilty* he wrote: "I'm struck by the organization in my writing—it's so strict that after an interval of several years the pickaxe hits the same spot. . . . A *system* precise as clockwork governs my thoughts (but I escape endlessly in this incompletable work)" (101).

By the late 1950s, Bataille's health was in rapid decline. If he had once been able to write, "pain shaped my character" (*Guilty,* 69), by 1957, it would increasingly shape his daily life. He was hospitalized twice that year, his illness having been diagnosed two years earlier as cerebral arteriosclerosis. But he was acknowledged as well. He published three different books with three different publishers more or less simultaneously: *Erotism* (Minuit), *Literature and Evil* (Gallimard), and *Blue of Noon* (J.-J. Pauvert). He was interviewed in *Le Figaro littéraire* (October 12) and *France-Observateur* (December 12), and again on television the following spring. During this time of sickness and celebration, Bataille drafted plans and notes for *Le Pur Bonheur, ou la part du jeu* and, in collaboration with the text designer J.-M. Lo Duca, began a major new book, *The Tears of Eros.*

In many ways, *The Tears of Eros* fulfills Bataille's long-standing ambition to write a universal history, a single volume encompassing all of the developments and reversals of human culture and consciousness, from the cave paintings to the concentration camps, by way of the sacred. He had given an outline for one such project the title *La Bouteille à la mer, ou L'Histoire universelle des origines à la veille d'un désastre éventuel* (The bottle at sea, or universal history from ancient origins to the eve of an eventual disaster).[78] The ambition to encompass all of history within a single narrative is a Hegelian one, but *The Tears of Eros* presents the night side of this narrative, the holes in the story. It is a history of representations and of pleasures, more a history of phantasms and of bodies than of minds. It is a history of consciousness as a history of erotic art. In a short text from 1955, titled simply "Aphorisms" (in this volume), Bataille wrote: "Although I know it, the pathetic movements of the arts remind me, ceaselessly, the object of my wait is not peace, but the immense delirium of the universe, in which the beating of my heart is mingled—demanding that I be a part of it." *The Tears of Eros* is another book of meditations, another practice of joy before death.

Yet, though *The Tears of Eros* itself presents the movement of a consciousness thinking against itself through the enjoyment of art objects and documents of religion and torture—precisely the mobile thought Bataille endeavored to seize in *Theory of Religion* and the other texts of *La Somme*—he also began making notes for a new book of aphorisms alongside his notes for *The Tears of Eros*. The notes gathered in "Outside *The Tears of Eros*" (in this volume)—though the term *notes* fails to describe these scratches or shards of writing—reaffirm the necessity of thinking against Hegel, the necessity of an impossible revolt. But they admit the impossibility of success. The project must be abandoned en route. In "The Congested Planet" (in this volume) Bataille recognizes that his plans will not be completed. In "Outside *The Tears of Eros*" he accepts the "necessity of abandoning the project while en route." The 1961 reedition of *Guilty* outlined *La Somme athéologique* as *Inner Experience, Guilty,* and *On Nietzsche*.[79] *Le Pur Bonheur* and *Le Système inachevé du non-savoir* had been abandoned en route.

His failing is a failing of the mind, occasioned by a failing of the body: "I don't have the necessary strength / in my mind Hegel isn't in question" ("Outside *The Tears of Eros*"). In the end, his writing, and not only his writing, became, despite itself, an affirmation of Hegel's value. *La Somme athéologique* is not so much a magnificent atheological summa as it is the dramatization of an immense failing, a tragedy.

What follows is not a book, certainly not *one* book. It is a book collected against itself, and against the other volumes of *La Somme. The Unfinished System of Nonknowledge* is a supplement to *La Somme athéologique,* but one that incompletes the work rather than completing it. Bataille's outlines, plans, and projects for *La Somme athéologique* overlap and remain contradictory, impossible, abandoned. *The Unfinished System of Nonknowledge* presents its reader with a collection of texts gathered against any single compositional trajectory.[80] It is left to the reader to follow the wayward paths of these texts from association to association, ensemble to ensemble, assemblage to assemblage.

Some outlines and associations: The 1954 reedition of *Inner Experience* became volume 1 of *La Somme athéologique* with the addition of *Method of Meditation* and "Post-Scriptum 1953," the later two of which, omitted from the English translation of the former, are included here. But *Method of Meditation* can also be read alongside the texts Bataille published as *The Impossible,* and both of these books might be read alongside *Inner Experience, Guilty,* and *On Nietzsche* under the general title *Par delà la poésie.* "Socratic College," "Discussion on Sin," and the "Lectures on Nonknowledge" offer a glimpse of Bataille at the podium, but each of these lectures/discussions referenced a different book of *La Somme*: "Socratic College" refers to *Inner Experience,* "Discussion on Sin" presents a chapter from *On Nietzsche,* and the "Lectures on Nonknowledge" read alongside *Theory of Religion* and "Nonknowledge" form *Mourir de rire, et rire de mourir.* "The Sovereign," "Post-Scriptum 1953," and "Aphorisms for the 'System'" all continue Bataille's reflection on his own contributions to modern thought and possible responses to his various critics—philosophical, religious, and otherwise. While "Initial Postulate," "Hegel, Death, and Sacrifice," "Hegel, l'homme et l'histoire," "Sommes-nous là pour jouer ou pour être sérieux?," "The Sovereign," "Nonknowledge," "Aphorisms," "Beyond Seriousness," "The Congested Planet," "Pure Happiness," and the "Notebook for 'Pure Happiness'" constitute elements of *Le Pur Bonheur, ou la part du jeu.* "The Absence of God" and "Aphorisms" both return to images and language developed in other texts and are both explicitly aphoristic, yet they are not of a piece with Bataille's other writings. Like several of the texts in this volume, they are perhaps best read in isolation.

In 1942, in *Guilty,* Bataille wrote: "Tears in my eyes at this idea of being waste! I'm whining, ready to pray, but just can't make myself" (69). This book comes to a close twenty years later with notes written before death, again with tears, this time of Eros, and again with a will toward prayer. Or rather, this time, with a willingness to accept the failings of atheology, and pray.

the

unfinished

system of

nonknowledge

Part I

Socratic College

Introduction

It is a banality to claim that there is a fundamental difficulty in human communication. And it is not hard to recognize in advance that this difficulty is partially irreducible. To communicate means to try to establish a unity, to make one of many; this is what the word *communion* means. In one way or another, something is always missing from the communion sought by humans, driven by the feeling that solitude is impotence itself. We must necessarily risk our lives: this implies entering into a movement connecting ourselves to other humans who are similar to ourselves. This is absolutely necessary for the life of the flesh. We would die quickly if we had not taken care to insert ourselves into a system of economic exchanges. It is hardly any less necessary for the life of the mind: the most profound difference may be related to the fact that the mind can die of inanity without any real suffering. But whereas economic problems are soluble in spite of everything, and it is relatively easy to reach a state of intestinal saturation, the mind that seeks to live on its own mental level must, in order to establish some spiritual link between itself and its equals, do more than vanquish a few difficulties. Even if it succeeds in this, the question of authenticity arises again. In the real world, this question is always posed, there is always something adulterated and insufficient in the spiritual contact between humans. This is why I think it is not too much to ask anyone who persists in wanting to live completely not to put on too many airs and, as there is always filth where there is life, to get used to filth. [*Crossed out*: All communication among men is rich with garbage. It is natural to want to avoid filth, garbage, ordinary trash. But a little simplicity reveals that a foul smell also marks the presence of life.]

I am not saying this to rid myself of a problem. On the contrary, I would like to get to the bottom of this difficulty—to try to reach the bottom on one point at least. I have had to search through recent events to understand certain aspects of everyday behavior as precisely as I could. I set out from the idea that men formerly sought glory to the point of having no intentions that might be compared to one another, overtly at least. Today, the concern for glory seems a very doubtful principle, it is even expressly vilified. It appeared to me, however, that contradictory attitudes were able to oppose themselves more or less consciously to this apparent vilification. In my view, the concern for glory is conveyed in the form of energy spent toward no other end than the pursuit of glory, this constitutes an attitude of little interest or familiarity to our minds. But, by glory it is necessary to understand effects that are clearly different one from another. In this way, I came to represent the consumption of tobacco as a purely glorious expenditure, having for its goal to procure for the smoker an atmosphere detached from the general mechanics of things. Smoking is not an exterior concern wherein physical factors alone would be at stake. The fatigued mind relieves itself in a self-affirmation as nonintellectual as possible. In this, smoking is nonetheless an expressly human attitude, and I do not think there is any comparable animal attitude. When smoking, the human mind not only surrenders itself to a squandering that is indefensible according to sound reason: it is above all a squandering deprived of meaning, deprived of any knowledge of itself; such deprivations allow absence to appear. We sacrificed to appease the gods or to reconcile ourselves with them, we buy jewels to affirm a social level or for seduction, we take walks in the mountains to make up for the excesses of the cities, we read poems for a thousand reasons: and even excluding exterior reasons, we can talk about these various kinds of waste; they enter from many sides, wrongly or rightly, within the intellectual connections that constitute us. Smoking, on the contrary, is the most exterior thing to our understanding. Insofar as we are absorbed in smoking we escape ourselves, we slip into a semiabsence, and if it is true that a concern for elegance is always connected to waste, smoking is elegance, is silence itself.

I was led to show that the search for glory—it is as if we were saying the dilapidation of energy and of the goods it produces, insofar as it is the negation of the avaricious isolation of the individual—is the means by which communication occurs between men. It seems certain to me that tobacco, even smoked in solitude, is a connection between men. But this isn't from an expenditure or a connection that is more inconsistent, or better situated outside of consciousness. If glorious expenditure is a connection, it is advantageous that it be the most transparent connection possible, that we should not stop at its limited aspects; it is advantageous that it be produced in the lightest way, without which no one would be aware of it. To those who do not grasp this interest, something is missing. In communication, something fragile, I don't know what, dies if one pushes it: communication demands that one slip. Is it not evident, nevertheless, that in becoming unconscious, impalpable, expenditure risks being as if it were not and its connection with being were negligible? It is possible that today men spend no less on smoking tobacco than our forefathers did on sacrificial animals. It is possible that expenditure won through the elegance and lightness of smoke: animal sacrifices must have been something heavy. Closer to us, luxury or military glory also lack lightness. But is it certain that tobacco completely satisfies the demand to which it seems to respond?

If it is a question of attaining glory, and beyond its heavy forms its transparency (which risks having a resemblance of its opposite), it seems to me that an elegant solution like tobacco has but one role: it designates a reef. And without doubt, it is the same with most elegance. Through elegance, we get away from heaviness, but lightness is paid for with insignificance. We avoid the excesses of the tragic. Above all, we avoid becoming comical. Meanwhile, before the inanity into which elegance slips, it would be surprising if one time someone cried out: "It is better to be heavy! It is better to be comical!" Elegance settles beside this reef, underlines it, and presents it as a pretext for not going further. Is this tolerable?

Truthfully, the concern for elegance is unbearable exactly when it strives to remain there. Maybe it is difficult to make oneself understood when, instead of simply answering the questions, one shows the answer in a movement. But I think I can say this: "Impossible to hold myself to weighty solutions, as much as to disengage myself from them without any more waiting and even to sacrifice myself to the demon of futility; it is no less possible beyond looking for the transparent path."

These are perhaps rather complicated linguistic precautions taken in order to express the necessity of a discipline, but I wanted to recognize first of all the indications of the unconscious. To no longer be able to take refuge in the calm of an ungraspable freedom, even to surrender to the excesses of inconsistency: not only was it necessary to go through this to the point of almost losing oneself, but I imagine the necessity of being continuously invigorated by it. Losing time, from the point of view I have adopted, is hardly a convincing notion. Just the same, this is no reason to defer.

And I propose not only going further, but I would like to show that the only thing possible now is going all the way, in the sense precisely contrary to the unconscious. That we intended to find the road to an interior life outside of designated paths, contrary to the Christian inundation; that we intended to attain glory in its transparency; or, more simply put, to break the glass that separates beings and to ground communication, we strike out against the lies of the past no less than against the inanity of the present. The past put the spotlight on glory and the present admits no more than some ungraspable forms of it—this is the distance that separates the bloody sacrifice from a cigar—but we are unable to return from our present discretion to the prophetic masks of antiquity. We can only lay ourselves bare, in the full light of consciousness. The only thing that is intended for us is to become conscious beings, conscious not only of all that we are but of the possibilities hidden at the depth of our being. We can only attain this transparency through a stripping bare that does not reserve the smallest piece of clothing. The return to draped phantoms and the flight into elegance are forbidden to us at the same time.

In this sense, the necessity about which I spoke earlier of being light—one destroys it by sustaining it—can only be translated in one way: in moving forward one must necessarily be resolute and quick, without ambiguity or hesitation. Boredom is in things done halfway. I can reproach myself for having hesitated, I do not believe it is possible for much longer. It is a question of emerging from the uncertainty in which we have been living, where elegance and bright colors leave inconsequential paths open. It is not bad to speak. Besides, it shows that we are not overly afraid of inelegance. But if one moves one foot forward as much as the other, without waiting. It is no doubt permissible for us to add to the liberal world's flow of words. It seems, however, that in regard to the world of the mind we can define this world in this way: we can indefinitely introduce new assertions without changing the meaning. If we want to escape from this impasse, we must return to the only systems of consequential thought, which are necessarily scholastic. I don't mean that human thought entering into the path of consequences can only be scholastic, but it must have scholastic form on one point. In the first place, what would becoming conscious mean if it could escape the scholastic Revelation and take refuge in inconsequence? The consciousness that we are able to have of being and of its possibilities would fundamentally have nothing to do with the change that we designate when we say of man that he is conscious, if consciousness did not entail a revision of values and *of behaviors connected to values*. Within the liberal world, so-called changes in value retain the fundamental belief in a certain equivalence, consequently in the innocuousness of everything. The new values can be satisfied with a new literary form: this form is precisely what allows juxtaposition without a war analogous to that of the museums. The scholastic form is opposed to the literary form in that it is of no interest to whomever uses it. For any one of the small human museums that the liberal world consists of, the scholastic form suppresses the temptation to add a rare piece to its collections.

I propose to elaborate an ensemble of scholastic givens in regard to inner experience. I believe that inner experience is possible only if it can be communicated and that it could not be communicated in a definitive way without attaining scholastic objectivity. Poetic or even simply literary communication is undoubtedly neither vain nor avoidable, but it involves the flight of consciousness and its dissipation into smoke. Given the preference we grant it, I'm inclined to be suspicious of the liberal vice, the horror of consequences, which overcomes us all. Only propositions reduced to a clear form—stripped of poetic artifice as much as possible—can truly engage consciousness and connect experiences, once referred to as mystical, to the baring of their processes. And these propositions cannot be the work of one person alone but must be the result of the elaboration of several people, simultaneously bound to the sharing of a profound experience and the provocation of that experience.

This proposition does not imply the rejection of different modes of expression but only of ambiguity. A portion of the expression of inner experience is necessarily poetic and cannot be translated into clear propositions, though I can clearly say that this is so. I can express this precise idea again: poetry is an obstacle to consciousness insofar as it is connected to the role played by thinking and expressing oneself poetically on a level where consciousness is possible. This role is probably one of the important factors of the stagnant elegance that I was talking about earlier. And because it is an obstacle to consciousness, it is also therein an obstacle to transparency. Once more, elegance persisting in the unconscious is stagnation. We only attain the accomplishment of transparency at the height of consciousness. All of these considerations are foreign to the present, to the total war in particular. However, at a time when powers on every side are linked together for maximum efficiency, it becomes natural to think that liberal forms have arrived at a state of obsolescence. In these conditions, unconscious elegance became touching, but the smoke that is connected to it will be dissipated no less quickly; even if it was not annoying and hostile in itself, waiting in the unconscious is no more than a means of moving toward liquidation. The circumstances themselves aid this success: in one way or another I am inclined to believe that we must go to the end of the possible, without which we would have nothing more than dissipation before us. I do not believe this evocation is misplaced within an introduction to apparently modest projects. I doubt that the possibilities of these times give modesty the same meaning it had in the still liberal world, which demanded modesty as it demanded insignificance and the equivalence of values. Whatever the task I am proposing might be, it supposes no present or ulterior ambition, disproportionate to the strength of a small group. It is only a question of placing the human mind on the level of reality. It is within our reach to destroy in us the remnants of our attachment to the wealth of the liberal world: these riches were illusory. The entirety of the question consists in knowing if what we are or at least what we can be will be sufficiently harsh within the world of consequences. In concrete terms, a few of us can form, with the will to go to the end of consciousness, a kind of organization or school, to which I propose to provisionally give the in part amusing title of "College of Socratic Studies," a college that would publish nothing, would have neither means of propaganda nor of overt assembly, but that would nevertheless attempt to absorb, in its lack of solutions, the activity that is most clearly outside of each of our activities.

For a few months, we meet from time to time to talk and we attempt to define an object of conversation corresponding to common interests. In the long run, it seems obvious to me that it is not easy to have a single consciousness among several people sufficient to what we do and to what we want. Everything is quickly muddled. The moment comes when one can no longer return to chance, when an effort is required if one does not accept renunciation. To express the impression that a certain number of long conversations gave me, I will say this: if what we are attempting were supported by the state, if certain sums of money were put at our disposal, we could no longer return to chance. This would be bothersome in one sense, because it is bad to no longer *be able* to benefit from chance. But it is equally bad not to *be able* to behave like those who regularly dedicate their efforts to their endeavors. Chance having served us poorly of late, I propose that we no longer count on it. We can only continue on the condition of a banal attempt. I think it would be best to concede this principle and hereafter to conceive of our meetings as do the groups meeting for Hautes Études at the Sorbonne. One of us can prepare a short presentation and the questions that serve as the focus of these presentations can be chosen in a logical working order. If it turns out that for a reason beyond our will we cannot meet for some time, the acknowledged principle would be no less likely to reorient the interest that each of us risks bringing to our common research. One thing alone cannot be postponed: it is necessary to specify the object of these inquiries as of this moment.

For lack of something better, I earlier proposed to qualify these meetings with the epithet *Socratic,* maintaining the pleasantry that justifies the choice. I confess experiencing a feeling of detachment from Socrates' thought. This thought cannot be separated from the idealistic position of the Good. Socrates is no less amusing a character, like an incarnation of the malevolence of "discourse." My proposition rests on his two famous maxims: "Know yourself" and "I know but one thing, that I know nothing." For my part, only a kind of happy irony, I believe, follows from these two maxims; however, they seem no less fundamental to me than they were for Socrates. The first is the principle of inner experience and the second that of nonknowledge, on which this experience rests as soon as it abandons the mystical presupposition. And it would no doubt be difficult to define the object of the proposed research better than while talking about "the experience of nonknowledge" or about "negative inner experience" being contrary to what is generally regarded as knowledge *[connaissance],* in other words contrary to the experience that man has of the exterior world while living.

Now, I will try to indicate how scholasticism, the object of which would be this negative experience and the elaboration of which would be the activity of the possible college, might be developed. On this subject, I will first concern myself with an initial step in this direction made last year in discussions similar to those that bring us together today. We had no intention of developing scholastic precepts at that time, but on several occasions Blanchot in particular formulated propositions of a rather accomplished design. I only took them up again several months later, from memory, while writing a book,[1] but I don't believe I distorted them noticeably.

Thus these propositions define what we referred to in problematic terms as the *spiritual life*—while it is, it seems, preferable to talk about *negative inner experience*: this experience, these propositions assert, can:

—*only have its principle and end in the absence of salvation, in the renunciation of all hope*

—*only affirm that experience itself is the authority (but all authority expiates itself)*

—*only be a contestation of itself and nonknowledge.*[2]

More recently, I have had occasion myself, Blanchot absent, to specify the meaning that should, to my mind, be granted to the second of these propositions. It means, I think, that "authority can only be founded on the questioning of authority."

On the other hand, the proposition concerning the absence of salvation (the first one) implicitly introduces the notion of the "impossible" on which I wrote a few months ago, discussing life placed at the level of the impossible that it encounters.

These first propositions concern the *sources* of experience. A second chapter, necessarily, would concern the *degrees* (methods, assemblage *[mise en œuvre]*). Finally, a third, the *exterior conditions,* in other words the connections between a "possible" world and an existence at the level of "the impossible." I do not believe it is necessary to expand this any further this first time: I prefer insisting on a principle that in my opinion results from what I have said about the sources of experience. I articulated some propositions formulated by one of us during discussions analogous to ours. They appear to me not only to indicate in which direction and in what form the research can be followed. Moreover, what seems to stand out is that these propositions imply something other than the usual studies and research: they suppose on the part of whoever formulated them a lived experience and represent, on the other hand, the sharing, the communication of this experience in opposition to lyricism and subjective effusion. It is this shared quality that justifies the conversations that bring us together, in my eyes; intellectual discussions without any other object only establish, I fear, profound misunderstandings among men, these misunderstandings no doubt only arise from an obscure thirst for isolation and for rivalry that passes unnoticed. It is in this manner that I can place only a secondary interest in the fact that a college like the one I propose should be connected to a given philosophical tradition, should even have the study of this tradition as one objective among others. A college of philosophers? Surely not; a life preserver thrown to philosophy in peril? Aren't those who fight for the dead already dead themselves? I don't want to exclude that which touches, be it from afar, on a specific object of research, or to lock myself up in dry scholastic elaboration. I nevertheless believe that a misery, liberalism, to which the interest in philosophy is almost fatally connected, is in flight like a contagious illness from our times. Besides so much in the material of tradition insists on poetry: in this way I would willfully link these scholastic intentions to the name "horrible workers" that one day in a letter Rimbaud bestowed on those in his wake who would explore the kind of obscurity wherein he himself foundered.

Outline of an Elaboration

If together we endeavor to elaborate knowledge of inner experience, it is necessary to specify in advance an outline prescribing a road toward this knowledge. An outline presents from the very beginning the inconvenience that it has a result in view. In particular from the scholastic perspective. It constitutes a set of coordinated propositions. It is therefore necessary to insist on the provisional and even artificial aspect of this way of beginning. The proposed set of propositions is essentially revisable and is so limitlessly. The sharing of the experience justifiably consists in revising this set and the revision will never be received as complete.

If a pure science were envisioned, this kind of groping would still be admissible. For a much stronger reason if the scientific goal is remote, if the knowledge is regarded as the means without which the experience would be impossible, the elaboration is no longer an end and the essential value judgments no longer rest on it but on the experience itself. All that one can say is that the value judgments implicate the elaboration with their point of view. This way of speaking is no doubt obscure but it can be reduced to a simple remark: if one abandons a particular point of view (like that of knowledge), everything maintains itself, everything is interdependent, everything moves together. What we can name inner experience undoubtedly exists and if we can of necessity fear not attaining an exact knowledge of what it is, at least we can attempt to live it: in this sense, even mistakes are valuable.

In this representation set forward as an outline, I will voluntarily part with the present, in other words from the state of relative deprivation and the threat of unhappiness in which we find ourselves. In itself, this state constitutes a contestation of the value that all experiences resulting from favorable conditions have. I cannot get drunk without alcohol, or have an erotic experience without associating myself with a partner who pleases me. It is likewise with the experience of the sacred, which supposes participation in some common movement (besides, on this subject the difficulty is not new). The fact that man can let himself be deprived of his exterior possibilities introduces the possibility of an inner experience in a fundamental way, *an experience resulting from the abandonment of man to himself, without the help of any happy factor coming from the outside.* This experience is therefore possible in a prison or in a camp—in the expectation of death or in physical pain. This definition and this corollary can serve as a point of departure.

This evocation of misfortune introduces the anguish likely to precede the moment when this misfortune comes to term and is, after all, more common than the misfortune itself. Thus, it is difficult to imagine experience other than linked to anguish. Anguish outruns even the threat of misfortune and can occur in any circumstance. In respect to misfortune, we might even say that it constitutes a favorable condition for anguish—as wine does for intoxication (but not a necessary condition). Anguish without reason is in any case much more significant for experience. But as there can be an element of bare inner experience in any erotic experience, in occasional anguish there is always an element of pure anguish, which we feel for no other reason than the fact that we exist. Therefore, it remains possible to reduce occasional moments of anguish to this pure element, singularly capable of being a positive point of departure from the experience.

From this beginning, the hardly evoked experience appears in relation to possibilities of joy and of suffering. It is the fact of a being eager for risk and fearful of suffering. But the desire for experience soon appears to be as much in contradiction with this avidity as with this fear. No inner experience is possible for those who allow themselves to be dominated by pleasure and pain. The consequence of the experience might be the loss of pleasure or the encounter with suffering. Experience does not generally propose greater pleasure or the rejection of greater suffering. Only Buddhists are satisfied with the principle of the struggle against pain; in this way, they are reduced to pure negation as a principle of departure though their practices put positive values at risk. Inner experience naturally exceeds the subordination of human life to the search for pleasure, to the flight from pain. It postulates a positive value beyond pleasure. This search, in its various historical forms, is the clearest indication in the sense of the existence of this value.

The essential difficulty begins here. The search for a beyond in relation to immediate interests appears from the beginning as a principle of contestation. All of life is contested by anxiety about this beyond.

But it is necessary to add immediately that this contestation can by no means be limited to what we commonly call life. If inner experience affirms the existence of a beyond and establishes this existence as a principle, it cannot stop its contestation there: this principle itself must be contested in turn and experience appears in this movement as a contestation without limit. From this principle, the definition accusing inner experience of the *incessant interrogation of existence by itself.*

It was natural that at the end of these interrogations we might attempt to locate an authority that escapes immediate contestation in the vaguest beyond and that we might personalize this authority as a God. Outside this hybrid historical affirmation, in part popular, in part scholarly, contestation again encounters the *poetic* and the *sacred.* But *poetic, sacred* cannot serve as preemptory affirmations that define God as would a petition of intoxicating principles. *Poetic, sacred* fall within the purview of discursive analysis: their reduction is inevitable. At the end of the reduction, experience alone subsists and, beyond pleasure, is only able to find value in itself. If experience appeared at this moment as the *poetic* itself or as the *sacred* itself or even, why not, as God, these values would remain connected to the contestation that the experience has made of itself. It would be a question of poetry contesting itself, of the sacred contesting itself, of God contesting himself. The pause that allows these possibilities to affirm their authority, to install themselves in existence, would disappear. Everything, authority itself, would be caught in a movement of interrogation without limit. There would be no other authority than in this movement, in this interrogation.

Without any doubt, when considering experience, this point of departure is the most important; this point of departure surpasses Christian limits and exceeds the principle of egoistic pleasure. On the other hand, it seems to me necessary to put the accent on this because of an enduring tendency of the mind to stabilize value, to misunderstand the necessity of a movement wherein everything disappears, wherein there is no possibility of satisfaction. In the end, is it hard to perceive that in the shortest pause everything sinks once again into enjoyment and into certainties that are taken up so that we might better possess this enjoyment?

Experience is posed in this way, first of all independently of the subject that lives it and of the object that it uncovers: it is as much the interrogation of the subject as of the object. But it is clear that it is by no means a question of the experience of an indefinite or limitless being. The experience is itself exactly the act of a particular and limited being. What I question in myself is no doubt being itself, but I cannot call being itself into question before having thrown myself against the limits of the being that I am. Experience is therefore first of all the interrogation of the limits of being, essentially of the isolation in which the particular being finds itself. In this way, it is in search of an exterior object with which it will attempt to communicate. Without doubt here we can see only the premises of inner experience proper. But these premises are inevitable and necessary to the fulfillment of the final experience. In a certain sense it is possible to look at the Christian experience as responding to the necessity of this first step. But it is a question of a correspondence of proximity. The degrees of the experience should be disengaged from these historical limits and as far as it is possible, it is advantageous for us to describe some possible forms of experience independently of the disorder wherein history has realized them.

The contestation of the limits of being initially throws itself against the servitude of the action, consequently at discursive forms of life, always engaged in the meaning of the action. Experience is in the first place a struggle against the spell in which useful language holds us. This struggle can begin on the discursive level but it can not obtain great results. The opposition offered by a new kind of vulgar discourse is usually ineffectual. The mind can resort to more powerful spells, like modifications of the physiological state. It can resort to processes that rupture one's intellectual equilibrium, to tragic thoughts. These solutions can even be presented as methods or techniques that it would be vain to underestimate. It seems to me, however, that these methods or these techniques can only call into question the limits of being, not being itself: they are therefore often connected to the position of an infinite, exterior being, situated beyond contestation.

A perceptible step is made if we substitute the unknown for the notion of this infinite, exterior being. But in all these steps it is necessary to see essentially only the means of *communication,* the means of making being slip beyond the limits of the isolated ego. Communication can be viewed as a margin open to possibility: through this margin being surpasses more and more distant limits, but in the end, lost in communication, being finds itself alone again, though it attains a kind of immensity. Just as the weightiest unknown finds itself only on the condition of going to the depth of knowledge, the unintelligible solitude of being finds itself on the condition of going to the end of communication, at the moment the mind attains a derisive summit where it is everything.

If you have been following me correctly, you see that the mind born of limited misfortune has, after a long hesitation, arrived at the comprehension of a limitless misfortune. But this operation demands peculiar conditions. Through these steps the mind can only be brought by luck (what Christians called *grace*). And luck is not in this case reduced to an exterior means. Luck can be considered as the object and even as the subject of experience. The interrogation that experience is necessarily appears as a gamble: it is the gamble of being, as much of the subject it is as of the object. Lastly, luck that *can* result from the gamble is that which alone *can* survive contestation, *luck* being the daughter of contestation and being unable to subsist without a new contestation, a new gamble. Without luck, an access to the level of the impossible—the comprehension of a limitless misfortune—would be quite closed off to the being. In other words, luck is necessary for the being to go to the end of its possibility and to support that which without luck would be impossible—would not even be perceived. In this, to support means to admire, to bless, but without stability, in an excessive state.

It is understood—I mentioned it at the beginning, I am saying it once more—that this insight is only an outline, in one way even it will never be anything but an outline. By this I mean, in the first place, that these propositions can be shattered, denied, reordered; and, secondly, that those propositions that would follow could be shattered, denied, and reordered in their turn.

Nietzsche's Laughter

The possible and the impossible are both in the world. We are troubled by the sky, the starry space in which we discover laws of harmony, general viability. In this domain, we can only have a presentiment of suspended horror, ungraspable to us. But we have a precise knowledge of our terrestrial domain that comes from the possible and the impossible. The possible is organic life and its development in a favorable setting. The impossible is the final death, the necessity of destruction for existence. This at least is irreducible: human conduct adds the exuberance of cruelty, useless disorders, war, torture, oppression, vice, prostitution, alcoholism, and, in the end, the multiple horrors of misery. For man, the possible is good, the impossible is evil. This is not only the opposition of the pleasant to the disastrous but a battle of irreconcilable principles: a laudable good on one side and an evil worthy of eternal hell on the other.

The moral qualification of evil indicates man's profound agreement with the possible. This also indicates a general belief in the domination of the possible in the world. This domination would be assured and would only be compromised by human vices. Only the word *God* means this to man, implying the existence of a sovereign perfection, governing all the things of the world. There is not an impossible if God exists, or at least the impossible is illusory: it is a test imposed on man, while the triumph of the possible is given in advance. Loss nevertheless persists: evil must be punished, the evil will suffer torture in hell. Hell is, in fact, the condensation of the impossible, the sanction of eternity added to the impossible. I can imagine no better indication of that which the suppressed "will to the impossible" becomes. Hell is that which makes the divine lie the fault of a child, a naïveté not intended to deceive.

The possible, so it seems, exists at the limit of the impossible. As if a conscious will sought the maximum of the impossible: it goes without saying that in this aim the possible is at first a necessity. The belief in hell is the same concept inverted, eternal hell being a minimum of the impossible, but, by chance, this minimum is infinitely greater than the maximum of the contrary notion. So the human imagination, like nature, climaxes with the impossible.

In fact, whatever God's absolute appearance might be, God is only a compromise among the contradictory wills of man. God is the mediation of the possible and the impossible. As such, the image of the perfect Being always slips in the human mind toward the impossible. In the order of profound concepts, God surpasses the categories of intelligence to the point of being beyond the possible and the impossible, equally beyond one as beyond the other. Thus Eckhart's inner experience gives God, as if by necessity, all the attributes of intellectual impossibility. And Angela of Foligno communes with God through the love of the demon. So much so that the will to reduce to the possible is limited to the terrestrial domain: heaven and hell escape it equally. But this follows from a slipping whose point of departure is the possible. Before everything else, the world, though this is not the way we receive it, should become the realm of the possible. For this, even death is rejected: the world in its depths is the world of the possible to such a degree that we only see a superficial appearance of it. But it has also been necessary that the possible depend in part on human will, so that the impossible could have been a responsibility here below. Personal salvation is the element in the system that expresses the escape from the impossible.

Our repugnance to living the idea of the impossible is so well ingrained in human weakness that the equilibrium of this system is fragile. The time came when we easily imagined struggling against the impossible, actually chasing it from the earth. Nature being good, the impossible adhering to human faults, why not remedy the situation here below? We must eliminate the abuses through which the wicked become guilty, in whatever way track the impossible down on earth, expel it forever. Human responsibility consists in devoting our lives to this travail. Thus alcohol introduces misery into this lodging, pale children, beaten women. We must expel the alcohol; it is our responsibility. And to such a degree that in the end only the possible remains.

But this realism, being a step above the old beliefs, went hand in hand with the ruin of our thoughts on the immortal soul and God. Beliefs were obliged to appeal to the beyond. Modern realism admits death, making human life, from the cradle onward, prey to an impossible nothingness. Likewise, in God, the only guarantee of the possible, in the name of which we struggle, is isolated.

The successes of realist ideas initially obstructed the perception that man was situated in this way before the impossible that he fled. It is true that this fundamental impossible appeared negligible in comparison with the horrors in which we were directly caught. Besides, we didn't make anything worse: death and the absence of God weren't new, they existed before disbelief. In the certainty of an indefinite progress, was it necessary to occupy ourselves with an aging child's play?

But God and immortality played such a large part in past human struggles that we can doubt if their eviction will remain without consequences. A great many men have let go of general guarantees for an immediate satisfaction. Today immediate satisfaction is wanting. Certain people think it is a question of a slight delay; others return to God; a small number, decidedly seeing humanity as the prey of the impossible, see a new attitude in anguish: evading nothing, living the impossible.

If God is dead, if humanity is no less forsaken than animals, who devour each other, it is no doubt laudable to ameliorate the human situation. But I imagine difficulties arising in the long run. The maximum attained, it is possible that humanity might be satisfied in the end: the majority are in fact easily satisfied, but are they really satisfied? And in their incapacity to perceive the impossible in themselves, at least I can perceive it in advance and without being entranced by blindness. An impossible exists in man that nothing will reduce, the same, in a fundamental way, for the happiest as for the most disinherited. The difference is in the elusion; happiness is no doubt a desirable form of elusion, but happiness can only defer the deadline. As we cannot limit ourselves to postponing this deadline, in the end we can only face the impossible. Putting life, that is to say the possible, in proportion to the impossible, is all that a man can do if he no longer wants to avoid it.

This task might one day receive—though not necessarily—consequences in the realm of action defined as *spiritual*. This is an old word
the precise meaning of which remains bound to forms of life lacking
neither narrowness nor ambiguity. I use it almost in a traditional sense
while specifying: the spiritual is what arises from ecstasy, from religious sacrifice (from the sacred), from tragedy, from poetry, from
laughter—or from anxiety. The mind is not completely spiritual. Intelligence is not. Fundamentally, the spiritual domain is that of the impossible. I will say that ecstasy, sacrifice, tragedy, poetry, laughter are
forms whereby life situates itself in proportion to the impossible. But
these are natural forms, in that someone making a sacrifice, writing a
poem, or someone laughing thinks nothing of placing himself in relation to the impossible; that someone makes a sacrifice, writes a poem
or laughs without really knowing what agitates him, even while avoiding it through sacrifice, poetry, or laughter. In becoming conscious of
the impossible, I place myself on its level, I can be or not be in ecstasy,
I can laugh, not laugh, have or not have a sacred feeling, poetic, tragic.
I no longer limit myself to suffering the impossible in things, I recognize it as such, I don't escape the impossible which makes me laugh,
and so on . . .

Traditionally, salvation occupied the central place in spiritual life.
But the will to salvation signifies the resolution to escape the impossible. Salvation is only a hybrid form. Salvation is fundamentally only
the principle of action (of the temporal) introduced into the spiritual
order. We must see it as an intruder. It is the same with God, even if
God slips necessarily, slips toward the impossible: Eckhart's God is the
same as the good God. God undoubtedly is such a moving notion that
we cannot reduce it to a platitude, to nonspirituality, to the possible.
Salvation saves itself only through anxiety. Without anxiety, it is the
perfect negation of the spiritual, entirely bound to loss.

What gives salvation its importance is not so much the end in itself
as the principle of an end introduced into spiritual life. The impossible
needs the possible from which to be disengaged. Salvation is the possible required by the mind for a confrontation with the impossible. But
in salvation, the possible is the end of the impossible: it is therefore the
evasion of the impossible. If the spiritual life demands the evasion of its
principle, it isn't what it claims to be. Salvation is only a commodity
despite which spiritual life, rarely, takes place, I mean the possible

attaching itself to the impossible. But the habit is so old that we no longer imagine spiritual life outside of the quest for salvation. If salvation isn't in question, what would the purpose of the spiritual life be? In other words what of the possible might we introduce into the impossible?

I explain myself in this way with the intention of giving Nietzsche's inner experience a significance that has not yet been drawn from it. On this occasion I don't feel the necessity to say everything that it is possible to mean by the impossible nor in what way ecstasy, sacrifice, and so on . . . situate the possible at the level of the impossible. This would take a long time and I have said it or will say it elsewhere. More than ever I want to address myself only to those proud beings, by no means bound by consequence to the possible, who have of the impossible at least the feeling that the tragic, the poetic, the laughable offer of it. I limit myself to these two propositions, already implicitly introduced: "Every impossible is that by which a possible ceases to be possible (as I said, without the possible there wouldn't be any impossible: the tragic is the attribute of the powerful)"; "at the extreme limit of its power, every possible aspires to the impossible (to what destroys it as possible)." I recall that the aspiration to the impossible is precisely the spiritual (as action is always an aspiration toward the possible). But again, at the moment when the will to salvation, like an intruder, is rejected from the spiritual, what is the possible without which there would not be an impossible?

Roughly, the impossible enters Nietzsche's life in the form of sickness, the sickness of a vigorous and robust body. As tragic as what *happened* appears today, Nietzsche's *future* around 1880 seemed better still. He himself says of the joyful cries of Zarathustra that we couldn't understand them without crying: at this particular moment he lived beneath the weight of what was *before him*. The most striking thing in Nietzsche's life is that he renounced Schopenhauer's philosophy at the moment when sickness justified its pessimism in his particular existence. He said no to life while it was easy: but yes when it took the form of the impossible. He could not forget himself, noting these few words around the time of Zarathustra: "To see tragic characters founder and *to be able to laugh,* despite the profound understanding, emotion and sympathy that we feel: this is divine."[1] In principle, laughing is the reaction the impossible offers when sympathy isn't personally at stake. Either the impossible overcomes indifferent people, or it overcomes beings to whom I am bound by sympathy. But without really putting them at risk, I can laugh at the impossible in humanity: the impossible leaves the essence of the possible intact. Laughing at the impossible as it overcomes me, laughing knowing I am sinking, I am a god who mocks the possible that he is. I no longer hold life to the standard of the impossible in order to escape it, as nature does in tragedy, in Aristotle's theory of catharsis. Zarathustra made laughter *sacred*. I can now say it with insistence, though laughter is frivolity, if Nietzsche had done it himself, he would have lacked this intention. The transparency and frivolity of the dance of the *amor fati* would not have been reached. To hold, without elusion, life to the standard of the impossible demands a moment of divine friendship.

Nietzsche left a lot to guesswork: he hardly addressed it in his letters. But what does the divine attained in laughter mean, if not the absence of God? One must go as far as murder and say not only "see founder" but "make founder." Nietzsche says this in *Beyond Good and Evil*: "At long last, did one not have to sacrifice for once whatever is comforting, holy, healing; all hope, all faith in hidden harmony, in future blisses and justices? Didn't one have to sacrifice God himself . . . ?"[2] Being divine is not only putting life to the standard of the impossible, it is renouncing the guarantee of the possible. Man's understanding of this notion is no more perfect than his understanding of God. God doesn't tolerate himself as possible. Man is constrained by this tolerance but God, the Almighty, no longer is. God's misery is the human will to appropriate God for humanity through salvation. This will expresses the imperfection of the possible in man, but the perfect possible that God is does not end before falling into horror and into the impossible. To die an atrocious, vile death, abandoned by everyone, abandoned by God himself, what else could the perfect possible aspire to? It would be foolish and small without this aspiration! Man, who is nothing but man, can be limited to the moment of his greatest thought, raising himself to the height of God: man's limit isn't God, isn't the possible, it is the impossible, the absence of God.

Nietzsche's inner experience does not lead to God but to his absence; it is the possible holding itself to the standard of the impossible, lost in a representation of the abominable world. The eternal return has the unique characteristic of precipitating this being, as in a fall, into the double impossible of Time. The impossible in the common representation of time is met only at the extremes of antecedent and future eternity. In the eternal return, the instant itself is in one impossible movement projected toward these two extremes. As much a truth on which to seat thought, the eternal return is a fable, but by way of the abyss? It cannot be closed again. Man's thought forcing him to embrace time is destroyed by this violence: considering time, man's pride can only throw him into vertigo, in response to which we see triviality. Offering vertigo, holding one to the standard of a fall into the impossible, is the only expression, whatever it might be, of inner experience, in other words, of an ecstatic revelation of the impossible. To achieve this effect it isn't necessary that we introduce the eternal return (and still less to ground it in science); this is, however, an intelligible sign—and an irrefutable critique of sleep. Nothing greater than this hypertrophy of the impossible.

But the myth, the symbol of the eternal return, cannot be considered in isolation. It is related to the conditions in which life attains the impossible. I've already said it twice: the impossible is only reached through the possible; without the possible, there would be no impossible. I'll go further: the impossible attained indolently through the neglect of the possible is an impossible eluded in advance: confronted without strength, it is only an obscene gesture. The will to salvation is only an intrusion in the spiritual order but this at least links the possible to the impossible. The impossible is the loss of self. How can one obtain that which being loses if not in compensation for gain? It matters little that the gain is illusory or smaller than the loss: deceiver or not, gain is the bait that makes loss accessible. If man renounces turning the vulgar possible toward the end he gains with the impossible, if he renounces salvation, what of the possible will he introduce into the impossible? This is the question I formulated earlier. Man is not God, he is not the perfect possible: first he must pose the possible. Salvation is miserable in that it leaves the possible in its wake, makes it the end of the impossible. And if I pose the possible in the beginning, really from the beginning? I am only opening the path of the impossible.

The hypertrophy of the impossible, the projection of each instant into the infinite, grants the possible a dwelling wherein it may exist without waiting—at the level of the impossible. What I am here and now is summed up by being possible: what I am is impossible, I know it, I place myself at the height of the impossible: I make the impossible possible, at least accessible. The virtue of nonavoidance consists in offering salvation *at the beginning* without making it an end but making it the trampoline of the impossible. The eternal return opens an abyss, but is the summation of the leap. The abyss is the impossible and the dwelling, but a leap introduced into the impossible, possible as it is, devoted from the beginning without the least reservation to the impossible. This leap is Zarathustra's overman, it is the will to power. The least constraint, and the jump wouldn't have taken place. The jumper, despite his impetus, would have his feet nailed to the ground. How could he not feel sorry for himself if he felt sorry for others? Those oppressed by the anxiety of eliminating the impossible from the earth cannot leap. The necessary quality for him who jumps is frivolity.

Nietzsche articulated an idea that would be understood only fifty years later, but would we have understood it were we capable of knowing the meaning of the leap, and at the same time, incapable of leaping? Nietzsche's leap is inner experience, the ecstasy in which the eternal return and Zarathustra's laughter are revealed. To understand is to make an inner experience of the leap, it is to jump. We've done the exegesis of Nietzsche in several ways. There remains, after Nietzsche, the experience of this leap. There remains only the clearing of the path from which we leap, to offer resounding cries into parts of the abyss. In other words, to create, in a practice and a doctrine, a form of spiritual life, unimaginable prior to Nietzsche, the way an empty word in the end unmasks the face of the impossible.

Discussion on Sin

Having wanted to define his position, solely in regard to sin, before an audience of Christians and non-Christians, Georges Bataille did so at Mr. [Marcel] Moré's home (on March 5, 1944) in a lecture that was later published in his book On Nietzsche, *with, however, some modifications as the following letter specifies:*

My dear friend,[1]

I don't know if I've said something to you about this at some point or another: The section of *On Nietzsche* titled "Summit and Decline" is pretty much the text from my lecture at Marcel Moré's home, though slightly modified. In principle, I limited myself to occasional formal changes, developing some passages.[2] And I've taken a difficulty raised in the discussion into account. I've introduced into the printed text the idea of the nothingness of boredom, which I only formulated at Moré's home in the course of the discussion, in response to Jean-Paul Sartre. The readers who refer back from *On Nietzsche* to the text you are publishing might be disoriented if they weren't warned.

Anyway, these changes are only of secondary importance; they don't concern the essence of this text in which I set out as if to go to the end of things. I imagine myself even today having sapped the foundation of popular morality, that what I expressly wanted to do to those who took upon themselves the burden of this morality, who gave it a sense of distress and from this distress, with me, pleaded against this morality. I don't know how I could overemphasize: "We want to be the heirs of meditation and of Christian penetration"[3] "... to go beyond all Christianity by means of a *hyper-Christianity [Überchristliches]* and without contenting ourselves with giving Christianity up."[4] What Nietzsche affirms, I affirm after him without changing a thing.

I regret having expressed myself badly about this during the discussion. Truthfully, I really agree with Hyppolite. If I use the word *sin*, it is not for simplicity's sake. In my eyes, it is without interest even to pose the problem of morality other than in light of historical experience. I require, in fact, "what the notion of sin has of the infinite." What concerns me in moral matters is the trembling lived by men who endure the path up to the end. Not a, long over, academic experience.

Without this understanding, how could I have perceived the fatality of a crime in terms of the ascension toward the good?

I sense that a rigorous hostility is waiting to go to the end of understanding. Something we've hardly done up till now.

Sincerely,
Georges Bataille

This might interest you: today, a *Surrealist* (Jean Maquet) is espousing, in *Troisième convoi*, an attitude similar to mine, doing justice to Christianity with utter hostility.

In attendance [at the lecture] were: [Arthur] Adamov, [Maurice] Blanchot, Bolin, Ms. [Simone] de Beauvoir, [Jean] Bruno, [Pierre] Burgelin, [Albert] Camus, Couturier, Father [Jean] Daniélou, Father [Henri] Dubarle, [Maurice] de Gandillac, [Jean] Hyppolite, [Pierre] Klossowski, Lahay, [Michel] Leiris, [Pierre] Lescure, [Jacques] Madaule, [Gabriel] Marcel, [Louis] Massignon, Father [Augustin] Maydieu, [Maurice] Merleau-Ponty, [Marcel] Moré, Mounir Hafez, [Jean] Paulhan, [Pierre] Prévost, [Jean-Paul] Sartre, and so on.

Below are: 1. An abstract of the fundamental propositions of Bataille's lecture; 2. A response by Father Daniélou; 3. The subsequent discussion.

1. An Abstract of the Fundamental Propositions

(Introduction). The questions introduced by Bataille concern "good and evil in reference to being or beings."

Good takes its place as the good of a being. Evil as a "bias brought . . . to some being. The good would therefore be the respect for beings, evil their violation." At first, this contradiction appears:

"The good is connected to the beings' contempt for their own interests." According to a secondary conception . . . "evil would be the existence of beings, insofar as this implies their separation."

Simple reconciliation: The good would be the interest of *others*.

I. *(Fundamental proposition). It is a question of opposing not good to evil but the "moral summit," which is different from the good, to the "decline," which has nothing to do with evil and whose necessity determines, on the contrary, the modalities of the good.*

The summit responds to excess, to the exuberance of forces. It takes tragic intensity to its limit. It relates to measureless expenditures of energy, to the violation of the integrity of beings. It is therefore closer to evil than to good.

Decline—responding to moments of exhaustion, of fatigue—grants all value to concerns for preserving and enriching the being. Rules of morality result from decline.

Bataille will show, in the first place, that the most equivocal expression of evil at the summit is Christ on the cross.

"Pilate's executioners crucified Jesus but the God they nailed to the cross was put to death as a sacrifice: crime is the Sacrificial Agent, a crime that since Adam sinners commit infinitely . . .

"The execution of Christ damages God's being.

"Things took place as if creatures were able to communicate with their creator only through a wound that lacerates integrity.

". . . God wounded for human guilt and men who wound their guilt in relation to God find, painfully, the unity that seems to be their conclusion . . . Humanity attains the summit of evil in the crucifixion. But it is precisely in having attained this summit that humanity ceased being separate from God. From here we understand that 'communication' cannot take place from one full and intact being to another: communication wants beings with their being *at stake,* placed at the limit of death, of nothingness; the moral summit is a moment of risk taking, of the suspension of being beyond itself, at the limit of nothingness."

II. *In "communication," in love, desire has nothingness as its object. It is like this with any "sacrifice."*

Generally, sacrifice is on the side of evil, it is a necessary evil, and it would be unintelligible "if men universally" only "communicated" between each other simultaneously with infernal or heavenly shadows. Thus desire—which is the connection in all communication, from sacrifice to sin—sovereign desire, gnawing at and feeding anguish, engages being, my being, in a search for that which is beyond it: nothingness. In this laceration, this painful feeling of a lack, I have a premonition of my absence through which the presence of the other reveals itself, provided that the other is also examining the edge of his own nothingness. *Communication happens only between two beings at risk.* Here we find a similar explanation for the works of the flesh and for sacrifice. The person carrying out the sacrifice and the witnesses to the sacrifice identify with the victim; at the moment of execution, they are leaning over their own nothingness. They understand their god slipping into death. *In this way the sacrificial gift puts the being of man partially at risk and allows it to be united with the divinity's being, which is also at risk.*

III. [*More often than the sacred object, desire has the flesh as its object and in carnal desire the game of "communication" appears rigorously in its complexity. In the carnal act, in desecration—and in desecrating himself—man crosses the limit of beings.*]

[So, what attracts desire in the being of flesh is not immediately the being, it is its wound: it is a point of rupture in the integrity of the body, . . . a wound that puts its integrity at stake, its rupture, which does not kill but desecrates. What the desecration reveals, is also what death reveals: nothingness, the corpse expresses nothingness. In sensuality as in death, nothingness *itself* is, moreover, not that which attracts us any more than it captivates the corpse as such. It is to the artificial aspects—the apparent severity of the dead—that pious respect, calm veneration are bound. Likewise, in sensuality, transposition is necessary for the appeal of nothingness, when "pretty, voluptuous nudity" is triumphant over the risk effected by desecration.][5]

If the nothingness of obscenity indicates the limit where being comes to be lacking, in temptation, the nothingness of the outside appears as the response to the thirst for communication. The meaning and reality of this response are easy to determine. *In temptation being finds itself crushed by the double pincers of nothingness. If it doesn't communicate, being destroys itself in the void that is life isolating itself. If it wants to communicate, it equally risks losing itself:* I communicate only outside of myself, only in letting myself go or throwing myself outside . . . "If I surrender in contemptible conditions I will be . . . fallen in my own judgment."

[Thus "the long resistance in temptation" reveals that much more that communication "occurs only insofar as beings, leaning outside of themselves, risk themselves, under threat of degradation. It is for this reason that the purest beings don't ignore the sewers of sensuality . . . They sense, in extreme aversion, what another exhausts."]

IV. Humans can only "communicate"—live—outside of themselves, and since they must "communicate," they must *want* this evil, this desecration which, putting the being within themselves at risk, renders them penetrable to one another . . . Thus: all *"communication" partakes of suicide and crime* . . . In this light, evil appears as a *life source!* Ruining the integrity of being in myself and in the other, I open myself to communion, I attain the moral summit. And the summit consists not in *submitting to,* but in *wanting* evil.

V. If evil appears "as a means through which we must pass if we want to 'communicate,' as a life source," this is only a fictional relationship: *even the notions of good or being interpose a duration, the concern of which is essentially foreign to evil—at the summit.* Communication, essentially, wanting being to be overstepped: *essentially, what is rejected in evil is concern for the future. It is precisely in this sense that the aspiration to the summit, that the movement of evil— constitutes all morality within us*—a morality with value only insofar as it moves us to put ourselves at risk.

The "popular morality" that appeals to merit and proposes *the good of the being realizing itself in the time to come* as an end in itself admits risk only *for a useful cause.* The nation, the amelioration of the fate of the poor, and so on. ["Popular morality" expresses nothing but a weariness whose greatest adversary takes the freedom of the senses for its object, sexual excesses—"a savage eruption toward an inaccessible summit" and whose "exuberance is opposed by definition to the concern for the future." Because no merit but a lot of reprobation is linked to it, the erotic summit restores luck, whereas the heroic summit attains, at the price of harsh suffering, the restoration of merit— although luck plays in wartime disorder.]

In common judgment, the essence of a moral act is being servile to some utility, to return to the good of some being a movement in which the being aspires to surpass being. In this way, morality is no more than a negation of morality.

VI. Nevertheless, the inordinate expenditures of energy in which the concern for shattering the limit of being engages us are unfavorable to the conservation of this being. Neither crime nor sensuality ordinarily respond to the desire for a summit. But "the torn regions" that they designate "nonetheless indicate the summit toward which the passions tend."

VII. [Christian ecstasy appears, then, *in a single movement participating in the furies of Eros and crime.*]

". . . A Christian mystic crucifies Jesus. His love even requires God to be at risk, that he cry out his despair on the cross. [The saint's crime par excellence is erotic . . .] Every time, desire is the origin of the moments of ecstasy and love that it is: at any point the movement always has the annihilation of beings as its objective. The nothingness at risk in mystical states is sometimes the nothingness of the subject, sometimes that of the being envisioned in the totality of the world . . . The mystical trance . . . exhausts itself in order to pass beyond the limit of being . . . Little by little, desire raises the mystic to such a perfect ruin, to such a perfect expenditure of himself, that in him life compares itself to the glare of the sun."

Nevertheless it is clear . . . that these ruins, these consumptions linked to desire are not real: in crisis, the crime or the annihilation of beings is representation. It is that a moral compromise "rejected the real disorders" (orgy or sacrifice) and substituted the realities of symbols (of fictions) before the desire persisting from a summit, "beings persisting in the necessity of finding in 'communication' the beyond of that which they are." [The sacrifice of the Mass, which represents the real death of Jesus, is still only a symbol in the infinite renewal that the church makes of it. Sensuality took form as spiritual effusion. Themes for meditation replace real orgies . . ."]

VIII. *The substitution of spiritual summits for immediate ones could not take place, however, if we did not admit the primacy of the future over the present, if we did not draw the consequences of the inevitable decline that follows the summit. Spiritual summits are the negation of what could be given as the morality of the summit. They arise from a morality of decline.*

"If I suppress consideration of the future, I am unable to resist temptation . . . To tell the truth, this state of happy openness is not humanly imaginable. Human nature *as such* cannot reject its concern for the future . . . We escape the vertigo of sensuality only while representing some good for ourselves, situated in a future time . . ." and we reach "the nonsensual, nonimmediate summits only on the condition of pursuing a necessarily superior end. And this end . . . must still be situated above the spiritual summit. . . ."

". . . Resisting temptation implies abandoning the morality of the summit, rising again from the morality of decline . . . As long as we are animated by youthful effervescence, we consent to dangerous squandering. But when these forces begin to fail us, . . . *when we begin to decline,* we become preoccupied . . . with accumulation . . . with enriching ourselves for difficulties yet to come. We act. And action, effort can only have an acquisition of forces as its goal. Thus spiritual summits . . . are linked to efforts to gain some good. Summits no longer arise from a *summit morality*: a morality of decline designates summits less by our desires than by our efforts."

IX. *Thus the mystical state is conditioned, commonly, by the search for salvation.*

. . . This link between a summit as a mystical state and the indigence of being . . . must be fallacious . . . A solitary ascetic pursues an end for which ecstasy is the means. He *works* for his salvation: . . . just as a worker works hard for his pay . . . It is insofar as he succumbs to human misery that an ascetic has the possibility of undertaking a lengthy work of deliverance . . . without the lure of salvation (or any similar lure), we would not have found the mystical way! Without this "crude artifice," humans could not have had a "conduct of decline (infinite sadness, the laughable seriousness required by effort)."

X. *We must go further. To formulate such criticism is already to decline. The act of "speaking" of a morality of the summit itself arises from a morality of decline.*

. . . "Speaking" . . . of a morality of the summit . . . the most laughable thing! . . . its construction "supposes a decline on my part" . . . the "summit proposed as an end is no longer the summit: I reduce it to the search for an advantage *in speaking about it.* By taking hopeless debauchery for a moral summit . . . I deprive myself . . . of the power to reach the summit through debauchery."

XI. *Like Kafka's Castle, in the end, the summit is nothing but the inaccessible. It slips away from us, at least insofar as we don't stop being human, speaking. Besides, we cannot oppose the summit to the*

decline like evil to good. The summit is not "what one must reach,"
decline not "what one must abolish." Just as the summit is, in the
end, nothing but the inaccessible, decline is from the very beginning
inevitable.

("The summit is, in essence, the place at the limit where life is
impossible.")

XII. Through history the *reasons* that a human being might have for
going to the summit (the good of the nation, justice, salvation, etc.) have
developed. *"But the difficulty is to go to the summit without a reason,*
without a pretext."

". . . Every gamble, every ascent, every sacrifice being, like sensual
excess, a loss of strength, an expenditure, we must justify our expendi-
tures every time with a promise of gain, be it illusory or not." Even
though a revolutionary action would establish the classless society—
beyond which a historical action could no longer arise—it seems that,
humanly speaking, the amount of energy produced is always greater
than the amount necessary for its production. Hence this perpetual over-
full seething of energy—which continually leads us to the summit—
constituting the malefic share . . . We would lack the motives for action
that hitherto offered pretexts for infinite squandering: . . . What would
then become of . . . the energy that overflows from us? . . .

XIII. Now, Bataille asks once again: *"Is there a moral goal that I*
might reach beyond beings?" and answers: ". . . following the slopes of
decline, I will not be able to meet this goal . . . I cannot substitute a
good for the goal that escapes me."

Bataille "urges" those who "possess a motive" to share his fate: his
hatred of motives and his fragility, "which he deems happy." The peril-
ous situation that is his luck, while he carries this final question within
him "like an explosive charge": *"What can a lucid man do in this*
world? Carrying within him an incontrovertible demand."

XIV. *(Conclusion).* Within hostile and silent nature, what becomes
of human autonomy? "Maybe the desire to know has only one meaning: to serve as motive for the desire to question. No doubt knowledge
is necessary for the autonomy that action—by which it transformed
the world—procures for humanity. But beyond the conditions of
doing, knowledge finally appears as a decoy, when faced with the interrogation that commands it. When this interrogation fails, we laugh.
The raptures of ecstasy and the fires of Eros are so many questions—

without responses—to which we submit nature and our nature. If I knew how to respond to moral questions . . . I would distance myself decidedly from the summit. It is by leaving the interrogation open as an inner wound that I maintain chance, a possible access toward the summit . . ."

2. Father Daniélou's Presentation

The few remarks that I am going to propose don't have the pretension of exhausting the problems posed by the text that has just been read to us. These problems have a definite object, for which this meeting has been arranged, to present a Christian reaction to Mr. Bataille's endeavor. Will this endeavor appear in total opposition to Christian thought? Will we be able, on the contrary, to underline certain rapports, or even certain contributions? I would like to provide a few elements of clarification to begin the dialogue that we will presently pursue.

The first characteristic of Mr. Bataille's attitude is of being "mystical." This attitude seems to me to be defined in relation to the moral attitude. The moral attitude is characterized by "the preoccupation with salvation." The mystical attitude supposes, on the contrary, that one accepts a risk; it is a call to enter into new, never-before-taken paths where one makes one's way "alone like a mineral," as Rille said. Thus the hierarchy of Mr. Bataille's values is not defined in relation to good or evil, but in relation to the mystical or the nonmystical—and the moral sphere is no doubt totally rejected from this last aspect, the mystical domain comprising what is beyond and what is well within morality. In this way he essentially has sin and ecstasy, carnal Eros and divine Eros for his domain. These elements constitute the sphere of the sacred and find themselves reconciled insofar as they are ways of accessing the sacred, although they remain antagonistic.

If one wants to further specify what characterizes this sphere of the sacred, first, it is a place of extremes; Mr. Bataille often uses this word. What brings the saint and the sinner together is being outside average paths, it is their singularity. And through this they exert a particular attraction inasmuch as they represent a rupture in the average order, of boredom, as long as they are subversive. Second, it is negativity: the two attitudes have this in common, that they tend toward a nothingness of being, that they are destructive of all limits, that they aim to dissolve every determination. This will soon raise the question of the equivalence between determination and limit. But it is correct that the sinner and the mystic deny everything that they encounter and that their desire maintains itself in a beyond. One last aspect of the sacred is finally that it is the sphere of communication, because it dissolves precisely the determinations of individual beings and because it permits fusion, like a kind of liquid state wherein there is no longer any separate existence.

That these descriptions might correspond at once to mystical states and to states of sin is an assertion that has already been made by either Origen or Gregory of Nyssa, when they justify the use of the word *Eros* to describe powerful mystical states. In fact, these states present the characteristics of excess, of negativity, of escape, and of fusion that define the sacred. But if there is a formal resemblance here that allows them to be reunited under a similar accolade, elsewhere there is the most complete opposition. And besides, this is nothing to surprise us, since it is this opposition itself which, in situating them at extremes, reconciles the mystical and the sinful insofar as they are extremes.

In one case, excess is in effect a surpassing of moral life, because of the fact that the soul is driven along unknown paths, which it follows without seeing, along which the soul submits to a theophony that elevates it above itself; in the other case, it is, on the contrary, the question of an ecstasy in the realm of perception, in which the soul is dissolved into the mirage of appearances. It is remarkable that the same words might express this double experience: intoxication, Eros, sleep, ecstasy are at once the most pejorative and the most laudatory. Negativity possesses equally contradictory meanings; in one case, according to the mystics, these are all perceptible images, all real desires that yield to the invasion of a light that radiates and purifies; in the other case, on the contrary, sensation totally absorbs consciousness in the moment. Likewise, finally, communication occurs in one case through the destruction of everything that is not of the most profound spiritual means; in the other, it is, on the contrary, this core itself that is disintegrated through sensual discharges.

In this way Mr. Bataille's classification brings together objects that are, in reality, contraries. One might say that there is a search for an equivalent to ecstasy within sin for beings who don't have the courage to confront the desert, the nights, the devastation that drive one to it. This is fundamentally, I think, the case with Mr. Bataille. But he won't grant me this in the least. And for a very distinct reason. For him, sin is in no way an inferior means of access to the sacred, but a privileged means. And why is this? It is that Mr. Bataille retains a distrust in regard to the ecstasy of the mystics, which he considers to be warped by a desire for salvation, so much so that it risks being solidified into a closed-off possession. Sin, on the contrary, always includes a despair that prevents it from turning back on itself, that maintains the open wound. This is important for Mr. Bataille, in whom one senses above all a horror of what would be a closed, self-sufficient world—and with this horror a will to prevent this solidification—this seems very inexact to me. No one is less settled than the mystic, whom God perpetually disturbs and prevents from turning back on himself, for whom all of life is progress and who achieves in ecstasy this total decentering of the self which is in fact that toward which we tend—and which puts them in complete communication with others.

Staying on this subject, sin is a means of access to the sacred. But in order to see it, it is necessary that we deepen our analysis of this notion. Up to now, in fact, we have defined the sacred uniquely by formal traits. But it also possesses a content that is precisely common to sin and to grace—which is their reference to God. What constitutes sin as such, what distinguishes it from failed action, from the πλημμέλημα,[6] is by no means the fact that it does not tend toward its end—or of being a *peccatum*,[7] a false step—in which case we would dismiss it and it would no longer be sin. It is that it offends God, that it is sacrilegious. This is what gives sin its absolutely irreparable, irrevocable character. Thus men are in the grip of sin and are totally powerless to break free from it on their own. "Everything that is not faith is sin," said Saint Paul. Becoming conscious of sin is therefore the decisive act that makes the encounter with the sacred possible—and the act that permits one to part from the sphere of moralism.

Moralism is indeed in one sense the great obstacle to grace. The reason for this is that it creates a self-satisfaction, that of the Pharisee saying: "Lord, I thank you for not being like other men, who are thieves, liars, and adulterers." On the contrary, sin, being a moment of awareness of our radical contamination and of our total powerlessness to free ourselves from this contamination, is the condition for our appeal to God. It is remarkable in this respect that Christ is surrounded by sinners in the Gospels: Magdalene, the adulteress, and the others. And Celsus, the adversary of the Christians, attacked the church in the [second] century, by reproaching it for welcoming brigands and the unchaste. This aspect of Christianity is strongly emphasized in Protestantism, to the point of making sin a constituent element of humanity during our terrestrial life. It is also fundamental in Catholicism.

But one sees how sin is connected to grace. Sin is connected to grace insofar as it destroys self-sufficiency, the spirit of avarice and of belonging. And on this point again, Mr. Bataille is correct. But here, sin only functions insofar as it is *hated*. It is through the presence in the soul of an irrevocable and hated evil that sin determines the experience of total powerlessness and provokes the return to God as the source of the desired grace. It is through the tragic duality that sin establishes in the soul, that is as alienated from itself, that sin becomes a means of salvation, inasmuch as it reveals this fact of belonging to self, discloses itself as guilty, and opens from then on to grace. This is by no means because, in itself, it esteems value, inasmuch as it subverts order, interest, or the establishment.

We must insist on this point so as to avoid any ambiguity, so as to avoid even that ambiguity which was at the heart of Mr. Bataille's lecture. The spiritual love indicated by Christ to the sinners—"I came not for the virtuous, but for the sinners"—is in no way complaisant in regard to sin. He aims only at destroying sin. It would be to completely divert the words of Christ from their meaning, using them to authorize excusing weakness. "There is a kind of hypocrisy which is worse than that of the Pharisees: it is to hide behind Christ's example in order to follow one's own lustful desires and to seek out the company of the dissolute. He was a hunter who followed souls to their burrows; he did not seek his pleasure with easy creatures. But as for ourselves, they are the cause of our undoing, and we do not save them."[8]

We see how sin is in a way an introduction to the sacred, insofar as it drives man to despair and forces man toward the act of faith, insofar as it brings about the transfiguration of the world. There is, therefore, according to the Kierkegaardian schema, innocence, sin, and glory. But glory and sin are two contrary realities that cannot coexist, yet are tightly connected. Mr. Bataille applies himself specifically to making them coexist. For him, once again, the sacred is defined by communication; communication by dissolution. Sin brings about dissolution. And through dissolution, which permits fusion, which is glory, fulguration, ecstasy. One could say that it is only a question of words, that it is about knowing what one means by the sacred; that from the moment one empties the sacred of its relation to God, there is no reason not to define the state of fusion in sin as the sacred. But Mr. Bataille claims that sin retains its guilty character—and therefore its reference to God.

If we look for the reason for this necessity for the presence of sin at the heart of grace, of slander in glory, it is, we will be told, that the triumph of one of the elements would bring a kind of stop, a reconstitution of being—and therefore the end of this state of disintegration, of dissolution, which is the very condition of communication, if communication is constituted precisely by the suppression of beings insofar as they are separate existences. But we can ask ourselves if this state of communicability is necessarily linked to sin. It seems to me that the fear of encountering a stoppage, of being enclosed in a definite order, is at the root of Mr. Bataille's thought on this point. From this point of view, God, insofar as God appears as the foundation of this order, seems to him to be a fixed reality and therefore also a limit.

I think this reveals an incapacity to conceive of, on the one hand, the absence of limits, and, on the other, the entire communicability outside sin. I think that the fundamental Christian doctrine of the resurrection represents precisely the realization of this limitless existence, the overstepping of the limits of biological individuality, a corporal state like liquid and therefore totally permeable and transparent. Mr. Bataille's often reproached negativity, this taste for nothingness sought beyond all beings, seems to me to express this need for the destruction of the individual body, which appears at once in sacrifice and in love, but which is less an appetite for the destruction of the body than of the limits of the body and, in connection with mortality, the fury of the mind to possess a body that participates in its mode of existence.

Second, I think that this fear of a stoppage in the possession of God also comes from a false conception of this possession. I completely understand what Mr. Bataille means when he sees the necessary condition of glory in sin, because sin destroys integrity and because this disintegration is necessary in order to put the being in a communicable state. I myself have encountered this problem. But I think that this condition is not limited to sin, or rather sin is the inferior state of this wound. In its most elevated forms, it is another wound, in other words, despair over not possessing God. Sanctity is the acceptance of this despair as the normal condition of the soul, in other words, total dispossession, through which the soul appropriates nothing for itself and corresponds totally with God.

A third point that seems noteworthy to me is that Mr. Bataille's conception of God corresponds to the God of the philosophers, which in fact seems perfectly sufficient unto itself. But the Christian god is this God in three persons that communicate completely with one another, so that no one possesses anything alone, but they all possess their nature together. Here we have the ideal model itself of communication in which everything that is communicable is communicated and where only personal distinction persists, necessary to make communication possible. Mr. Bataille will possibly say that this reservation is enough to prevent communication in the way he intends it, for which one would require the dissolution of people themselves. But on this point, it seems to me that there is no longer communication, in the sense that, in order for it to be shared, it is necessary that there be something to share—and in order for the integrity of a being to be destroyed, it is necessary that the wounded being persist.

This raises the question that seems to me to be fundamental in our discussion. For Mr. Bataille—I don't know if there is some influence from Buddhist thought—the personality is conceived as a limit that prevents communication. There is identity between the destruction of the limits and the destruction of the ego, the existence of the ego being an obstacle to the passage wherein nothing exists but a state of fusion that is communication, wherein there are no longer any separately existing beings. Every person is egoistic and egoism can only be conquered completely with the disappearance of the person; when sin disintegrates someone, who attains his integrity—and through this renders it communicable. Here there is an equation, which I reject, between the person and the limit. Biological individuality is closed, but the person who can communicate completely, who is limitless, who can be totally immanent to another, is not.

These remarks relative to the notion of sin could be pursued in relation to other theological notions used by Mr. Bataille. I am thinking in particular about the notion of sacrifice that is so important to him, and furthermore about his powerfully beautiful passage on the sacrifice on the cross as a means of communication. Sacrifice is envisioned by Mr. Bataille as the sacred crime, and therefore as an evil that is the means to a good, in other words, communication. The idea that the death of Christ makes God communicable is rich in meaning. But one must not forget that Christ's death on the cross is a sacrifice insofar as it is offered by Christ for the sins of the world—and that it is therefore, in a figurative sense, that one might say that it is the sinners who put Christ to death: in this sense it is because of them and for them that Christ freely offered his life.

I have left the moral and philosophical problems raised by Mr. Bataille's text entirely aside. From the ground on which I have placed myself with my appreciation of the mystical bearing of his attitude, I will summarize my thought. I think that in the negativity, the excess, the communication, the sacrifice, the mystical values, Mr. Bataille might contribute to a revaluation. I think these values take their full meaning only insofar as they are mystical, not only in form, but in content. I think that what leads Mr. Bataille astray from this higher realization is an obsessive fear of spiritual comfort that he believes he senses on this point, and of self-satisfaction. I believe that Christ's message, on the contrary, is a message of gratuitousness and of luxurious expenditure.

3. Discussion

M. DE GANDILLAC: Before returning to and developing the dialogue begun in the two presentations that we've just heard, it would perhaps be fitting to hear the perspectives of several of our friends here today who will enrich our discussion and direct it in various ways. First, I will offer the floor to [Pierre] Klossowski, who would like to introduce an absolutely essential question into the debate, that of the ambivalence of the sacred.

P. KLOSSOWSKI: Given its nature, the particular question posed by Bataille does not pertain to the following crucial problem.

Given that the sphere of the sacred is the sphere of ambivalent relations with God as determined by sin, does Christianity definitively complete and sanctify this sphere? In this case, Bataille would certainly bring a precious contribution, a renewal, a reclarification of our authentic religious behavior. Does it not, in fact, seem as though our theology has abandoned this sphere, through overrationalization, and, in regard to the unspoken fact of our relations with God, those concerning sin in particular, that redemption would no longer appear except as judgment day, a simple settling of accounts.

If it is a terrible thing for man to fall into the hands of the living God, as the Gospel said to the Hebrews, as Bataille correctly informed us, all while pretending to not know this God, to have fallen into the hands of the living God is above all to recognize oneself as guilty before him. But, for Bataille, *not being guilty is not really being at all*. To be guilty or not be, that is the question, because being without guilt, for Bataille, is not expending, it is not being able to expend, and to have nothing to give is to be annihilated by the One who gives all, including what we are.

I think therefore that what Bataille disapproves of as the *morality of decline* is being pure and simple. Thus, it will be even more intolerable to be *this kind of* being before God. Being, for Bataille, is being bored. This is really Heidegger's *Langweile*.[9] Being guilty, on the contrary, is gaining interest against God.

Guilt, in fact, distracts us from this servitude that is the fact of being, comforts the burden of motionless being, and engages humanity in movement for movement's sake, which is never anything but an offensive movement against God. And the advantage of this movement is that man no longer has the feeling of being a simple creature, that God is no longer simply the creator, but that a contestation between God and humanity offers humanity the chance to come out victorious. And the pivot point of this offensive movement is always sin. Thus the constant necessity for sin, the positive function of the generative crime of communication.

Now, I've come to the second term of this alternative. If Christianity, on the contrary, delivered us once and for all from the ambivalence of the sacred, it has, with this act, uprooted sin insofar as pivot of our relations with God. The gift is then being and not guilt. And yet, what is terrible in the fact of falling between the hands of the living God is that our relationship with God can no longer be ambivalent. It is that the pivot of our relationship with God can no longer be sin, but the fact of being as such before God.

Responsibility begins here. We must stop being guilty in order to become responsible. And although it is certain that the religious stage is transcendent in relation to the ethical stage, the religious person's transcendence doesn't integrate the ethical any less. The ethical finds itself religious, and this is why an act conforming to natural law can be a sacred act in the Christian sense of the term. But this really horrifies Bataille, because for him the sacred, so as not to integrate the ethical, so as to disintegrate it, will at the same time be confused with the ethical. This is why his a-theology implies a valorization of evil that is as necessary to him as Macbeth's crime scene is indispensable to the integrity of Shakespeare's drama. Here we are moved entirely into the category delimited by Kierkegaard as the *Interesting*.[10]

G. BATAILLE: What Klossowski has just said seems to me of primordial importance in the sense that the indicated difference is really, or so it seems, something developed throughout history, opposing the period anterior to Christianity to Christianity itself. What seems striking in non-Christian sacrifice is, in fact, that the sacrifice is accepted, that precisely the sacrificial crime is taken on by those who claim its benefit, whereas in Christianity, those who benefit from the sacrifice are simultaneously those who curse it and deflect the blame onto the other. There is a will in Christianity not to be guilty, a will to situate the guilty outside the heart of the church, to find a transcendence of humanity in regard to guilt.

It seems to me that there is some childishness in the nostalgia for a primitive state of things; if the pre-Christian attitude was surpassed, it seems to me that it should have been. However, insofar as I still believe in the possibility of granting the following attitude its development even in the present circumstances, it seems to me that this attitude might in fact approximate more closely that of the human who, not being Christian, took on the totality of this act, at once the cause and the consequence of sacrifice. When the executioner who approached his victim had no possibility, other than through rather rough comedies, which, consequently, held nothing in reserve, had no possibility of escaping the feeling of guilt that they affirmed by the very fact that the ax fell on the head of the victim, it seems to me that the ancient sacrifice was more complete, was the same as sacrifice would be if it were accepted by the Christians who would willfully plunge themselves into sin and think it impossible to avoid descending into the abyss for redemption to be accomplished. This would avoid, it seems to me, what appears to be the essential obstacle of Christianity. If it is true, on the other hand, that Christian sacrifice is itself lost in a beneficial world that appears to me even with regard to the City, to represent a kind of perfection in being, I mean this in the way you meant it earlier, in the Being that is only boredom, that is only the fatality, within which we find ourselves finally enclosed by limits, limits from which we can without doubt escape, but within which the air becomes more and more unbreathable. The air breathed by someone who remains enclosed in the Christian sphere proper might become, through certain openings, relatively fresh at times, but I'm obligated to incriminate the whole. And I'm obligated to reveal that this air has become unbreathable. We all know it and the Christians themselves denounce it. There is, in the fatality within which Christianity is enclosed, in its boredom, something that dominates the present Christian situation, when we are facing the spectacles that the surviving church still offers us, with its disarming aspects of piety in bad taste, of bigotry, and of everything that has become so shocking in the survival of the present Catholic world as seen from the outside. Is it lawful to suppress this aspect of things in one fell swoop? I don't believe that it is. I don't know what flame continues to burn, here or there, within this development. That no one denies it, but that this absence of flame, that this outwardly raging boredom is connected to this dismissal of guilt, to this complete separation between Christianity and the world of sin, this seems to me to be rather shocking evidence given that what does Christianity finally lead to? Nonetheless, on one side, there is the absence of boredom, which is the Christian world. I mean that, of course, it is only a question of the Christian world taken in its complete and gross reality, but, in the end, things are no less there.

FATHER DANIÉLOU: I believe, rather, that the church has disgraced itself in order to allow itself to be invaded by sin, since, by sin, we mean that which is an obstacle to communication, which is to say egoism and folding back on oneself. Perhaps in the Middle Ages there was less separation between the church and the world of sin and perhaps the church was less boring, it's possible; I don't see, for my part, how the invasion of sin would make Christians less boring.

G. BATAILLE: I am not proposing the salvation of the church, but I am bound to note what, unfortunately, others have noted.

P. KLOSSOWSKI: I think our world is crushed by the feeling of guilt and that, in its powerlessness to become conscious of its responsibility before God, it remains enclosed in boredom. I grant you that, insofar as certain members of the church partake in this sickness of the present world, they are "boring" just as the present-day world is "boring."

Why is the world of sin boring? Because it likes its sin without wanting to know it. You always talk to us about the explosion of the world of sin. This world is truly tarnished.

G. BATAILLE: It has sometimes seemed to me that the Christian world was more particularly boring from the side on which sin was absolutely lacking.

M. DE GANDILLAC: Didn't Father Daniélou allude to this boredom when he spoke earlier about "spiritual comfort"?

FATHER DANIÉLOU: For me, spiritual comfort is itself sin.

M. DE GANDILLAC: We are playing with words a little.

FATHER DANIÉLOU: Everyone plays with words. The word *sin* creates an ambivalence.

J. HYPPOLITE: What's serious is therefore not sin, it's mediocrity, which is neither grace nor sin.

M. DE GANDILLAC: But this mediocrity doesn't have the tragic meaning of sin felt as such. We radically transcend the sphere of boredom as soon as we enter the sphere of dramatically conscious guilt.

J. HYPPOLITE: There is a historical obsolescence here that is ineluctable.

M. DE GANDILLAC: We shouldn't transpose the debate onto an institutional level. What we are looking to define here is more an experience that, in every hypothesis, will only ever be the act of a small minority, that will always remain inaccessible to the anonymous and banal masses.

A. ADAMOV: What shocks me the most in the discussion is the tone of Bataille's voice: it seems to me absolutely authentic. The Egyptians were right in making the intonation "of the voice alone" the preliminary condition for the enunciation of all truth. It is very rare, in our day, to simply hear a man speak with an intonation that is truly his own, that conveys a personal experience.

I recognize that Bataille is right when he says that it is the absence of sin that makes the Christian world so boring. But, for me, the notion of sin is inseparable from that of existence independent of any distinct sin. When you think of the etymology of the word *ecstasy*:[11] to be thrown outwardly, you will understand what I'm saying. Ecstasy alone, in throwing man outside of existence, allows him to recover the state from which he has been excluded.

On the other hand, as Klossowski acknowledged earlier, Christianity in our day no longer has a sacred character. Klossowski, dreaming no doubt of a new historical era in which the religious sense would be displaced, sees this as good. But if I glimpse this good, I also see the evil that it implies.

If religions have failed, it is because they have lost their sense of the identity of opposites. Everyone today attacks reason in the name of the irrational. This comes from the fact that rationalism, by the very fact that it is grounded on the principle of noncontradiction, carries within itself all the arguments that one might oppose to it.

Returning to Christianity, I find it very significant that this principle of triumphant reason in the end chased demonic figures from the cathedrals. That Christianity still has a meaning for some men, that it is a real aid to them, this changes nothing. We have entered the night. Still wanting today to belong to a defined religion, in the name of the religious spirit itself, I am saying that this is not possible.

FATHER MAYDIEU: I would like to make two remarks. If I appear to eliminate joy in Christianity, this is because, for many, Christianity is no longer creative. At least, this is the impression that one has during a bourgeois Mass. But there are, on the contrary, places in which

Christianity is essentially creative. In Paris, in a time during which so many people were as though hypnotized, I saw a triple creation within a very small circle:

1. A popular university created on the outskirts of Paris, right next to an SS second officer's school, though it was forbidden by the regulations;

2. An organization created by an abbot, the chaplaincy of the prisoners of war, then the chaplaincy of civilian prisoners. This, with an enormous amount of courage;

3. Finally, just recently (and this is a problem raised by a book that, after all, is not without its faults: *France, pays de mission*)[12] I saw a group of priests (six or eight poor priests, some having money) having given everything and a group of laypersons create, make a Holy Order come about, though it will not be definitive (you know that there are initiatives for Holy Orders, a Holy Order sometimes takes a long time to be born), but making a new order arise as the Mission of Paris.

The second point that I would like to bring up relates to sin. I think we have a lot to learn from sinners. First of all, because we are all sinners; further, I think that there is sometimes a richness in sin that the "wise" man (I'm taking wise in the bad sense of the term) eliminates. Like Daniélou, I think that Christians wouldn't become more distracting if they began to founder in the world of sin, but that they should maintain contact with what we call the world of sin, the world to which they belong, to become conscious of what sinners are. What shocked me in the Parisian mission was the notion of a new apostle, what they call the "intermediary militant," meaning the Christian apostle who, instead of leaving the milieu to which he wants to return Christ's testimony, remains in solidarity with this milieu with all its characteristics and shortcomings. One should go drink, not for pleasure, but because one wants to drink. It is insofar as we will communicate with those who have this same life, these same aspirations, and these same worries that we will be capable of bringing Christ's message to them. In these places of apostleship that take life into their reality, it seems that one sees joy stand out. I have never seen boredom there. I entered into the Holy Orders late. It so happens that I used to frequent the world of sin, I must confess that I was bored there . . . On the contrary, since I put on these clothes, I have never been bored. All the same, fifteen years without boredom, that's not bad.

P. BURGELIN: I have nothing particular to add except that I've been bothered, in some respects, by certain disassociations that have been made, for example, by the opposition of Morality and the Mystical, without leaving a third path. These two paths conceived as opposed, squarely and absolutely, and then, nothing else.

It seems to me that there would be a place, although, for my part, I'm not at all clear on this question, for looking for a third path, which would in my opinion be the path of Faith, which would be neither the path of the Mystic, nor especially the path of Morality.

You should develop this point. I'm stating my annoyance faced with this choice between ecstatic eroticism and pure morality.

M. DE GANDILLAC: When Adamov spoke earlier about a logic of the contradictory and of a possible dialectic, I thought of Karl Barth and I wondered if a true Barthian would pose the problem in the same terms; I would like to know if Mr. Burgelin felt the same sentiment.

P. BURGELIN: For my part, I don't see it at all. In particular, what bothers me is perhaps the idea that one can search for ecstasy, further, that ecstasy is given to someone, this is truly possible, but that one can direct one's life in a systematic search for ecstasy, that's something that shocks me. In any case, from the Christian point of view it seems to me that everything comes from God and nothing from man and that, consequently, a search that comes from man has no kind of meaning in these matters. That Christianity is boring or that it isn't, this is a question that doesn't move me in any way. That has nothing to do with me. I wouldn't, myself, pose the question on this level. There would be a number of points like this. I have been a bit troubled by the opposition that Mr. Bataille made when he identified, in sum, the notion of value and the notion of salvation, the notion of perdition and the notion of grace. Here again, I wouldn't feel at all ready to pose the problem in this particular way. At first, because I would of course make a radical cut between the notion of value and the notion of salvation. And then, because perdition seems to me to be too close to normal human life for me to be able, in this context, to speak of chance, chance always seeming like something necessarily exceptional.

It is precisely because the world of perdition is the "normal" world that the idea of separating the Christian world and the world of sin shocks me, for my part, deeply.

There aren't two worlds; there is only one world, and this is obviously the world of sin. In the world of sin, grace insinuates itself when it can, but that is another problem.

L. MASSIGNON: I was very struck by Mr. Bataille's simple, directly confessional tone. He spoke like a man, like a man who has an experience, and yet one should introduce a little bit, I won't say philosophy, but there is the body and the soul, there is, after all, the question of the death of the body. You spoke of the death of the body in the form of ecstasy. You conceived of ecstasy as a something that was sought after. But ecstasy is not sought after. Ecstasy is sought by Plotinus, but not by the Christians. I deny Plotinus the title of complete mystic. This search for ecstasy is an intellectual search, pushed to its paroxysm. Is this what you're looking for? It seems that you are looking for something more direct from the human assembly that makes attraction, the inner taste of life, intervene. You don't want to define ecstasy with the sign of intelligence. Ecstasy is a physical failing. It isn't through a concerted intellectual desire but through a hollow taste, an abandonment of the desiring will, that one will seek ecstasy. Ecstasy is a negative thing. It reveals the deficiency of the body. This might be the way it is for a saint. It is generally like this for a saint. But the saint's sanctity isn't consecrated at this particular moment. It's found even in a suspended state because it is a mark that the body must die. It's a kind of disjunction. A mysterious disjunction. It isn't even necessary to make a *dolorism*[13] of it by supposing that, having experienced ecstasy, one would desire to experience it again. This is a kind of disjunction that prepares one for the death of the body (except for Christ, whose body was immarcescible).

There is another death about which you said a lot when you touched on extremely direct and profound things within us; this is a kind of spiritual death, what your predecessor in this, Nietzsche, called "the death of God." But here again, after the death of the body, there is a kind of spiritual death so that one may be reborn. I believe that it really is necessary to pass through this; this is the kind of death wherein mystics entirely surrender themselves to God and God withdraws the mystic from himself. But one must not consider this kind of withdrawal that mystics submit to from God as a rhetorical figure. It is a terrifying reality and mystics express it as much more harsh than hell. I think that this spiritual death about which you speak cannot be experienced more strongly than by the mystic who believes in God, because, even through this, if you will, dialectically, he is attached to a kind of nothingness that exceeds him. In the nothingness of his summit, it is a thing that is beyond hell, and I don't think that this is about literature, in any case.

Nevertheless, there are two perspectives: first the perspective of the separation of the body and the soul, the death of the body that is prefigured by ecstasy, then, this kind of death of the spirit that is anticipated by abandonment. Two or three times you alluded to Christ. Nonetheless, with an infinite trepidation for your avowal, but also with personal love, we must return to these two kinds of death again: Christ's agony and abandonment precisely prefigures these two kinds of death, of the end of the body and of a kind of abandonment of the spirit: "why have you forsaken me . . . ?"

For humanity, that we may cross and go to this summit that I persist in believing real—not that we are driven there by an attraction that we might have brought on but because we are called to it, that we haven't sought it out, it sought us out—there is a kind of magnetic attraction. This is what makes the vocabulary of the mystic similar to your own. This is something more profound than ourselves. This can only be consummated by these two kinds of death. There is a distinction between the body and the soul that has been at the base of this debate. We know that we have a personality, and we know that there is a difference between our body and our soul, but up to now I don't think this distinction has been indicated by a technical term in this debate.

G. BATAILLE: Obviously, I've tried to avoid, in a completely systematic way, the use of notions like those of body and soul; they are completely foreign to the general notions that I might have on the level of ontology.

L. MASSIGNON: Even of inner experience?

G. BATAILLE: I don't see the necessity of making this duality of the body and soul intervene in the description of the inner experience or of the mystical experience, from the moment when the latter is not itself built on these notions, as is the case, it is true, in Christianity or in the entirety of mystical experiences.

L. MASSIGNON: Nevertheless, ecstasy is not a thing of the soul. It is a purely physical thing, in the signs that one finds of it. You yourself have noted and analyzed everything that the Président de Brosses[14] indicated in what he recovered of the ecstasy of Bernini's St. Theresa. I don't see any reason to attribute to ecstasies, like those of Saint John of the Cross or of Saint Teresa, a value so closely connected to the body.

I don't think that the experience of the distinction between the soul and the body is a purely academic distinction. I have the feeling that this is something that we must traverse in the form of rupture and disjunction.

G. BATAILLE: In any case, I am, for my part, completely foreign to it. I am as stunned by what you've said as by what Burgelin said, perceiving—and it is principally for this reason that I wanted this meeting to take place—that, in the different experiences that could be had in a mystical life, the same difficulties have appeared today as those that I wanted to underline in their most exaggerated form. You, without my wanting it, brought these fundamental difficulties to our attention when you said—and Mr. Massignon took this up where you left off—that, in fact, we are unable to seek ecstasy. This is a principle that appears to me to dominate the situation. Nevertheless, from Mr. Burgelin's point of view, I mean from the Protestant perspective, I don't think that the thing is transgressed; it isn't like this in the Catholic world, for example, or, no doubt, in other worlds where the mystical experience has been known, from the moment when there has been mystical experience. This experience exists, although we must make this basic reservation in advance, it exists in the form of a project, and even in the form of a textbook. Treatises on these circumstances exist everywhere. Books with the aim of communicating experience, of facilitating, therefore, the path toward it, exist everywhere. Of course, I'm not saying that these books should not have existed; I'm not saying that the mystics, having had their experience, having perhaps felt the need to describe it, should have thrown their books into the fire: I suppose, however, that they have all been tempted to measure the authenticity of their experience. I imagine that the problem that I'm looking to raise today must have been a sort of dominant problem for them. There is something repugnant, perfectly sickening even, in the fact of wanting to communicate the experience not because one can escape the possibility of communicating it—the need to communicate it is too strong—but because, while communicating it, one communicates it to others as a project, one communicates it to others while indicating to them the path that they can follow, one communicates it to others already as the embryo of a degradation of the experience. It seems to me that there is a certain interest in noting, as you've done, that this feeling must have been felt by others in domains that might seem rather divergent indeed.

M. DE GANDILLAC: Maybe we will come back to this aspect of the question. For the moment, it seems like a good idea to offer Hyppolite the floor as he would like to question Bataille on the ambiguous theme of nothingness.

J. HYPPOLITE: Earlier, during Bataille's presentation, it seemed to me that rather diverse sources had been cemented together by an inner sincerity but that, philosophically, they seemed quite different to me. One among them, which was rather Nietzschean, was connected to the problem of Morality, the other posed an ontological problem, which is of a different order. I would simply like to know if this need to go beyond the self, which was consequently the negation of our own being, locates nothingness in our desire or beyond our desire. There are two opposed perspectives here depending on whether it is we who are nothingness, if desire is within us, if nothingness is in the desire itself, or, on the contrary, depending on whether we go into nothingness to escape ourselves. There is a situational problem here that appears rather complex to me.

G. BATAILLE: When I use the word *nothingness,* I put myself on the ontological plane, and by this I'm referring to that which is situated beyond the limits of being.

J. HYPPOLITE: Are we being or is being outside of us?

G. BATAILLE: When I speak of a being, I'm speaking of a particular being and I'm designating myself in particular and generally the egos of others as well. In relation to this ego, there exists an absence of this ego, which one might call nothingness if one so desired and toward which desire doesn't exactly carry us as though it were toward an object, since this object is nothing, but as though toward a region through which the beings of others appear.

J. HYPPOLITE: Notice the importance of this for the question that was put forward earlier; you described this ecstasy; this need to leave the self, as a sort of annihilation of your own being.

G. BATAILLE: No, I didn't describe it, I simply said that, in non-Christian ecstasy, one might have encountered, at any point, the annihilation of being. And, referring to such diverse possibilities, I used a rather vague expression and I don't think I could have done otherwise, other than by dragging out the phrases that I used. By this I simply wanted to indicate that nothingness can be found at any point in the experience, and nothingness is always the annihilation of being, the point at which being annihilates itself.

J. HYPPOLITE: Suppose that nothingness is in us, that it is specifically in desire itself, in what you call being. Wouldn't this rather profoundly reverse the roles? Wouldn't the need that we have of escaping ourselves be a need to escape our nothingness, if nothingness was contained in desire itself?

G. BATAILLE: You're talking about notions that are completely foreign to those that I have developed. It is possible that nothingness is in fact within our desire. I'm not looking to deny it in any particular way. It would be rather contrary to the position that I generally take. But there is always that, developing a certain number of ideas, to which I gave what coherence I could, this notion you're now talking about didn't occur to me and remains quite outside my horizon.

J. HYPPOLITE: It leads to very different valorizations of the beyond.

G. BATAILLE: No doubt.

J. HYPPOLITE: Because there is nonetheless a choice implied in the terminology that you've employed, calling nothingness what is outside and being that which we are.

If, on the contrary, the void is within us and if it is the being that we are looking for outside, wouldn't this profoundly modify your position?

G. BATAILLE: That would modify everything.

J. HYPPOLITE: If you have chosen this terminology, doesn't this choice convey in advance a certain position that doesn't arise from a purely phenomenological description of things?

G. BATAILLE: Like every kind of choice.

Naturally, I tried to offer a faithful description of an experience I had, and it seems that if we are limited to the first experience, we can admit to what I've proposed; if we push the experience further, we can no doubt perceive in desire that we are nothingness. I acknowledge that, for myself, I still don't clearly grasp the possibilities of moving forward in the way that you are talking about. I still don't clearly know where it leads and I don't see how this path that would lead me I don't know where could be situated in relation to the one that I've just spoken about.

M. DE GANDILLAC: I think we would all like to know Jean-Paul Sartre's opinion on this problem.

J.-P. SARTRE: What struck me above all is that you say that there is a beyond being, which is nothingness. But it's you who baptize it as such. If you baptize it as such, it's that you have in yourself the possibility to make the thing appear as nothingness. Where does this possibility come from? If you're full, you don't carry nothingness inside you; otherwise you would not name it as such.

G. BATAILLE: I carry nothingness within me as negation.

J.-P. SARTRE: Where does the possibility for you to have negation come from? We return to the idea of desire. If desire isn't in a sense nothingness, if in yourself you don't have the possibility of making nothingness appear, what is outside of you is in a sense nothing. It is equally a plenum. You cannot name it or make it appear. You have just made it appear as nothingness, you've had that possibility.

During your presentation, you seemed to present being as full being and to present what is outside as the void. I wonder if Hyppolite wasn't right and if the fact even that you've called it nothingness; doesn't bring about a reversal of positions.

G. BATAILLE: All I can say is this: these preoccupations, which I haven't set aside, and which I have from the very beginning recognized as being able to have meaning in what I've advanced, did not occur to me when I constructed this conception, which is relatively simple in relation to the possibilities you are evoking. And, no matter how, being appears for itself as a plenum at any moment, however contestable this first notion might in other ways then appear, and, at another moment, it is the absence of being, the fact that outside me is no longer me, can be called nothingness.

Naturally, I'm not prejudging, in this way, the possibilities of pursuing this analysis. I'm also not prejudging the consequences that such an analytical development might have on the description and on the entirety of what I sought to introduce.

J.-P. SARTRE: I see that the consequences are rather important because, if you've admitted this, one could say that you sought being and not nothingness and that ecstasy is a loss in being and not in nothingness. This is a position that we should examine. These are the two possible positions: either we are plenitudes and what we seek is nothingness, or we are voids and what we seek is being.

G. BATAILLE: To tell the truth, this brings me back to a certain point that I put forward in the first place. It seems that, in the dialectic of my presentation, the movement that you indicate is rather sharply implied. First of all, being, which seeks something beyond itself, doesn't expressly take nothingness for its object but another being. Only this other being, it seemed to me that it could only be reached through nothingness, and nothingness, at this moment, must coincide up to a certain point with a kind of depreciation of the being that desires, with a kind of annihilation of the being that desires since this being that desires is represented as boredom, and that in boredom there is always the cognizance of a void. Besides, I'm not, at this moment, trying to do anything other than respond, in the same way one tries to plug a hole and only roughly, but with this response it seems possible to sufficiently indicate that not only could the perspective that you now describe be integrated into my own description, but that it could be integrated as information.

J. HYPPOLITE: Because of the notion of sin? This isn't certain. It is always possible, but it is ambiguous. And if desire must be supported by being and communication is made by being instead of by nothingness, that would change everything.

G. BATAILLE: The question of being is at risk in the dialectic I talked about, which opposes the ego and the other, and it is correct that I always envision the other as the object of a desire, that the ego is the subject of desire and that this subject of desire is a priori a contestation of itself inasmuch as it is the desire of another. At the same time that there is a plenum in being, there is also the feeling of a void, since it is this feeling of the void that repels it toward the outside.

I admit feeling as if I'm talking about these things only in an approximate and improvised way. They don't disturb me, that's all I can say.

J. HYPPOLITE: If I intervened on the subject of this reversal, it's that it had seemed that your notion of sin and your notion of ecstasy, of the two forms of eros, the mystical eros and the sensual eros, that these two notions were connected to your conception of nothingness.

G. BATAILLE: They are connected to my conception of nothingness in the sense that the passage through nothingness is precisely sin. It can be sin from two points of view; the act of seeking your own nothingness beyond yourself is already a sin.

J. HYPPOLITE: Seeking your own nothingness!

G. BATAILLE: Your own nothingness. This movement already describes the movement of the fall. At the same time, the other being that is absorbed by desire and that can be perceived through nothingness must, in order to be so perceived, be attained in its own integrity, must be in some way communicating with its own nothingness.

J. HYPPOLITE: In nothingness, we communicate one with another. But if this nothingness is in us, isn't sin already in us?

G. BATAILLE: Sin is simply the veil of beings, not exactly nothingness. Even if nothingness is in us, nothingness wouldn't necessarily be sin since sin is the damage done to beings. But, the nothingness that is within us remains there without there being any violation of our integrity any more than there is a violation of the being within us when we don't escape it or when our integrity isn't violated by someone.

P. BURGELIN: Sin, for you, is an act and not a state?

G. BATAILLE: There can also be a state resulting from this act. The state of decomposition, for example.

M. DE GANDILLAC: Isn't sin first a refusal?

G. BATAILLE: To tell the truth, the multiplicity of situations is such that one can always envision that at some moment sin assumes the look of a refusal.

P. BURGELIN: And not essentially?

G. BATAILLE: Essentially, no. I conceive it as an act. To tell the truth, this doesn't follow, this narrowness of mind doesn't follow from the church's description, in which sin is presently greed . . .

M. DE GANDILLAC: Historically, the fundamental sin is first presented as a voluntary and conscious refusal.

G. BATAILLE: That's not exactly the conception I have developed.

J. MADAULE: Sin against the Holy Ghost.

G. BATAILLE: That's an obscure notion, for me, as it is, I think, for most people.

M. DE GANDILLAC: Allow me to make my question more specific: it seems that you see sin as a quite essential means for being to escape a certain bourgeois comfort, a certain hardening, a certain self-satisfaction, a complacency in one's self and one's boredom. But this liberating sin, is this sin for you, meaning essentially the refusal of an offered gift, or do you rather envision sin as a series of acts through which life expresses itself, the taste for adventure, the taste for risk?

G. BATAILLE: I haven't claimed to speak about sin in the self, or to speak about sin in the quite specific and general sense in which the Catholic church describes it; besides, I wanted to depart from a less than simple notion that associated crime and sensuality. It was in these representations of crime and sensuality that I sought to situate what I call sin.

M. DE GANDILLAC: In fact, the word *sin* is so linked to Christianity that it is difficult to use it in another way, without first defining this other meaning. This is why I venture to question you. This is why I asked the question. In the Christian perspective, it seems that sin is essentially neither crime nor sensuality. That it's a question of Adam's sin or a question of Satan's sin, which are nonetheless fundamental, here you find refusal and disobedience, revolt and ambition, but not sensuality, nor crime.

G. BATAILLE: Without doubt.

M. DE GANDILLAC: Murder only appears with Cain. Consequently, it is not a primitive act.

G. BATAILLE: It's just that I'm having trouble seeing what sin might be as far as the value that it assumes for the soul, if it's not an act. If I refer to my own experience of sin, either through personal memories, or through an awareness of the other, I have the impression that we connect the horror of sin to a positive action, to the idea of an intervention that is simultaneously a fall, because this act makes us pass from one state to another, from a state of purity to a state of decomposition. And, in my mind, what's more, from a state of autonomy and folding back on oneself, to a state of opening, of injury.

J. HYPPOLITE: This is grace itself; what you are valorizing as much as sin in the act of self-denial is the act of succeeding in denying the closure of oneself on oneself, which you valorize either in the form of sin, or in the form of ecstasy; and with this act, you oppose this escape from the self, this negation of the self, to a morality that you envision on a Nietzschean level as a kind of greed, like the result of decadence, of a vital deficiency because of which we attempt to anticipate and to accumulate.

G. BATAILLE: That's right.

J. HYPPOLITE: You are therefore opposing an act that is an escape from the self to a morality that is entirely centered on the preservation of one's own being.

G. BATAILLE: That's right.

J. HYPPOLITE: Escaping the self which, by the fact of calling it nothingness, facilitates the assimilation of sin and of what the Christians might perhaps call grace.

Doesn't the use of the word *nothingness*—see why I insisted on this terminology—just to refer to what is outside us, make your assimilation of sin and of grace easier, for example, than your opposing one and the other on the level of a Nietzschean morality against the conservation of the self?

G. BATAILLE: This assimilation doesn't seem easy to me since I'm not making it, and, if I'm not making it, obviously, this is so as not to give precedence to the notion as one of grace, which might interfere with the rather fragile construction that I've developed today, but which comes up in quite a different form, in the form of luck. I'm not, therefore, preoccupied with knowing if grace, insofar as it intervenes in the soul of someone who has an experience, came from without or within. I picture it as luck, and luck includes the ensemble of the elements in question. Consequently, luck is unable to come about, either from within or from without. Luck is the coincidence of the ensemble of elements, coincidence as possibility is open. And, in this sense, obviously, there is finally an assimilation of grace and of sin, because luck makes sin possible and luck alone. But luck cannot be identified with sin itself, because it is simply the ensemble of coincidences that make it possible.

J.-P. SARTRE: I would like to know why Bataille uses the word *sin* and if he couldn't maintain the same ideas without the notion of sin, which seems to me to refer to values that he, however, rejects.

G. BATAILLE: It seemed to me possible to use the term so as to simplify and simultaneously to accentuate the debate.

J.-P. SARTRE: You don't believe that at this moment you're making the debate possible, whereas it would have been impossible?

G. BATAILLE: It doesn't seem so. What Father Daniélou said a little while ago obviously went in the direction of the possible debate.

J.-P. SARTRE: When Father Daniélou talks about Christian sin, it has a very distinct meaning for him. When he asks if sin is closer to God or offers a larger opening to humanity, it has a very specific meaning for him, a meaning that refers, moreover, to the whole of Christian life. When you talk about sin, it seems that you're talking about entirely different things under the cover of the word.

G. BATAILLE: Entirely, and that's what I don't believe. It seemed that there was a possibility of throwing a bridge across the two uses. I don't doubt that this would be to build a bridge and that, consequently, from the point of view of a certain logic, it is an absurd notion. But isn't it that often enough these bridges thrown across elements that are put in question don't have much value? It seems that they intervene constantly. Why wouldn't they intervene in a debate?

J.-P. SARTRE: When you say *sin*, you personally, implicitly, accept the existence of a certain number of values. But in relation to what? Do you really accept values? You spoke of sensuality and crime; how is crime a sin? Because it is a violation of beings? Who forbade the violation of beings, for you?

I don't see why, according to your principles, one wouldn't violate beings as one would drink a cup of coffee.

G. BATAILLE: It's obvious that I spoke a bit quickly and that I should have gone into very specific considerations. Sin is defined, on the one hand, by God's commandments. It's obvious that, from God's commandments, I've retained only a part; I have, on the other hand, elided the fact that I referred to a universal experience of the separation of acts into good and evil.

J.-P. SARTRE: That changes everything. There's a good for you. And, in that case, you're beginning to want this good, to position it so as to no longer want it afterwards. That becomes a moral and metaphysical position that is sustainable elsewhere but that is very difficult and that is sufficiently different from the one that you've maintained for us this evening.

G. BATAILLE: You've stated my position exactly. Following this reasoning, I adopt definitions that exist, generally speaking.

J.-P. SARTRE: And these definitions of the good, as, following this reasoning, you've adopted them, are drawn specifically from a moral world that you, however, challenge, so that just as you commit the sin, you are on a level where this morality loses all meaning for you. It's no longer a sin that you commit, it's . . .

G. BATAILLE: You're exaggerating my position when you say that I challenge it. No doubt I introduce a point of view from which these notions must be challenged. Still, these notions, I offer them first as existing, as the foundation of the reactions that contest them.

J.-P. SARTRE: Once you contest them, they fall completely outside you, and sin stops being sin even then. You escape from them and you are denying them by the very act itself. You cannot simultaneously regard what you do from the perspective of the morality that you are contesting while calling it sin. One might say a "revolutionary act," an act that rejects all of Morality; this offers a curious way of maintaining a morality even while denying it, and, on the other hand, even if we accepted this morality, we would have the idea of a wrong and not necessarily the idea of sin.

G. BATAILLE: It seemed to me that there was a kind of irony in the act of maintaining in this way notions of good and evil that I didn't believe in. I don't think I attached any other meaning to it. It's possible that this should be considered vicious and, besides, irony is, by definition, vicious.

J.-P. SARTRE: In fact, morality must not torment you much when you commit a sin. And sin effectively becomes less agonizing and less tragic.

G. BATAILLE: To tell the truth, it seems that you sin by way of an exaggeration in the logical sense. We are not the simple beings that logic would insist we are. Logic would insist that we separate ourselves, that we divide, that we put this to the left, that to the right, and in reality, we are this left and this right. There's someone within me who, if, for example, he killed someone, would feel that the act he had just committed was abominable. This is strong in me, I don't doubt it, not that I've had such an experience . . . I have the very distinct feeling that if I committed this act, I would fall into a kind of hole and I would have the experience of sin, I think. This doesn't prevent me from transgressing the possibilities I've just described, from envisioning a beyond in relation to these possibilities, and a beyond that implies, precisely, the feeling of sin or the feeling of evil that I might have had.

A. ADAMOV: Don't you think—I'm sorry to change the subject once again—that if a man is led, by naming certain conditions, to commit an act condemned by morality, let's say he gives in to a particular kind of debauchery, an orgy, for example, that this man will necessarily know demoralization—whether he believes in sin or not? Demoralization flows even from the nature of his search. It is the unavoidable consequence of the dispersion that this search involves.

J.-P. SARTRE: I think, if I establish this demoralization as a value, I would make another kind of morality evident even in this value. This is something that bothers me to the same extent: do you or do you not attribute a value to the states obtained through sin or in sin? For example, to the ecstasy of the sinner. If you attribute value to them, you set forth another morality. Likewise, we can very easily obtain a kind of disintegration, with narcotics, but if we seek it, it becomes a value.

G. BATAILLE: I've pretty much indicated my position on this subject. I spoke of a morality of the summit, which I opposed to a morality of decline, and finally I concluded by simply noting that, from the moment when I spoke of the morality of the summit, I was, in reality, speaking in the name of the morality of the decline.

J.-P. SARTRE: That makes the position rather delicate.

G. BATAILLE: It makes the position perfectly weak, perfectly fragile. And it is exactly in this sense that I spoke from beginning to end. I spoke only of an untenable position.

J.-P. SARTRE: Significantly, you have said "when I speak": and you skillfully made the fault fall on language. But there is, on the one hand, the presentation that you're making and, on the other hand, your concrete research. It is this research alone that interests me. If the language is distorting, then you are at fault. We are at fault when listening to you. What counts is the time, the moment when, without speaking or speaking the least possible amount, you realize sin. This moment exists, and it is this moment that is important. It isn't here today, but we are talking about it. You cannot seek its realization without establishing a value.

G. BATAILLE: Naturally, I pose values and I have indicated that in posing values in several ways I have ended up in an inextricable situation.

J.-P. SARTRE: Then it's no longer a question of a contestation of morality by an I-don't-know-what that would be beyond morality. This gives us a coexistence of two moralities: one inferior, the other superior.

G. BATAILLE: Naturally, and the superior one is obligated to renounce itself because, at a given moment, it perceives that its own values have developed in the name of the inferior morality. Consequently, it renounces itself and disappears, and everything enters into the night.

J. HYPPOLITE: That makes a third morality; this renunciation itself is a third sense of value.

G. BATAILLE: The movement of contestation having begun in the second, there isn't any difference between the second and the third; it is the contestation that follows its course. One perceives, at a given moment, that contestation cannot stop on itself and that it is like an acid that corrodes itself.

J. MADAULE: The value is nothing, in sum, but the contestation of every kind of value. There is only one value that is the contestation of values, that of being superior or inferior.

G. BATAILLE: Exactly. This is what it's a question of in the end.

J.-P. SARTRE: We agree. But it is a morality, the morality of the search.

G. BATAILLE: From the moment we said it, we said too much.

J.-P. SARTRE: Finally, it is not the second morality that falls into the abyss in order to make a third, it continues. These are the avatars of one and the same morality; when you perceive that you are seeking values for moral comfort, you abandon them, but your demands remain the same and you are always on the same plane.

G. BATAILLE: In all moralities, whatever they are, the values have only been created by the clash of two systems: the system of contestation, on the one hand, and the positive system of the separation of good and evil, on the other—what I call, on the one hand, the decline and, on the other, the summit.

What seems serious to me is that, from a point, it is possible to be deprived of the faculty to describe a good and an evil that would be sufficiently persuasive that one might maintain the other side of things, what I call the ascent to the summit.

In order to ascend to the summit, one needs a pretext, in other words, in order to give oneself up to contestations and to a system of the contestation of oneself, so as to realize these violations of the integrity of the being that I was talking about, one needs a pretext that is borrowed from notions of good and evil and, in this way, one can practically say that the die is cast. This is what, on the whole, Father Daniélou emphasized earlier when he showed that the Catholic church described quite different possibilities, that Christianity, with sin, enabled us to prevail upon the state of things that is no longer sin and to situate the Christian outside sin in this way. But, specifically, at a given moment, that I sought to reveal—it seems that the present conditions are given for this—that this possibility is lacking, that, consequently, man was forced to choose between two paths: one that would consist in self-annihilation, in renouncing any kind of escape outside himself, in sum, in fabricating an economy of rational expenditure, which would be limited to the production of the sum of energy necessary for fabrication, which would consequently eliminate everything that is pure waste from life, pure expenditure, pure luxury, pure absurdity; the other, according to which it would maintain an expenditure, a luxury, a waste that would have no more reason for existing than itself. Besides, it seems to me that this moral problem is easier to conceive and easier to perceive in extremely crude forms because, in fact, there is nothing more banal than saying, about such luxury, about such waste, that it happens for such and such reason, that it is for this or for that that Mr. or Mrs. So-and-so has a party, that it is for this or for that that a group or a tribe has a festival. But after a certain moment, we can no longer say that. It would seem that we get away from it (I say "we" because I am under opposing appearances) so reasonably that we finally come to lose the faculty of granting a motive to our expenditures. We haven't so much gained the faculty of giving these expenditures a limit that would reduce them to the value of energy necessary for production. No. There still exists a considerable overflow, an overflow that it is necessary to expend as we wish, and the moment comes when, in order to expend this overflow, one will no longer have any kind of motive because it will seem to be nonsense.

J.-P. SARTRE: Sin, according to you, has a dialectical value, meaning that it disappears from itself; it has the role of pushing you toward a state wherein you are no longer able to recognize it as sin.

G. BATAILLE: Naturally.

J.-P. SARTRE: Whereas, according to Christians, on the contrary, even if it escapes, sin remains what it is. Consequently, this is not at all the same notion. It is something that appears at a given moment, that serves as an aid, that brings you to a kind of scandal, from which you then arrive, through contestation, at a state that is the one you are seeking. At this moment, you can no longer take it for sin.

G. BATAILLE: As in every dialectic, there is a surpassing and not a suppression. Now, I'm referring to the Hegelian dialectic, I'm not making a mystery of the fact that I am Hegelian more than anything else, without being Hegelian through and through.

The notion of sin connected to action is easily recognizable as Hegelian negativity, the negativity that is action.

J. HYPPOLITE: For Hegel, I'm not sure that it doesn't lose its characterization as sin. Is it sin that returns itself to negation or negation that returns to sin?

G. BATAILLE: It seems that the negativity that is action is always destructive.

J. HYPPOLITE: As Sartre was saying, your discourse uses Christian language and has a Christian ambiguity; this is possibly Hegelian as well. Did you need this for your humanist ethics?

G. BATAILLE: I needed it for this discussion, so that the present debate would be facilitated.

J. HYPPOLITE: Certainly not only for that, this isn't only to facilitate a debate. You need this Christian notion of sin for yourself, for the morality of the summit.

G. BATAILLE: I used it in my book with more prudence than I have today, and much less often. Today, I have emphasized it to a large extent.

J. HYPPOLITE: The question is: are you able to do without this language? Could you transcribe your experience without it?

G. BATAILLE: It wouldn't be easy. I would have to paraphrase.

A. ADAMOV: In any case, instead of *sin,* you could say *fault.*

G. BATAILLE: The ambiguity would remain.

J. HYPPOLITE: Fault is not the same thing; fault is situated in the morality of decline, it isn't of the same order as sin.

G. BATAILLE: This notion seems convenient to me because it refers to states lived with a great intensity, whereas, if I talk about faults, abstraction intervenes.

FATHER DANIÉLOU: I think that without this notion your work would completely lose its coloring, and, in a sense, it's an element that seems quite essential to your work. I have the feeling that Sartre, earlier, was trying to enclose you in his own position and that, in reality, you exceed that position precisely in what constitutes you as yourself, which is this kind of refusal to allow yourself to be enclosed in any position. I have the feeling that if you no longer had this idea of sin, you would immediately lose what particularizes your own position. I don't know if I'm expressing myself clearly enough. This is a point that I don't think you can let go of without practically abandoning, almost completely, your position.

J. HYPPOLITE: After reading your book just once—I don't know your work—my impression was the following: someone who absolutely needs the Christian position, because, in order to dispute the Christian position, the Christian position is indispensable. This isn't a question of another language, it's a question of the ambiguity of this Christian position, an ambiguity that we can reproach you for from the Christian side just like any other. That's your originality. If I omit it, I would no longer have your book.

G. BATAILLE: Your impression is quite correct. All the same, I think that what's incorrect is the illusion that I gave of needing this position in order to deliver myself to sacrilege and, in this way, find a moral life that I would not have found without sacrilege and, consequently, remain within the Christian orbit. Besides, it's obvious that I set myself up for this accusation, as my mistake. I don't think I anticipated that it should have been so distinct. I really thought you'd notice something else, what I might call informality. If I've been informal, it is because I don't care, it's because I am enclosed nowhere, it's because, beginning to end, I felt a feeling of ease that surpasses all the common rules for these situations.

I must say that I haven't felt in the least bit sacrilegious, that I didn't care, that all that I hold dear is not being enclosed by any notion, passing beyond notions infinitely, and, so as to be able to surpass them in this way and prove myself to myself—and if necessary prove this informality to others (up to now I haven't been too successful)—I needed to close myself off or to depart from situations that closed other people off in the past. It seems that I couldn't find anything else. If I had been in another country, if I had been in the Orient, or if I had been in a Muslim culture, or Buddhist, I believe I would have set out from quite different notions. I departed from notions that had the habit of closing certain people off around me, and I made light of it. That's all I did. But I expressed it very badly. I think that I particularly failed to express the gaiety with which I did this. This might be inherent in a profound difficulty that perhaps I failed to convey and that I still encounter today:

beyond a certain point, burying myself in my troubles, I found myself betrayed by language, because, in terms of anguish, it's rather important to define what might be felt as an excessive joy. If I expressed joy, I would be expressing something other than what I felt, because what I felt was, at a given moment, informally related to anguish. But it's important that anguish be appreciable, that informality be anguish, and the informality is, at a given moment, as it comes no longer to know how to express itself, as it comes to let itself be expressed, on this side, in a normal way. Furthermore, it seems that someone might realize this difficulty rather easily, even in a matter-of-fact way, by showing this: that, no matter how, language is inadequate, language can't express an extremely simple notion, for example, knowing an idea of a good that would be an expenditure consisting of a pure and simple loss. If, for humanity, I am obligated to refer to being—and you see immediately that I'm introducing a difficulty—if, for humanity, at a given moment, loss, and loss without any compensation, is a good, we are unable to reach the expression of this idea. Language is lacking because language is made of propositions that make identities intervene, and after the moment when, considering the excess to be spent, we are no longer obligated to spend for profit, but to spend for spending's sake, we can no longer contain ourselves at the level of identity. We are obligated to open ideas beyond themselves. I think that this is probably one of the most singular of the positions that I developed. Taken together, in a quite general way, the people that I endorse are open as opposed to closed. What distinctly separates me from what Father Daniélou said earlier is that he is, in the end, obligated to endorse individuals who, no matter how, close themselves off. I mean an individual who is closed despite his desire to be open, and this is all too noticeable in the history of theology. If I refer to Gregory of Nazianzen in particular, it seems particularly striking. But it's always that, no matter how, the movement is more powerful than one's regrets. No matter how, the being closes himself off, and the being of God, and the being of the church are closed beings, while those beings that I endorse are open, meaning fundamentally ineffable beings, beings that can't be described as such, since, in being open, they are hardly beings; they are continuously decompositions; because thought itself fundamentally cannot apprehend them, but is destroyed by them.

J. HYPPOLITE: What also struck me about your book was, on the one hand, the problem of luxury, of complete expenditure; and, on the other hand, that of communication. What you gain in expenditure is communication.

G. BATAILLE: Exactly.

J. HYPPOLITE: While you never attain communication through a moral project; you attain communication only through expenditure. Is it therefore communication that we are looking for in expenditure? Or is it expenditure alone? Do you place a value on communication to be obtained through expenditure, or do you make expenditure the supreme value? It's very different. If it is through expenditure, through surplus, that I obtain communication with other beings, what is essential for me is this communication. Expenditure is only a means, or rather, is expenditure the main point?

G. BATAILLE: It seems that, in real life, it is impossible to separate these notions since, in expenditure, desire brings a being that is other and, consequently, no longer expenditure itself, but communication.

J. HYPPOLITE: All the same, there is an ambiguity in these vitalist notions of expenditure.

Could you have written your book in the vitalist language that you employed in the example of the productive society? Could you have written your whole book, enclosed all of your thought in this language alone: the accumulation of reserves, the reserve of energy, and, on the other hand, expenditure?

The word *communication* can have two meanings. It can signify the negation of the self, and I lose myself in this annihilation . . . or it can signify finding another "me," another being for itself. This isn't quite the same thing. This is the same problem as that of nothingness that you set up earlier. Is this communication communication with another me, a "for itself," and why does expenditure make this communication possible for me? In the sense of "he who wants to save his soul loses it"? Is this it? Fundamentally, it's that in wanting to save myself I am lost: in losing myself I attain the other me. So that communication is superior to expenditure. Expenditure is only the means of attaining communication.

G. BATAILLE: You've quickly isolated the differences between two kinds of communication that are on the order of the differences that we isolated between closed beings and open beings just a moment ago. Communication can, in fact, direct the open being or it can direct the closed being. In the second case, we should speak of union, or rather of the desire for union. We can speak precisely about desire for union and we end up nearly cutting ourselves off in ourselves after such a union. We find this just as often in the theme of marriage as in the theme of the church. The theme of marriage can be opposed to the pure, mystical life. Earlier you introduced these two notions in an adequate way. In maintaining the difference in beings, I don't see the possibility of inserting, with regard to value judgments, any great precision in regard to the difference between expenditure and communication. The value judgment that I am introducing rests on the difference between the closed being and the open being. But it cannot rest on the difference between communication and expenditure, which appears to me to be more of another way of speaking about the same thing—with differences obviously between these two ways of speaking—than differences that could support a value judgment.

J. HYPPOLITE: This is very serious, because it seems that what I desire in expenditure is really communication with others. One can't attain it in marriage, or in the church, or in a closed being; but communication for you ends up signifying negation alone; it is no longer positive communication, no longer a positivity that would be the negation of a negation. The use of the word *communication* as we find it, for example, in Jaspers or in a few others, means not only my negation, but again finding another me, or entering into a relationship with the other. And that has quite another meaning than the negation of the self alone.

G. BATAILLE: I wouldn't say negation exactly, I use the phrase "putting into question." Obviously, I argue for the interrogation of oneself and of the other in communication; and it is not only a question of the communication that would result in a union that precisely I would in turn put into question.

J. HYPPOLITE: Absolutely in agreement.

G. BATAILLE: Questioning is not exactly denying, because questioning is living just the same.

X: What struck me is what Bataille said just now. Bataille identified the world of sin with what he calls the absence of boredom and he opposes it to the Christian world that he characterizes as the world of boredom.

Well, inasmuch as I am a Christian, I must recognize that there is a certain truth to what you say, but this opposition wouldn't exactly be justified because one can't oppose the Christian world as such to the world of sin, because the church is composed of sinners. These notions interpenetrate one another. We are, all of us, sinners and we can't not recognize it. But, on the other hand, if we oppose the church to the world of boredom, to the world of sin, it might in this sense be justified in saying that there is a certain Christianity—if you will, a Christianity of Pharisees—that opposes sin with something rather boring, something that isn't weighted to counterbalance sin, virtues, for example, a certain morality, and that, surely, is a world of boredom.

Father Daniélou, in recalling Kierkegaard's saying according to which sin is connected to grace insofar as it destroys suffering, demonstrated that sin is a pivot, insofar as it maintains the place between ignorance and grace; in this particular sense, it seems that if one can oppose something to sin, it's not virtues, but grace. You say: for you, sin is a certain escape from the self. One can recognize a certain value—negative, if you like—that designates a final goal, a goal that we must attain and that we can't attain down here. Sin maintains such a place in us! We are living uniquely in sin. We live in sin so that we stop seeing it. We breathe it as we breathe air. This sizable place that sin maintains in us is just the one that should be maintained by grace toward which we are called and in which we realize ourselves. We realize ourselves in coming out of ourselves. In order to realize ourselves as people, it is necessary to escape ourselves, escaping this tiny envelope that we must break, which is our suffering, the suffering of an individual. There are two exits: one is sin, the other is sanctity. It seems that the exit through nothingness that you were talking about is a false exit, precisely for lack of another, which is the only valid one for the Christian: the exit toward the fullness of grace.

G. BATAILLE: I'm astounded by Father Daniélou's mention of Kierkegaard, on this subject; he said that the church always saw the great sinners as people who were kind of neighbors to sanctity. Here I will add that it is lawful from quite another point of view to see the great saints as people who were very close to the largest of sins. Perhaps one might consider, on one side and the other, the saints and the debauched as failures, as people who failed, and I think that in truth they each have their reasons. The accomplishment of humanity, the totality of humanity, supposes simultaneously sanctity and the sin of sanctity in one human being, not really as what would be the best for him, but in some way as his goal, which is to say his impossibility, this maybe to which he is definitively driven.

FATHER DANIÉLOU: I think it's this tragic tension between sin and sanctity that brings together the saint and the sinner, as opposed to those who remain in the realm of morality.

G. BATAILLE: It seems that what differentiates me most expressly from you is the abandonment that I must make of any kind of good worth realizing on earth, of every kind of action that might appear to me as being done before, which deprives me of every possibility of stability from the moment I no longer have the support that you have, the support that carries you down the path of the closed being, that carries you away sometimes despite yourself, if it's a question of yourself, and sometimes wanting it, if it's a question of the church in its entirety. From the moment when this point of support is lacking, it suddenly becomes impossible to qualify sin as the church does; it also becomes impossible to find the least amount of stability because what one encounters crumbles on all sides. There are only words in the night, exchanged by chance, with a single devotion: luck. One must say, this is one of the most painful devotions, the most expensive, the one that leaves you at the mercy of the worst, whereas, all the same, the Christians at the mercy of grace don't seem to be so underprivileged. It seems that Christians have spoken a lot about grace and about the unhappiness that it risks making appear at every instant, since it can be lacking, but it is always that those who spoke about it are the ones for whom grace generally isn't lacking. And this seems rather astounding because, definitively, in the Christian system, in this system which is founded, in this system which is ordained with the order of things, one can't see why grace would be unavailable to someone who merits it.

FATHER MAYDIEU: It isn't when grace is lacking that this instability is produced, it is on the contrary when there's too much grace that it's necessary to locate a stability that is no longer ordained by the order of things. No longer being obligated to such or such an act precisely, the Christian should endlessly invent new acts, go beyond a good that overtakes all good. It isn't when grace is lacking, it is when it is overabundant that the Christian rejoins some of the requirements that you have just been outlining.

G. BATAILLE: It seems that in the excess of grace, one rediscovers a situation neighboring the ones that I pointed out.

FATHER DANIÉLOU: "He who loses his life . . ." is an evangelical expression.

G. BATAILLE: With the exception that I can't accept the term *evangelical*. Which changes everything.

FATHER DANIÉLOU: You don't accept it because you interpret it in a certain way. Salvation doesn't mean—it is on this point that one clashes with you—it doesn't mean greed, possession, turning back on oneself, it means quite simply, orientation, value. It seems that the weak point of your thesis is this identification between greed and every value.

J. HYPPOLITE: We are coming to express your conception very clearly—better than I had understood it at the beginning—of two terms on the ontological level: the Other and me. There are only these two terms. For a Christian, the Other is qualified; despite everything, it is above all determination, but above everything is God, who is not closed.

M. DE GANDILLAC: Negation by transcendence.

J. HYPPOLITE: The problem of nothingness is really fundamental here.

M. DE GANDILLAC: Whether one puts the accent on negation or on transcendence, each one will have different forms of spirituality. But neither in one case nor in the other am I completely sure that you can corner the Christian, as you seem to, on one issue alone: as consciously or unconsciously seeking closure.

I think the attempt at a spiritual stripping away has always been described by those who've lived it in an intense and authentic way as a total spoliation, including even the renunciation of any search for a God that could be defined in a perfectly positive way, the way one might know the program of salvation precisely in advance. The mystic tends toward a plenitude that corresponds to no project in the correct sense of the word and which is a kind of empty promise.

FATHER MAYDIEU: As an example of instability, one might cite the parish priest in Ars, who must have seemed to be the most stable man, the most certain to those he counseled, but who, according to him, no longer knew what he should do. He was the parish priest and he wanted to enter a convent. The great saints are always beings who are unsettled by their plenitude.

G. BATAILLE: What will happen if, founded on an order of things that truly is clear, you attain instability in spite of everything? What will happen to those who don't have this foundation from the beginning? What can one foresee of what will happen to them thereafter? Furthermore, it seems that they are generally destroyed. And why would they not be? Unless human existence really has a faculty of ceaselessly going beyond itself and of torturing itself up to the limits of torture, such that being born again indefinitely, despite the pains that we will have experienced and in spite of the instability that will be continually felt as such, existence follows its course as something perhaps rampant in a certain sense, triumphant in another, without which one can draw nothing from it, perhaps even know nothing about it.

M. DE GANDILLAC: I wouldn't want to ask you an indiscreet question, but I feel more at ease with you now, because we've all been convinced by your tone. As Adamov was saying, if there were those among us who might occasionally doubt the profoundly authentic character of your experience and of your whole book, this suspicion has absolutely been dispelled by the tone even of our conversation. I think I can ask you this question in all sincerity: isn't there in fact a certain contradiction between the informality that you were talking about earlier, this kind of joy and indifference, and despite everything, the tragedy of the situation in which you willfully enclose yourself?

G. BATAILLE: It doesn't seem so to me. I don't perceive this contradiction.

M. DE GANDILLAC: You don't live your contradiction in a permanent way.

G. BATAILLE: Nietzsche says that it's necessary to perceive tragedy and to be able to laugh at it. It seems to me that this is a rather complete description of these possibilities.

M. DE GANDILLAC: There are two laughters.

G. BATAILLE: On the subject of Nietzschean laughter, one thinks of mocking laughter. I spoke of laughter, and was portrayed as forcing it.

M. DE GANDILLAC: That's another laughter, which isn't peaceful laughter.

G. BATAILLE: It isn't peaceful laughter; forced laughter is the most foreign to me.

M. DE GANDILLAC: Romantic irony . . .

G. BATAILLE: I can only speak of a vigorously happy laugh, vigorously puerile.

FATHER MAYDIEU: One sees this encounter between tragedy and laughter in Christianity. And Claudel made a variation in the Passion when he applied the text of the wife to the Virgin Mary: she laughed at the new day . . .

G. BATAILLE: That is more Claudelian than Christian. It is astounding that it's difficult to cite passages from the Old and New Testaments wherein someone is laughing. The Bible is truly a book in which no one ever laughs.

FATHER MAYDIEU: But, there is a strong woman. This isn't the same laugh as the one you're talking about.

I really liked what Burgelin was saying about the call of faith. Whether it is faith or ecstasy, it seems that morality is justified only in what exceeds it.

G. BATAILLE: In any case, you are safe from what awaits me, at least in your spirit.

M. DE GANDILLAC: The Christian is the least safe.

G. BATAILLE: I speak about it gaily. I don't mention it in order to complain.

M. DE GANDILLAC: I would love to know Gabriel Marcel's opinion.

G. MARCEL: I would have too much to say. I am especially in agreement with what Hyppolite and Sartre said.

The only thing that I will say continues one detail: I think one can perceive not informality but the will to informality in Bataille's book. I think there is a big difference between the two. At least there is from the perspective of the reader.

G. BATAILLE: Earlier I said that I had succeeded rather badly in expressing this informality. I don't think I'm in any condition, today, to do better.

M. DE GANDILLAC: This has more to do with the perspective of the book than the perspective of the conversation.

J. HYPPOLITE: I would also like to make a distinction between the perspective offered by the book and that of the conversation. I didn't know your work, I have truly come to understand your position better here than in your book—insofar as you will grant me that I have understood it. Did we want to enclose you in a system that was much too logical for you . . .

G. BATAILLE: I don't think so.

M. DE GANDILLAC: Mr. Massignon had to leave us before the end of the discussion. If he had been able to take the floor again, he would have reproached Hyppolite and Sartre for having locked you up in the framework of a purely abstract logic that doesn't correspond to your experience.

G. BATAILLE: I don't see why I would deny the contestation offered on this level. Besides, it isn't so uncalled for. I don't see why it wouldn't be relevant to other points of view.

J. HYPPOLITE: I wanted to hold you to it in order to show the logical surpassing in your experience. Written in another language, you work would not produce the same impression, if, for example, you did without the Christian concepts that perhaps you could, logically, do without. Your book would have been infinitely less interesting to me if it had been written differently. I'm not talking about the interest in "informality." But, in spite of everything, you could perhaps logically do without these Christian concepts. It seems, however, that the experience would be lost. There is a depth in your experience that surpasses every logical system.

G. BATAILLE: It seemed to me that most of my friends decided to refer to an exclusively non-Christian world, if you will, to poetic experiences. It seemed to me that I succeeded in escaping this narrow-mindedness through frequent references to the Christian world and by perceiving, by not hesitating to perceive, possible connections, in spite of an opposition that I believe is fundamental and that seems to have been underlined quite violently, because, all things considered, with the exception of a very small number of representatives of the church and of Christianity in general, I doubt that anyone could calmly hear what I was able to say today.

However, whatever this difference, to which I still attribute the greatest importance, might be, I don't regret that the possibility of a bridge over an otherwise extremely deep abyss might have appeared possible today, the possibility of a bridge across which we might pass—it isn't a question of passing from one side of the abyss to the other—but of a bridge that we might reconcile with itself, which would permit the perception of the continuity of an ongoing human experience, a continuity from the pre-Christian era to Christianity, and from Christianity to other possibilities.

M. DE GANDILLAC: Doesn't this bridge, which you are completely correct in perceiving, imply a form of communication that is precisely the one that we are testing in this moment, which is completely different from the one that you described as the only possible form of communication, another communication than that of mutual destruction?

G. BATAILLE: This doesn't exclude mutual destruction.

M. DE GANDILLAC: Is friendship a possible thing for you?

G. BATAILLE: Certainly not. Friendship on the plain we're talking about isn't possible. My relations with Christianity can't be friendly relations; they are purely and simply hostile.

M. DE GANDILLAC: I was talking about friendship in a much more general sense.

G. BATAILLE: Why not? A little friendship in the awareness of a complicity.

FATHER DANIÉLOU: All the same, it seems to me that there are a certain number of things that we reject together and that permit the unity of the debate.

G. BATAILLE: The unity of the debate depends on your placing mystical life before the church, which is at bottom the main point of my position.

FATHER DANIÉLOU: Yes, in the sense that you oppose mystical life and the church, as that which is open and that which is closed.

But this formula is obviously unacceptable if we grant these words their true meaning.

G. BATAILLE: In relation to you, I feel like the opposite of someone who, calmly from the shore, watches ships that have lost their masts. I am sure that the ship is demasted. And I must insist on it. I'm enjoying myself, and I'm watching the people from the shore laughing, I think, much more than someone else watching the demasted ship from the shore, because, in fact, in spite of everything, I can't imagine someone so cruel as to be able to perceive, from the shore, the demasted ship with a very free laugh. Foundering is something else, we can dedicate ourselves to it with great pleasure.

J. HYPPOLITE: It's Zarathustra's laughter.

G. BATAILLE: If you like. In any case, I'm surprised that some people could see it as so bitter.

J. HYPPOLITE: Not bitter.

G. BATAILLE: To tell the truth, I'm unhappy myself.

G. MARCEL: All the same, it's a story that ended badly . . . A simple historical reference.

G. BATAILLE: Then what?

G. MARCEL: Was Nietzsche still laughing in Turin? I'm not sure he was.

G. BATAILLE: On the contrary, I think he was laughing at that moment.

M. DE GANDILLAC: We aren't talking about laughter in Turin.

G. BATAILLE: But what does anything mean at that point?

Part II

Method of Meditation

If man didn't sometimes *sovereignly* close his eyes,
he would end up no longer seeing
what is worth being looked at.
—René Char, *Leaves of Hypnos*

Foreword

My ambition in the following pages is the most remote ever known.

However worthy of interest a political task might be—or anything else etched in such bold ideas—(in such moments, I think, I judge, imbued with the sense of my limits: the humility of a comical character, indifference to oneself, the happy negation of sloth liberates me from hesitation): I am aware of nothing intended by man, by a man who reduces himself by giving in to some subordinate operation (some operation that differs from that which arrests me, from a *sovereign operation*).

I imagine that I would weaken the affirmation of my fate were I to explain myself further. And I would willingly limit this foreword to these few words, but I believe the moment has come to dissipate, if it's possible, the misunderstandings created by the disorder of my books, when they touch on the subjects discussed below.

I

I situate my efforts beyond but alongside Surrealism.

A daring, defiant demand manifests itself under the name Surrealism. It was confused, it's true, often letting loose the prey for the shadow. The present confusion, general settling (today, which is the least demanding?) sometimes appears preferable to me. Nevertheless, Surrealist ambitions persisting, I don't think I could say exactly what I just said. And, anyway, I am astonished by today's revelations: with rare exceptions, I see neither intellectual consciousness, nor temerity, nor desire, nor force around me. Still, I am able to speak only with exasperation.[1]

II

My method is at the antipodes of "Yoga."

In principle, a method of meditation would have to address the teachings of yoga (Hindu concentration exercises).

It would be pleasant if some manual existed, stripping the yogis' methods of their moral or metaphysical beliefs. These methods, moreover, could be simplified.

Prolonged calm, deep breathing, as in sleep, like an enchanting dance, slow concentration, irony, thoughts toward the void, a skillful juggling of the spirit on meditational themes, the sky, the earth, and the subject successively collapse, this could be the object of teaching. Removed from this discipline, such a description would help us attain the "ecstasy of the yogis."

In action, the value is appreciable in that it isn't the shortest means of escaping to the "sphere of activity" (if you prefer the real world).

But this is exactly why it is the best *means*. On the subject of yoga, the question is rigorously posed: if *resorting to means* defines the sphere of activity, how can we ruin this sphere, when from the onset we speak of *means*? Yoga is nothing if not this ruin.

III

My reflections are founded on a "privileged" experience; nevertheless, "to go the furthest possible" has no meaning once one has recognized the primacy of a "continuum."

By *continuum*, I mean the continuous surroundings of the human group, opposed to a rudimentary representation of indivisible and decidedly separated *individuals*.[2]

Among the criticisms made of *Inner Experience*, that which gives "torture" an exclusively individual meaning reveals the limit, in relation to the *continuum*, of the *individuals* that have made this criticism. There is a point in the *continuum* wherein the trial of "torture" is inevitable, not only undeniable, but, situated at the extreme limit, this point defines the human being (the *continuum*).

IV

Nothing separates me from man in general; I take the totality of what is upon myself.

The common exclusion of the worst (folly, vice, indolence . . .) seems to me to denote servility. The *servile* intelligence serves folly, but folly is *sovereign*: I can change nothing with it.

V

The essential is inavowable.

What is not servile is inavowable: a reason to laugh, to . . . : ecstasy is the same. What is not useful must hide itself (under a mask). Addressing himself to the crowd, a dying criminal was the first to formulate this *commandment*: "Never confess."

VI

The apparent laxity of rigor expresses only a greater rigor, to which one had to respond in the first place.

This principle must be inverted again.

The rigor apparently affirmed here and there is only the effect of a profound laxity, of the abandonment of something essential that is, in any case, the SOVEREIGNTY OF BEING.

Part I

Contestation

The idea of silence (the inaccessible) is disarming!

I am unable to speak of an absence of meaning without giving it a meaning it doesn't have.

The silence was broken, when I said . . .

Some "lama sabachthani" always ends the story, betrays our inability to keep our mouth shut. I must give meaning to that which lacks meaning. In the end, being is offered to us as impossible!

This immense folly, this arrogant childishness, this boorish futility of laughter, and the entirety of an ignorance frozen in servile mania returns to me from every side with an identical response: *impossible!* Man, the being that is here, is in every sense the *impossible* incarnated. He is the inadmissible and admits only, tolerates only that which makes him deeper: inadmissible, intolerable! Lost in a maze of aberrations, of deafness, of horrors, eager for tortures (eyes, fingernails ripped out), endlessly thrown into the satisfying contemplation of an absence.

Whether one dares to hope for escape, amending this, cursing that, denouncing, condemning, decapitating, or excommunicating, depriving (it seems) of value (of meaning) that which others . . . , one engages some new platitude, new ferocity, new hypocritical bewilderment.

But how (I ask everyone) could I renounce your folly? When I know that, without it, I would not be! What would I be—what the rocks or the wind are—if I was not an accomplice to your errors?

I am a cry of joy!
This isn't a mistake, it isn't horror that fans my flames.

I think the way a girl removes her dress.
At the extremity of her movement, thought is shameless, even obscene.

Under no circumstances is an excessive conflagration contrary to the murderer, to the usurer, to the teacher. It forsakes neither the lost girl nor the "man of the world." It completes the movement of foolishness, of insipid jest, of cowardice.

Meditation I

An important person, I demand an audience.

With a kick in the behind, the minister leaves me in a huff.

Enraptured, I enter the waiting room: the kick transports me, marries me, penetrates me; it opens within me like a rose.

Meditation II

I find a glistening worm between two graves.

In the night, I place it in my hand.

The worm looks at me, penetrates even my shame.

And we lose one another in its gleam: we commingle, one with the other in the light.

The wonder-struck worm laughs at me and at the dead and I marvel equally, laughing at being divined by a worm and by the dead.

Meditation III

The sun enters my room.

It has a thin neck of flowers. Its head resembles the skull of a bird.

It grabs a button on my jacket.

Strangely, I take hold of button on my shorts.

And we look at each other like children:

> *"I take you,*
>
> *you take me,*
>
> *by the beard.*
>
> *First . . ."*

•

Every problem is in a certain sense a problem of the *use of time.*
This implies the preliminary question:

—What do I have to do (what must I do or what is in my interest to do or do I desire to do) here (in this world where I have my human and personal nature) and now?

Writing, I wanted to touch the depth of these problems. And having given myself this occupation, *I fell asleep.*

My response expressed the day's fatigue. But this image remains faithful to my view of the world. This profoundly expresses the nature of the being in the operation of knowledge: the being cannot be indifferent that an inclination counters the desire to know.

If it is being striving to reach its limits, philosophy must first resolve a primary problem in the person of the philosopher: Is this occupation (this striving to attain one's limits) urgent? For me? For humanity in general?

The fact that it isn't for a large number of people is usually attributed to *primum vivere* (that is, "to eat"), on the one hand; on the other hand, to some insufficiency on the part of those who have the time for philosophy (not intelligent enough, weak character).

If philosophy is only one science among many, only with a different domain, the urge is to consider it a *subordinate* task, where the calculation of inconveniences and of advantages is brought back to judgments foreign to the problem at stake. But if it is knowledge with no other end than itself, the calculations brought back to other ends deprive the operation of its exceptional character (emasculate it, align it with minor activities, and willfully restrict it from knowing). From this: the professorial tradition of philosophy and the accumulation of materials that in no way resemble the sovereign operation. And not only do these kinds of work not lead to this operation, they turn away from it (blind, prevent knowing its urgency).

The criticism Hegel addressed to Schelling (in the preface of the *Phenomenology*) is no less annoying. The preliminary work of this operation isn't within the capacities of an unprepared intelligence (as Hegel says: likewise it would be senseless, if one were not a cobbler, for one to make a shoe). This work, in its mode of application, nevertheless inhibits the sovereign operation (a being going the furthest that it can). Specifically, this sovereign character demands our refusal to submit this operation to preliminary conditions. The operation takes place only if urgency appears: if it appears, it is no longer time to begin works in which the essence is subordinated to ends exterior to oneself, which are not ends in themselves.

Scientific work is more than servile, crippled. The needs to which it responds are foreign to knowledge. They are:

1. The curiosity of those who do crossword puzzles: a discovery fails to provoke interest, the search for truth supposes a "pleasure of not knowing" (Claude Bernard):[3] scientific truths fundamentally only have value when *new*; we measure the novelty of old discoveries after centuries;

2. The needs of the collector (to accumulate and organize curiosities);

3. Love of work, intense output;

4. The taste for a rigorous honesty;

5. The worries of an academic (career, honor, money).

At its origin, often enough, a desire for sovereign knowledge, to go as far as one can go, a desire so quickly born, nullifies itself, by accepting subordinate tasks. The disinterested type—independent of application—and the persistent use of empty words make the exchange. Science is practiced by men in whom the desire to know is dead.

For now, I am not trying to define the *sovereign operation*. It is possible that I have spoken of it without even knowing it. And if necessary I would admit that speaking of it as I did is childish (it indicates an inability to gauge my possible effort). It nevertheless remains for me, having imagined it, to reveal to myself the lure of subordinate operations.

Now I have to start over:

Servility ordinarily specifies its limits: to contribute to the advancement of mathematical sciences, or of others . . . From limit to limit, one happens to pose, at the summit, some sovereign operation. And I add: the path that leads toward this summit is not the subservient operation. One must choose: one is unable to subordinate oneself to some ulterior result and "to be sovereignly" at the same time. (Because "to be sovereignly" means "not being able to wait.") Although an authentic sovereignty demands that they have been as complete as possible, I am unable to escape from subordinate operations. At the summit of intelligence there is an impasse where the "immediate sovereignty of the being" decidedly seems to alienate itself: a region of sovereign folly, of sleep.

Beyond a certain point, foolishness is inescapable. My intelligence offers me the comfort of stupidity (a calm certainty). The idea is breathtaking. Still, it suffices to be indifferent: begin a friendship with odious chattering, with silences, with terror, with whims. A friendship that you cannot imagine. Nothing seems more foolish to me than the sovereign contempt for others to which my position condemns me. My sense that I am losing myself in a void opens illumination to lightness "without form and without mode." I would gladly define ecstasy: feeling gay but anguished—from my immeasurable stupidity.

•

I no longer sustain this poignant emotion, this light as if airy intoxication, linked to excessive tensions.

My feelings already enclose me as in a tomb and yet, above me, I imagine a song similar to the modulation of light, from cloud to cloud, the afternoon, in the unbearable expanse of the skies . . .

How can I avoid the intimate, never-ending, horror of being? . . . This heart crying a thousand tender joys, how can I fail to open it to the void?

My joy extends an ungraspable game to infinity. But I know the
night is falling. Black tapestries fall on all sides.

Long, sad death, smothered silence of a tomb, under a living,
wormy grass, underlines this sense of airy lightness, this gaiety lost to
the height of stars.

And nothing . . .

•

I WALK WITH THE HELP OF FEET, I PHILOSOPHIZE WITH THE HELP OF
FOOLS. EVEN WITH THE HELP OF PHILOSOPHERS.

I incarnated the ungraspable.

If I lead being to the extreme limit of reflection, to its misunder-
standing of itself, like the infinite, starry expanse of the night, I FALL
ASLEEP.

And the IMPOSSIBLE *is there. (I am* IT.*)*

How could I fail to recognize philosophers from all eras whose
never-ending cries (powerlessness) say to me: YOU ARE THE IMPOSSIBLE?

How could I lack, who better than I, an adoration for these voices
echoing the misunderstandings that men have of themselves and of the
world in the infinite silent expanse?

Sleep of reason! . . . and, as Goya said: THE SLEEP OF REASON CRE-
ATES MONSTERS.

The essential is the aberration. The biggest comedy . . .

What is the worst aberration?
That which we ignore, gravely holding out for wisdom?
That from which, when we see it, we know there is no escape?

•

From extreme knowledge to vulgar understanding—generally the
most divided—the difference is nonexistent. In Hegel, our understanding of the world is one of the first things we understand (the *first*
understanding to occur, not Hegel himself, decides the key question for
him, touching on the difference between madness and reason: "absolute knowledge," on this point, confirms the vulgar notion, is founded
on it, is one form of it). Vulgar understanding is in us like another *tis-*

sue! The human being is made not only of visible tissues (bony, muscular, skin), but of a tissue of understanding, more or less extensive, appreciably the same in each of us, found equally in all adults.

Works preparatory to philosophy are (negative) criticisms or growths of tissue.

In a sense, the condition in which *I would see* would be on leaving, on emerging, from "tissue."

And without doubt I must say immediately: this condition on which *I would see* would be dying.

At no moment will I have the possibility of *seeing it*!

The philosophers that one opposes to me are just so many ways of weaving within the fabric of the tissue, stupidity is the only contribution that agrees with me. Rigorous stupidity (linking them to this series of ruptures that undo the mirage in which activity encloses us, making us laugh ceaselessly) is the window through which *I would see,* if it was, from the start, the sleep (death) of intelligence (of the apparatus of vision).

The sphere of known elements wherein our activity inscribes itself is only the product of our intelligence.

A car, a man enters a village: I *see* neither one nor the other, but the tissue woven by an activity of which I am a part. Here where I imagine *seeing* "what is," I *see* the *links subordinating* the activity that is there. I do not see: I am in a tissue of consciousness, reduced to itself, to its servitude, the freedom (the sovereignty and the primary nonsubordination) of what is.

This world of objects that transcend me (in the emptiness within me) encloses me in its sphere of transcendence, encloses me in some way in my exteriority, weaving a network of *exteriority* within me. In this way, my own actions annihilate me, opening a void within me, a void *to which I am subordinated.* Nevertheless, I survive this alteration by binding ties of immanence (returning me to indefinite immanence, which admits superiority nowhere):

1. *Erotically.* I see a woman, I draw her out, strip her from the sphere of objects linked to activity—*obscœna* are immanence itself, we are generally absorbed, integrated in the sphere of objects, but with genitalia, we still hold on to an undefined immanence (as if with an indestructible, hideous, hidden root); (otherwise genitalia, erotic connections, it's true,

are perishable: no matter to whom we bind them, common activity tends to substitute those objects that are subordinated to us for erotic connections . . .).

2. *Comically.* We are carried in the stream of hilarity: laughter is the effect of a rupture in the link of transcendent connections; these comic links with our equals, continually broken and continually retied, are the most fragile, the least heavy.

3. *Bonds of kinship.* We are connected to our parents by our birth, and bound thereafter to our children.

4. *Sacred bonds.* Uniting ourselves with the fundamental immanence of a whole of which we are a part; beyond that, as in each relation of immanence, indefinite immanence (the limitations of the group define the hybrid character of the ensemble that is united by the bonds of immanence); as with finite objects, these ensembles have the possibility of transcendence (the community transcends its members, God, the soul of the faithful, thus introducing new voids in the interior of the domain of activity); they substitute themselves for pure activity, they subordinate themselves to the chain of objects, they propose themselves as an end, but, conceived in the transcendent mode of the objective world of activity, in the long run, no longer differing from this world, these ensembles are its sumptuous doubles.

5. *Romantically.* Touching on the love of nature (of savage nature, hostile, foreign to man); the exaltation of eroticism from the heart, the cult of poetry, of poetic laceration; giving value to fiction to the detriment of the *order of things,* of the official and real world.

•

The domination of activity is accomplished more than corrupted by the domination of the state, this "empty block," introducing into the inert conscience a dominant share of stark elements (transcendent, of another nature, colorless).

In myself, the state opens a sad and dominant void that, truly, gives me a polluted disposition.

Activity dominates us (and likewise the state) in making acceptable—possible—that which would be *impossible* without it (if no one worked, if we had neither police nor laws . . .). The domination of activity is the domination of the *possible,* is the domination of a sad void, a decay in the sphere of objects.

To subordinate ourselves to the POSSIBLE *is to let ourselves banish stars, winds, and volcanoes from the sovereign world.*

God subordinates himself to the POSSIBLE, *diverts chance, renounces the choice to exceed limits. The star exceeds divine intelligence. The tiger has the silent and lost grandeur that God lacks. Man is genuflection . . .*

Fear extends the shadow of God over the world like a Catholic school uniform over a perverse adolescent girl's nudity.

Whatever fever carries it, the love of God announces: (1) an aspiration to the state of an object (to transcendence, to definitive immutability); (2) the idea of the superiority of such a state. The order of things asked of God not arbitrarily but essentially is SUBMITTED *to the principle of the* POSSIBLE: *The* IMPOSSIBLE *is no longer my disadvantage, it is my crime.*

One says of the content of the word God *that it exceeds the limits of thought—but no! It admits a point, a definition, limits. This narrow aspect is even more striking: God condemns the shame of the child (if the guardian angel sees him in the wardrobe); he condemns the limitless right to silliness and to infinite, discordant laughter, which, since it is neither God nor matter, nor the identity of God and matter—since it is unbearable and yet there, impossible—screaming! impossible—to the point of wanting to die!*

•

We alleviate the empty character of the transcendent world through sacrifice. Through the destruction of a vitally important object (the alteration of which, resulting from an utilitarian use, was painfully felt), we shatter the limit of the *possible* in one moment: The *impossible* was, at this point, liberated by a crime, stripped, unveiled.

Earlier, I said: "My own actions annihilate me, opening a void within me, a void *to which I am subordinated*. Nevertheless, I survive this alteration by binding ties of immanence . . . 1. *Erotically* . . . ; 2. *Comically* . . . ; 3. *Bonds of kinship* . . . ; 4. *Sacred bonds* . . . ; 5. *Romantically*. . . ." I have shown nothing except the necessity of forming these connections, "to shatter the limit of the *possible* in one moment." A bond of immanence demands a preliminary laceration from the transcendent system of activity: such as stripping someone bare, childbirth, putting to death . . . (In the realm of comedy, a joke reveals the impossible at the heart of the possible. In principle, the romantic impulse erects laceration, not without vain ostentation.)

•

At the limit of silence, to speak in the heavy dissolution of thought, lightly slipping into sleep—without sadness, without irony, without surprise—responding softly to the demand of the night, already brings not the absence but the disorder of these processes.

Often enough, sufficient leisure is left for me to order my thought, in obedience to the rules. But today I express this movement: "Sleep invades me . . .": It is more difficult! In other words, I arrive at the sovereign operation, wherein thought accepts no subordinate object and, losing itself in a sovereign object, annihilates the demand for thought within itself.

If my book means, "you, the most intelligent man, this new Hegel . . . (or any other), are nonetheless the most stupid, narrow, and nailed to the 'possible' by inertia . . ." (how can I conceal that, generally, existence seems under water to me, subsumed in stupidity—in error? That is its condition; this is the condition of consciousness, at the limit of the laughter that denounces it . . .): I don't mean that I . . . "You are more intelligent, but I anesthetize my intelligence in order to relieve myself of yours."

Reassured: "Humanity aspires to stupidity . . . more than to philosophy (a baby leaves us enraptured)."

•

I don't worry about myself: I would love to count on the other (the distribution of being in numerous individuals has little importance).

But I have known no interrogation more tiring than mine.

On all sides, I perceive, as the fruit of labor, a naive freeing of power connected to the capabilities of man exerting his intelligence!

With a puerile carelessness, we grant *possibility* to existence (the possible nature) that everything contradicts in the end: this is the result, this is the postulate of labor. When I am laughing or having an orgasm, the *impossible* is before me. I am happy but every thing is *impossible*.

The simple truth:
Servile activity is *possible* (on the condition of remaining enslaved, subordinate—to other men, to principles, or even to the necessity of production—human existence has a *possibility* in front of itself).

But sovereign existence is in no way, for even an instant, separated from the *impossible*; I will live *sovereignly* only at the *heights of the impossible* and what does this book mean if not:

LEAVE THE POSSIBLE TO THOSE WHO LOVE IT.

In spite of everything, my life was also an immense chore. In paying this price, I got to know a, to my taste, sufficient share of human *possibility* (which today allows me to say: "the *possible*, yes, I bowed my head!"). Nevertheless, what gave me the power to write was having, sometimes, loved *doing nothing* even more.

I see hardly anything in idleness (rather, I imagine I have an excess of vitality). At thirteen years old (?), however, I asked a fellow student who was the laziest in their studies? It was me. But out of the whole school? Me again. In those days, I made my life difficult, *by failing to write under dictation*. The teacher's first words docilely took form under my pen. I remember my childhood notebook: I quickly limited myself to doodling (I had to maintain the semblance of writing). I was unable to do the homework for the coming day because I had not listened to the text: under redoubled punishment, I lived for a long time as the martyr of indifference.

What is an accomplishment if it isn't granted in a privileged experience? It is a moment of silliness in the end.

And the master himself, *if he so commands,* is subordinate to his own orders: sleep and laughter, at the summit, mocking him, detach themselves, forgetting. So much anguish in indifference? But whom can one believe? Do these words announce the raptures of ecstasy?

. . . some words! They exhaust me without respite: nevertheless, I will go to the source of the miserable possibility of words.

There I want to find that which reintroduces—in a point—the sovereign silence that interrupts articulated language.

Part II

Decisive Position

Principles

1. If I wish it, *to laugh* is to think, but this is a sovereign moment.

2. To say that in laughing I open the depth of worlds is a gratuitous affirmation. The worlds' open depths have no *meaning* in themselves. But for this reason I can bring other objects of thought into contact with these depths.

3. In common knowledge (which philosophy surpasses, but to which it is connected), every object of thought corresponds to a solid. This point of departure is such that no other is conceivable: knowledge proceeds from the solid, poised as the known, which one assimilates, so that one may know that which is still unknown.

4. Every operation returns thought to the position of a subordinate solid. Not only through its particular end but through the method followed: the solid object is an object that one can make and use: *is known as what one can make and use* (or what we assimilate, so as to know it, to that which we can make and use).

Good sense returns the world to the sphere of activity.

5. Returning to an attitude (long affirmed), I will now say:

—that I haven't received (accepted) a subordinated world that wanted me subordinated;

—that I saw the revelations brought by a burst of laughter as being the essence of things, to which I freely assented;

—that I made no distinction between laughing at a thing and possessing the truth; that I imagined seeing no object at which I didn't laugh;[4]

—that it wasn't only comic themes, but the existence of "what is" in general, and myself in particular, that made me laugh;

—that my laugh engaged me, thoroughly delighted me, and had no limit;

—that I already had a vague awareness of the overturning I brought about; I thought that, having explained laughter, I would know the meaning of man and the universe, that having left laughter, on the contrary, unexplained, knowledge avoided the essential;

—but all of this with authority.

6. Today I add:

—I do not *see* the object that does not make me laugh but only its relation to the sphere of activity (the relation of this object to a solid—to what we are able to make and use);

—likewise, common knowledge returns objects to solidity, in the moment of their subordinate activity: I am able to return them to the sovereign moment when I laugh.

7. To return objects of thought to sovereign moments supposes a sovereign operation, different from laughter and, generally, from all common effusion. This is the operation in which thought stops the movement that subordinates it, and laughing—or, abandoning itself to some other sovereign effusion—identifies itself with the rupture of those bonds that subordinated it.

8. The sovereign operation is arbitrary and although its effects legitimated it from the point of view of subordinate operations, it is indifferent to the judgment of this point of view.

9. Descartes's "I think" is connected, in spite of everything, to our consciousness of not being subordinate, but:

—this consciousness is unable to exist at the point of departure of objective knowledge;

—Descartes understood that, in its developed—and *subordinated*—form, beyond the "I think," thought has no basis in itself, but only in the manipulation of solids;

—the relation of objects to thought free of chains is a point of arrival, before which a multitude of operations developed without thought ever having any other "object" than a subordinated one (in principle, the idea of freedom designates the ability to choose between two or several subordinations).

10. In a sovereign operation, not only is thought sovereign (as it is if we laugh) but its object is sovereign, and recognized as such, independently of its insertion in the useful order: what is, is subordinate to nothing, and, revealing itself as such, makes us laugh, and so on . . .

11. The sovereign operation, had it been possible only once, science returning objects of thought to sovereign moments[5] remains possible (does not present any insoluble difficulties).

It encounters some obstacles nevertheless:

—Not only does the sovereign operation not subordinate itself to anything, it is indifferent to the effects that might result; if, after the fact, I want to attempt the reduction of subordinated thought to sovereign thought, I am able to do it, but the authentically sovereign has no cure, at every moment it disposes of me in another way (this is what I said in the first part);

—The voluntary subordination of operations of subordinate thought to the sovereign moment, although it does not introduce any particular presupposition (like a theology or a philosophy)—but only the arbitrarily chosen position of a moment of being (to which one will be able to relate, or *not to relate,* objects of thought)

—No longer allows thought to proceed haphazardly as science commonly does, advancing only where it can and, for lack of means, placidly leaving decisive problems to be resolved. *From the beginning* I had to operate in a global way, *from the beginning* to succeed in propositions chosen for a reason other than the possibility of establishing them. An approximation, even an error, was apparently better than nothing (I was able to return to this point through what followed, in any case, I couldn't free a void): the description I had to make could only have carried the ensemble of the tableau. This method proceeded from the authenticity of my process, this authenticity imposed itself, and if I may describe an outward aspect of it, to speak of it, I could not *prove* it through considerations that only a subordinate mind would know to introduce.

12. Some consequences of such usage of thought proceed in another way from the possibility of a misunderstanding: knowledge relating objects to the sovereign moment in the end risks being confounded with this moment itself.

This knowledge that one could call free (but that I prefer to call neutral) is *the use of a function detached (free) from the servitude that is its principle: the function related the unknown to the known (to the solid), whereas dating it from the moment when it detaches itself, it relates the known to the unknown.*

13. What I've just said seems to oppose itself to the fact that without a sketch, at least, of neutral knowledge, a sovereign operation could not be represented. I may, if I so desire, have an attitude, a sovereign manner, but if I *think—when a man cannot distinguish himself from his thought*—in principle, I take the subordinate character of common operations of thought into consideration. Sovereign thought (without which basic sovereign moments finally insert themselves in the order of things) wants a conscious coincidence of a sovereign moment and an operation of thought. But if some movement, some first attempt at neutral knowledge, *begins* a sovereign operation, the possible developments of this new mode of knowledge are distinct.

The sovereign operation *engages* these developments: they are the residue of a trace left in the memory and of the subsistence of these functions, but, insofar as it takes place, it is indifferent to and *mocks* this residue.[6]

The Sovereign Operation

14. Essentially, neutral knowledge, within the common domain, overturns the movement of thought. In a sense, it is also a new domain, but this is a secondary aspect (this new domain might just as well, without making a difference, allow nothing to appear that might differentiate it from other domains). The movement that founds the sovereign operation is also founded on it. But above all (any effort, at any hour, appears as vain to me, *like works to a Calvinist*), this operation is the end, *it is the path of an experience.*

15. In the first place, this discipline is a *method of meditation.* Its *teaching* is closer to the teachings of the yogis than to that of the professors. The smallest, inexact image of a sovereign operation is the ecstasy of the saints.

16. In order to describe it better, I would like to situate it in an ensemble of apparently sovereign behaviors. Other than ecstasy, these are:

—intoxication;

—erotic effusion;

—laughter;

—sacrificial effusion;[7]

—poetic effusion.[8]

17. This descriptive effort tends to specify the movement through which different objects of thought are related to its action, though, in itself, it is already obligated to establish the relationships of some objects of common thought to the sovereign moment.

18. The behaviors I have just listed are effusive in that they demand muscular movements of little importance and consume energy without any other effect than a kind of interior illumination (that sometimes precedes anguish—even, in certain cases, entirely limits itself to anguish).

19. Previously, I designated the sovereign operation under the names of *inner experience* or the *extreme of the possible*. And now I designate it under the name *meditation*. Changing words signifies the boredom of using whatever word it should be (*sovereign operation* is, of all these names, the most fastidious: *comic operation,* in a sense, would be less misleading). I like *meditation* better despite its pious appearance.

20. In laughter, sacrifice, or poetry, even partly in eroticism, effusion is obtained through a modification, willing or not, in the order of objects: poetry makes use of changes on the level of images; sacrifice, in general, destroys beings; laughter results from diverse changes.

In drunkenness, on the contrary, and willingly, the subject himself is modified: it is the same in meditation.

21. Drunkenness and meditation still have this in common: the vague effusions of each are connected, are able at least to be connected, to other determined effusions. The change in the object—erotic, comic—in drunkenness appropriately responds to the modification of the subject. This is limitless in meditation. The origin of the effusion is

no less, in the two cases, the activity of the subject: in drunkenness, a toxin releases it; in meditation, *the subject contests himself,* hunts himself (capriciously, often even gaily).

22. In meditation, the overwrought subject looks for himself.

He refuses himself the right to remain enclosed in the sphere of activity.

Still, he refuses exterior means: toxins, erotic partners, or alterations in objects (comic, sacrificial, poetic).

The resolute subject looks for himself, gives himself to himself, meets himself in an auspicious shadow.

And more completely than with a toxin, he puts himself, not objects, at risk.

23. Meditation is a comedy in which even the meditating person is comedic. But also a tragedy in which he is tragic. But the comedic in a comedy or the tragic in a tragedy are limited, whereas a meditating person is prey to the comic or tragic without limit.

24. The closest effusion to meditation is poetry.

Poetry is a natural mode for the expression of tragedy, of eroticism, of the comedic (even before heroism): it expresses great squanderings of energy through word order; poetry is the power of words to evoke effusion, through the excessive expenditure of its own forces: in this way, poetry adds to the determined effusion (comic, tragic . . .) not only the flow and rhythm of verses, but the particular faculty of disordered images to annihilate the ensemble of signs that is the sphere of activity.

If one eliminates the *theme* and if one simultaneously admits the negligible interest of *rhythm,* a hecatomb of words without gods or reasons for being is, for man, a major means to affirm, with an effusion *deprived of meaning,* a sovereignty on which, apparently, *nothing encroaches.*

The moment when poetry abandons *theme* and meaning is, from the point of view of meditation, the rupture that opposes it to the humiliated stammerings of the ascetic. But in becoming a game without any rules, and in the impossibility, lacking a theme, of determining violent effects, the exercise of *modern* poetry subordinates itself, in turn, to *possibility.*

25. If poetry wasn't accompanied by the affirmation of sovereignty (offering a commentary on its absence of meaning), it would be like laughter and sacrifice, or like eroticism and drunkenness, *inserted* in the sphere of activity. *Inserted* is not exactly *subordinated*: laughter, drunkenness, sacrifice, or poetry, eroticism even, subsist in a reserve, autonomous, *inserted* in the sphere of activity, *like children in a house.* In their limits they are sovereign minors, unable to contest the *empire* of activity.

26. It is clear, at this point, that the question of power was posed and poetry was unable to avoid it. In the end, it is only an *evocation*; it changes only the order of words and cannot *change the world*. The feeling of poetry is connected to the nostalgia to change more than the order of words, the *established order*. But the idea of a revolution *resulting from* poetry leads to one of poetry *in the service* of a revolution. I have no other intention than to make evident the drama dissimulated under the words: *limited, poetry was unable to affirm complete sovereignty, the negation of all limits: it was, from the onset, condemned to insertion; escaping these limits, it had to bind itself (to attempt to bind itself) to the contestation of the facts of the order of things.*

27. Now, what does the contestation—political, in fact—of the established order mean? It claims power and could, theoretically, do this in the name of that which exceeds servile necessity (this used to be the principle of the poetic revolution). They act differently, this is a fact, but one must not contradict them. The *major* positions of political sovereignties (understood: those of the past, founded on heroism and sacrifice)[9] were nothing less than *minors* inserted into the sphere of activity. The classical idea of sovereignty binds itself to that of commandment.[10] Every activity was subordinated to the sovereignty of the gods, of God, of monarchs; but each activity was more distorted by this than by the sovereignty of a burst of laughter or of a child. Because by *engaging* the order of things, this became its purpose and it was no longer independent. In these conditions, the sovereignty that would like to remain sovereign quickly abandons *power* to those who want to maintain it authentically with ineluctable necessity.

28. Sovereignty is revolt, it is not the exercise of power. Authentic sovereignty refuses . . .

29. Complete sovereignty differs from minor sovereignty in this way: it demands adherence without reserve from its subject, who must, if possible, be a free man, having, in the sphere of activity, real resources.

30. From the outset, the sovereign operation presents a difficulty so great that one has to look for it in a slipping.

The slave-subject of Christianity attributed (returned) sovereignty to the god-object, whose project wanted to see that one grasped oneself, in effect, as an object of *possession*. The god of the mystics is free (relatively) by definition; the mystic is not (on the contrary, he is even willingly submissive to moral servitude).

31. A Buddhist is more proud. The Christian submits himself, in suffering, to the empire of activity, believing he reads therein a divine will that *wants* his subordination. The Buddhist denies this empire, yet behaves in turn as a slave: he considers himself as fallen, and he must situate the sovereignty that he wants for himself in the other world. He engages himself equally in the contradictions of *work* in view of a sovereign moment.

32. But man only has to do the work, if for no other reason than to assure and repair his forces. Ascetic work is bound to the condemnation of every sovereign moment, this is not the moment it pursues! Whatever its power of seduction and whatever successes, in spite of its principles, it has known, the mystic tradition, burdened by subordinate presuppositions, is also a platitude, ambiguous, a foot stuffed in a shoe.

33. We can in no way fabricate a sovereign moment from a servile state: sovereignty cannot be acquired. In the sovereign operation, I can become conscious of it, but the operation *supposes* a sovereign moment; it is not able to fabricate it.

34. This sovereignty cannot even be defined as a good. I value it, but would I value it if my certainty of it were equal to my ability to laugh at it? On such a summit (this is rather the eye of a needle), I am able to live on this condition: in that at every moment I say, "Sovereign? But why?" I define a neutral knowledge, describing sovereign moments: my sovereignty welcomes this knowledge the way a bird sings and I know no gratitude for my work.

35. I am writing in order to nullify a game of subordinate operations (it is, when all is said and done, superfluous).

36. The sovereign operation, *whose authority results only from itself—expiates this authority at the same time.*[11] If it atoned for it, it would have some point of application, it would look for an empire, for duration. But authenticity refuses this: it is only powerlessness, absence of duration, hateful (or gay) destruction of itself, dissatisfaction.

37. Still, I want to define it a little more precisely at the limit. Not that I must or could speak . . . , but *it speaks,* gathering at one time the totality of the "meditating person" . . .

What it says is the object of the next chapter . . .

Part III
Nudity

In the end everything puts me at risk, I remain suspended, stripped, in a definitive solitude: before the impenetrable simplicity of *what is;* and the depths of the world opened, what I see and what I know no longer has any meaning, any limits, and I will stop myself only after having advanced the furthest that I can.

Now I am able to laugh, drink, abandon myself to the pleasure of the senses, deliver myself over to the delirium of words; I can sweat in torment and I can die: if I had dissolved the entire world in me, I would remain subordinate to necessity, I cannot risk myself more than in joy, torture, or death.

I risk myself if sensuality or pain project me beyond a sphere where I have only one meaning: the sum of the responses I give to the demands of usefulness; I am at risk when, at the end of the possible, I tend so strongly toward that which will overturn what the idea of death pleases in me—and I laugh, taking pleasure in it.

But the smallest activity or the least project puts an end to the game—and I am, lacking play, brought back into the prison of useful objects, loaded with meaning.

•

.. ..
.. .. this is, still, the *instant* .. ..
.. ..
· · · · · · · · · · · · · this, presently, neither my absence nor me, neither death nor light—and my absence and me, death and light—a light laugh rises in me like the sea, fills the absence immensely. All that is—IS TOO MUCH.

●

. . . It doesn't matter anymore, I am writing this book *clearly* and *distinctly*,[12] I wanted it to be what it is.

●

In the plenitude of ravishing, when nothing counted but the instant *alone, I escaped the common rules. But only in order to find them again quickly, unchanged; and, similarly that, in the burst, the ecstasy—or the freedom of the instant—disappears to possible utility, even the useful being, which defines humanity, appears to me bound to the need for material goods, and, I imagine, to give them falsely superior ends. My method is at the antipodes of elevated ideas, of salvation, of all mysticism.*

Part III

The Absence of God

If, in the night, the sidewalk vanishes beneath my feet, for a brief instant, my heart sinks: I have a weak idea of the absence of God.

•

The ignorance of the man who hasn't seen God *in all his glory* is profound, but more profound if God doesn't reveal to him that HE DOESN'T EXIST. Similarly, I know a woman only by loving her, but I turn away from her in the same instant, if she doesn't die. And I misunderstand every object that, not having dazzled me infinitely, doesn't deceive me infinitely.

There is neither being nor nothingness, if my object attains ecstasy in me, and there is no affirmation nor any negation that seems so senseless to me.

•

—You wouldn't read me if you knew.
—I know.
—Would you answer if you knew?

•

I am talking to my likeness: an uneasiness fills the room and I know that he will never hear me. My words poorly announce the melancholy of being neither God nor an oyster.

•

I have no truth but silence, in the name of which I am speaking as, awakened in my sheets by bedbugs, I would scratch myself. What I want: the interminable night of absence, an eternity of sick words, tediously repeated despite myself, my powerlessness, the mortal illness of words, my tears, my absence (more pure than my tears), my laughter, sweeter, more malicious, more empty than death!

●

Going mad, at the heart of hollow and infinite possibility, God, in the glare of lucidity, dreamed of being an invalid gnawed by bugs. Then he became a bug that the invalid, having lit the light, found in a fold of the sheets and crushed between his nails. This invalid fell back asleep and dreamed: he dreamed of pouring sand, having neither summit nor bottom, neither rest nor tolerable possibility. He wasn't able to wake up, or to cry out, or to die, or to stop this movement of elusive terror. This sleep endlessly awakened by anything was neither absence, nor anything, but a confusion full of rage.

●

For a fly fallen in ink, the universe is a fly fallen in ink, but, for the universe, the fly is the absence of the universe, a small cavity deaf to the universe and in which the universe is lost to itself. Would the fly be to God what the hole in a tickled ass is to the voluptuary? Who conceals it from what it *is*? Leaves it open and faltering?

Initial Postulate

As experiential truth, I am able to crudely advance this proposition:
If, in a given moment, I escape anxiety about the following moment (and about every moment that will follow),

—on the aesthetic plane, I attain the purest form of ecstasy (which justifies the known descriptions; conflagrations, excessive joy);[1]

—I place the only value that is not subordinated to anything else on the aesthetic plane (even in the idea of God, the almighty engages an action extended through time and in proportion to which I was asked to appreciate the *creator*—and this implicated the entire hierarchy of moral values related to works: if Christianity departs from this, it is a paradox);

—on the level of knowledge, I interrupt by definition the development of the possibilities of knowing by clear distinctions (it is a powerlessness and an external consideration if *after the fact* I say: "I place," "I attain," "I interrupt": if *I placed* whatever it was in *the moment*, I would subordinate it to this position the way a worker puts the final touches on the finished object).[2]

From this beginning, I perceive the possibility of a discipline that is different from those that, traditionally, limit the domains of the human mind. A certain number of isolated approaches have separately responded to this discipline, which, unlike philosophy, theology, aesthetics, morality, does not have a distinct constitution, though it can accept one. External to philosophy, such apprehensions do not allow themselves to be reduced either to aesthetics or to morality—thus the doctrine of "time regained" in *Remembrance of Things Past*, that of automatic writing or of the goal[3] of Surrealist activity in André Breton's *Manifestoes*, and still others, and, always indissoluble from such disjointed teachings, the processes that preceded them, accompany

105

them, or are their proposed goals—and they indicate the possibilities of an ensemble external to the previously established frameworks. These apprehensions intend neither the good, the beautiful, the true, nor God, but an immediacy that does not need operations connected to moral, aesthetic, scientific, or religious research. Thus no one could say that Proust or Breton are philosophers, and if they proceed in their privileged way, no one could even limit their means to those of art. To qualify them as religious would also introduce confusion: the object of religious desire only appears in association with some justifiable end (salvation is less weighty).

These given pathways indicate the first steps in a discovery that permits a level entry into the domain to be defined—in which we live without ever recognizing it. Envisioned methodically, this domain seems simultaneously accessible from several sides. We don't dispose of even one mode of apprehension, unless it is vague apprehension, of the moment. We must continuously choose between immediate interests and anxiety about the future: the moment is at stake in the smallest desire. But it is ordinarily represented by a shifty lawyer, who expects everything from the judge's weakness and timidly asserts the rights of juveniles. The appeal of the present moment consists in its puerility: I am a man who knows he prefers the future. And as large a share of life as the erotic and comical moments may be accorded, they occupy the place for us that relaxation does for children. Reason subordinates the heroic moment to services rendered. The poetic and the tragic are highly esteemed, but only as the ornaments of minds consecrated to higher ends. The religious, like the heroic, is justified by an ensemble of services (insofar as the confused term designates something that can be isolated), and ecstasy, the purest form of the religious, which offers less that might be subordinated, is related to the infinite negation of the fleeting moment: in sum, this hardly changes; whether one speaks of the Eternal or of nothingness, one acknowledges a common inability to place value in the perishable.

If I do so now—not without groping, following those who began— I institute a new order of thoughts and behaviors. The apprehension of the instant, without an indulgent concession and without justification, supposes a new discipline. I must:

—acquire knowledge that is as clear and distinct as is possible of the domains defined by the words *erotic, comic, poetic, tragic, ecstatic* . . .

—determine how they respond to the desire for the moment, how they leave the door open to reservations in view of the future, how they implicate, in opposition to the value of immediacy, miserable calculations . . .

—without the hint of obligation and, without any *reason* (other than this one: what is put off for later will be reduced, in the end, to the perishable moment or is only a lure assuring my "servitude"), to *live* erotically, comically, poetically, tragically, ecstatically . . .

—subordinate all thought concerning the erotic to eroticism . . . all thought about drunkenness to drunkenness, and so on, the way a theologian subordinates theology to God. The discipline thus represented differs in fact from philosophy or from science in the same way that theology differs from it. But God is still a compromise. God brought the divine attribute of immediacy to an object—conceived on the model of objects in the sphere of activity. God is the reduction of immediacy to the necessity of power. So that theology—itself never subordinated to the experience of God—never had anything over philosophy but the rights of an arbitrary sovereignty, founded rather on a deformed, but accessible, experience, on the experience of revelation, granted a few times for everyone, that in fact became inaccessible (the experience of revelation engages the deformation of every later experience, reduced in advance by faith to being at the same time desire for and fear of the immediate). It is only by reducing the instant to the instant, the ecstatic to the ecstatic, and, at least during the instant, *sine glossa,* that without revelation I create a discipline—logic and a-logic, ethics and immorality, aesthetics and negation of the aesthetic—which has the immediate as its object, the heir of theology. In the Middle Ages, making philosophy the *ancilla theologiae* was not folly: *in a constituent way, philosophy is an ancillary activity.* From the moment one stopped making use of it, obligating it, it was only a floating mass, coming apart and being put back together again, responding to the silence of the sky by a drifting discordance of abstruse discourse. It can't, in fact, resolve anything. And even the absence of a solution cannot be reached through it. It is only on the condition of defining the objects of thought that thought does not grasp—the way the immediate or the tangible object is or the way God was—that it abstains from reducing the world to thought (which arranges a chain of endless subordinations). The most perfect—Hegel's—nevertheless has this result: a system so riddled with servitude, so burdened with equality in relation to what follows from it, that nothing ever has any meaning except in relation to something else, that, the totality attained, all things considered, and the circle closed, it would no longer differ from the immediate: on the contrary, I suppose that it is insofar as this servile totality is rebelling, perfectly *impossible*[4]—one imagines the perfect rebellion to be the most calm—that it *slips* to an *impossible* freedom, to a free dementia of the immediate.[5]

Furthermore, the fact that philosophy is ancillary has another aspect. If a man takes himself to be a philosopher, if he also accepts being taken as such, this goes further than being a pastry cook or a singer; he renounces being a "whole man." A pastry cook, a singer, cannot claim to be a "whole man" as a singer or a pastry cook. The philosopher, insofar as he wants to be a "whole man," wants it as a philosopher. But in proportion to his pretension, one must see forthwith that philosophy is only a specialized activity: the "whole man" only justifies his character when it is lost in immediacy; he loses it each time when, in view of an ulterior motive, he is limited to a determined activity. It is the philosopher's contradiction to be brought to confuse a miserable *instrument* with the totality of being. This is his contradiction and also his misery. To such a degree that he is held in a profound way to this laughable attitude. He hardly has any trouble effacing himself before the dangerous shadows evoked by theology: but before the puerile caprice of the moment! Because the whole being, the immediate, which has no other end than itself and cannot exceed the moment, does not escape the limit of the puerile except in exceeding that of the possible. If he wants power, the almighty is open to him, but the almighty of the instant, this is the *amok*,[6] this is the height of powerlessness.

In the *Second Manifesto*, André Breton, relating the *amok* to the totality, offers a very beautiful, but disarming expression: "The simplest surrealist act," he says, "consists of dashing down into the street, pistol in hand, and firing blindly, as fast as you can pull the trigger, into the crowd. Anyone who, at least once in their lives, has not dreamed of thus putting an end to the petty system of debasement and cretinization in effect has a well-defined place in that crowd, with his belly at barrel level."[7]

In sum, the discipline I am dreaming about would be to philosophy what a whole man is to the philosopher—or even, if you will, if he were a theologian, to God himself! This proposition gives rise, of course, to the jest: the best thing is a silent, angelic, feeling of divine mockery. The inaccessible nature of the totality of the instant motivates less remorse than humor (simultaneously angelic and black). Thus: intellectual superiority, reducing the adversary to silence, implies an unsupportable task, betraying the principle that it brought to triumph: I pull the rug out from under myself. And so what: I'm free, powerless, and I will perish: I ignore the limits of obligation *in every way*.

Part IV

The Consequences of Nonknowledge

January 12, 1951.

At the end of yesterday's lecture,[1] Jean Wahl spoke of the subtle relations that might present themselves between Hegel's work and what I have to say today; I am not certain that they are very solid. Nevertheless, I find that the sense of Jean Wahl's announcement was close enough for me to emphasize it.

I ran into A. J. Ayer by chance last night and we found enough interesting things to talk about that our conversation lasted until nearly three o'clock in the morning. Merleau-Ponty and Ambrosino took part and, in the end, I believe that the transaction took place then, during that conversation.

It so happened, however, that the conversation took a turn such that, everything being in an agreeable place, I had the sensation that I was beginning my lecture; I apologize for making a distinction between a bar and a lecture hall, but such is the embarrassment of beginning.

In the end, we had the opportunity to talk about a fairly strange question. Ayer asserted this very simple proposition: the sun existed before man. And he couldn't even doubt it. It so happened that Merleau-Ponty, Ambrosino (a physician), and myself were not of the same mind on this proposition, and Ambrosino said that certainly the sun had not existed before the world. For my part, I don't see how anyone can say that. This is a proposition that indicates the perfect non-sense that a reasonable proposition can assume. A common meaning must have a meaning within all meaning when one asserts any proposition that in principle implies a subject and an object. In the proposition: there was the sun and there were no humans, there is a subject without an object.

I must say that yesterday's conversation [with Ayer?] was a scandal.

There is a sort of abyss between French philosophers and English philosophers, which isn't there between French philosophers and German philosophers.

I don't know if I made the unacceptable nature, for man, of the proposition according to which there existed something before him plain enough. Honestly, it seems to me that insofar as we remain within discursive considerations, we might indefinitely say that there could not have been a sun before man; however, this also might make us uneasy: a proposition that isn't logically doubtful, but that makes the mind uneasy, induces an imbalance: an object independent of any subject.

After having left Ayer, Merleau-Ponty, and Ambrosino, I ended up feeling regret.

There is no possibility of considering the existence of the sun without humans. We think we know when we say it, but we know nothing. This wasn't the privilege of this proposition. I can talk about any object, while I am before the subject. I am positioned before the object as before a foreign body that in one way or another is a scandal for me, because of the fact that objects are servile; a constant relation between the object and myself. Any object enters in me inasmuch as I make myself dependent on objects. One thing that I cannot doubt is that I know myself. In sum, finally, I asked myself why I was taken in by this phrase of Ayer's. All kinds of facts about existence wouldn't appear questionable to me. In other words, the nonknowledge that I am talking about, in search of its consequences, is everywhere.

To specify what I mean by nonknowledge: that which results from every proposition when we are looking to go to the fundamental depths of its content, and which makes us uneasy.

I will set out from an opposing proposition, not the kind of review of knowledge that could appear systematic, but from my anxiety about acquiring the maximum amount of knowledge: in fact, it is quite clear that inasmuch as I have a satisfiable curiosity about the unknown domain that can be reduced to a known domain, I cannot say what Hegel called absolute knowledge. Only if I knew everything could I aspire to knowing nothing, if discursive knowledge was in my possession such that I could aspire in an ineradicable fashion to have arrived at nonknowledge through it. Insofar as I know things obliquely, my pretension to nonknowledge is an empty pretension. If I knew nothing, I would have nothing to say, so I would keep my mouth shut. Nonetheless: even while recognizing that I cannot succeed in absolute knowledge, I can imagine myself knowing everything; in other words, I can neglect in myself the curiosity that I still have. I can say to myself that if I continued my search, I would not learn anything else that was important. There would be a chance, therefore, to change myself through significant knowledge, but this sort of turn won't let itself be surpassed: supposing that I knew everything much better than I do now, I wouldn't be rid of the uneasiness about which I am speaking. Whatever proposition I make, it will resemble the first one. I will find myself in the presence of this question, one could say of the question posed by Heidegger. For my part, the question has for a long time seemed insufficient and I sought to articulate another: why is there that which I know? Finally, I don't believe that we can translate this in a perfect way with formulas. It seems to me, however, that the fundamental question is posed only from that moment on, when no formula is possible, when we listen in silence to the absurdity of the world.

I have done everything to know what is knowable and I have looked for that which is unformulatable in my depths. I myself am in a world I recognize as profoundly inaccessible to me: in all the ties that I sought to bind it with, I still don't know what I can conquer, and I remain in a kind of despair. I recognize that this feeling is rarely tested adequately. I was fairly surprised that someone like Sartre didn't feel this feeling in the least bit, much less the rest of the world. He said something like: if we don't know anything, we don't need to say it twice.

This is the position of someone who doesn't know what is in the locked trunk, the trunk there is no possibility of opening. At this moment one typically uses literary language, wherein there is no longer anything that one must say. Only silence is able to express what we have to say. Therefore, in a troubled language, in a perfect state of despair, in a sense at least, incomparable to that of those people who look for something and don't have it; this is a much more profound despair, that we have always known, that is linked to the fact that we have a project in mind, a project that cannot be completed, that we are on the point of being frustrated such that we are essentially attached to our object. This despair is equivalent to despair over death. As foreign to death as ignoring the contents of the trunk I was talking about earlier.

We can picture death for ourselves. We can at the same time know that this representation is incorrect. Any proposition we assert on the subject of death is always tainted with a minimum of error. Nonknowledge in particular concerning death is of the same nature as nonknowledge in general. In everything that I have just said, it would seem to me very natural that each one of you has seen a purely singular position; this supposes an exceptional being (being that situates itself outside of the normal position). To tell the truth, this way of judging myself is quite consistent with humanity today. Nevertheless, it seems possible for me to say that it has not been like this, considerations that might appear rather frivolous.

A sufficiently contestable hypothesis: the position of people whose precise object is knowledge. When one knows that one knows nothing, it helps a lot; one must continue thinking in order to discover the world of someone who knows that he knows nothing. The world of those who have pushed intellectual limits is a very different world from the world of those who have confidence (children). A profound difference. These remainders compose themselves even with nonknowledge, in sometimes disconcerting syntheses, because from their point of view one must admit that they are no more satisfying than the first position.

It seems a good idea to refer to an experience as common as sacrifice (in another order of ideas than in my other lectures): the difference and the similarities of nonknowledge and of sacrifice. In sacrifice, we destroy an object, but not completely; a residue remains and, after all, from the point of view of science, nothing that happens matters. However, if we take these symbolic values into account, it is possible to represent the alteration, caused by this destruction, in the notion from which we began. The immediate satisfaction offered by a slaughtered cow is either that of a peasant or that of a biologist, but this is expressed in sacrifice. The slaughtered cow has nothing to do with all these practical conceptions. In all this, there is a limited, but solid understanding. When one surrenders oneself to the ritual destruction of a cow, one destroys every notion to which the simple life has accustomed us.

Man needs to give himself a perspective on nonknowledge in the form of death. These are not typical intellectual acts. There is always trickery. We all have a sense of death and one can suppose that this feeling is significantly at risk in sacrifice. A profound difference between Catholics and Protestants: Catholics still reduce the experience of sacrifice to a sort of symbolic emaciation. Nevertheless, one must not exaggerate the distance: traditional sacrifice and Catholic sacrifice, sacrifice of soma and the Mass. The fact of saying certain words over a piece of bread is just as satisfying for the spirit as the slaughter of a cow. Fundamentally, there is a common enough search for horror in sacrifice. In this regard, it seems to me that the mind takes as much from destruction as it is able to stand. The atmosphere of death, of the disappearance of knowledge, the birth of this world that we call sacred; in this there is the possibility of saying that the sacred is the sacred, though, at this particular moment, language must at least submit to a moment of suspension. Furthermore, there is the leitmotif of this explanation, that all these operations are badly done, debatable. All this is unsteady, for one very simple reason: the only way to express myself would be by keeping my mouth shut, thus the vice about which I spoke. This is at antipodes to what is troubling in the initial proposition, in the phrase that motivated my discussion with Ayer. Uneasiness experienced as well, the persistent uneasiness of one who searches for knowledge. Faced with nonknowledge, I experienced the feeling of performing in a comedy, of having a kind of weakness in my position. At the same time, I am in front of you as a babbler, offering all the reasons I would have for keeping my mouth shut. I can also say to myself: I might not have the right to keep my mouth shut, another difficult position to support.

It remains simply that nonknowledge does not suppress sympathy, reconcilable with the science of psychology.

From the moment one knows that the hope of salvation must truly disappear, the situation of someone totally rejected (the difference between the situation of the lecturer and that of the servant shown the door in a humiliating manner), a painful situation because one cannot accomplish any project that is stained by a kind of death. When one arrived at this kind of despair and one continues to exist in the world with the same hopes and the same instincts (with human and bestial aspects), one suddenly notices that one possesses the world much more profoundly than others. These possibilities are in fact offered much more often to those that abandon knowledge (a walk in the fields with a botanist). Every time we give up the will to know, we have the possibility of touching the world with a much greater intensity.

If you are facing a woman, as much as you know her, you hardly know her, in other words you have an "understanding" [connaissance] of her that borders on knowledge [savoir]. Insofar as you seek to know a woman psychologically without letting yourself be carried away by passion, you distance yourself from her. Only when you seek to know her in relation to death do you draw nearer to her. Inevitable contradictions follow: when you approach a somber being, you are called to deny the feeling of "perishability." In love, the will to project the loved being into the imperishable is a contrary will. It is insofar as a being is not a thing that it is possible to love that being. Insofar as it resembles the sacred. As the loved being can be perceived only when projected into death, the imagination of death results.

Moreover, it goes without saying that if one can, in the act of conceiving aspects of the present life, assure a foundation for nonknowledge, one comes to give it the most magnificent point of view: one has distanced oneself profoundly from nonknowledge. Love cannot be a success. In its effort to glorify a human being, this glorification is reduced to this world of practical knowledge.

Now that I have shown this first consequence of nonknowledge, I have again lost the right to talk about it. I have reentered categories of knowledge while straddling nonknowledge.

We can pass indefinitely from this consideration to the other; one is no more valid than the other. I would be saved only if I attained the impossible.

Nevertheless, there is a perspective in which we will be able to perceive a veritable triumph of nonknowledge: that of the end of history. Hegel's position in this respect is quite open to criticism. History must necessarily be finished to talk about it: Hegel's announcement of the end of history was a mistake, as it accelerated after 1830. However, we can speak freely about the end of history. The position I have demonstrated would tend to be closed. The last man would find himself in a situation that would be complete nonsense. If we consider our death to be similar to that of the last man, we can say that history is circular. He who would be last should continue the undertaking: it's certain that the night must fall with him, crush him, bury him. We can almost say that this would be the final leap.

It also seems to me that I let you believe I was able to permit, in all of this, a part to be played by destruction. In my opinion, the situation of the world does not imply tying oneself to the impossible. The surrender of all research in this sense is complete freedom.

There is no need to entangle oneself with strictly moral considerations, but to entangle morality with intensity.

There is a kind of denouement in this situation. At the moment of abandoning everything it isn't necessary to be rich. It so happens that we are in the moment of the Gospel, in the state of grace of which the only criteria is intensity.

Aspects of trickery become indifferent. There is no meaning in death or in the meaning connected to a project. In this sort of possibility of negation from the place where salvation finds itself outside everything,

everything is open at the limits of the moment, even if I was the last man and dying.

If I succeed in living sensitively in the moment, I escape every difficulty, but I am no longer a man (to be a man is, in other words to live with the future in mind), nor have I any recourse to animality in this sort of situation, which demands considerable energy, available to very few people.

No value judgment: I am unable to arrive at the least condemnation of those that know, that live in the world wherein I myself live, in the world in which I can no longer live.

Discussion

J. WAHL: Discussion is difficult since you yourself said that you like to contradict yourself. You said "aspire to" nonknowledge. Thus, you are searching for it, it is a kind of ideal for you?

G. BATAILLE: I think I could, with difficulty, avoid this search for nonknowledge representing a moment.

J. WAHL: Your attitude is ambivalent: you are desperate and you want to be this way.

G. BATAILLE: The will affirms itself in contradiction.

J. WAHL: Is it not necessary to surpass the antithesis of knowledge and of nonknowledge?

G. BATAILLE: This synthesis is essentially indefinable. There is no knowledge of the moment, nòr any means of entering into the moment by detours with a result in view and from the perspective of the original process. There is, however, a necessity of distinguishing the original process from the secondary process.

x: It's a perpetual deception between knowledge and nonknowledge. You must make a proposition in an attempt to consider yourself not as an object but as a subject, and in that case "I would assume silence."

G. BATAILLE: That's the most perfect consequence . . . but you haven't been lecturing.

x: To speak about the zone of clarity and of light is to surpass knowledge and nonknowledge: the path of simplicity. You can draw metaphysical and moral consequences from nonknowledge if you want to.

G. BATAILLE: You are clarifying the fact that what I said outlines what I was obliged to say because I've spoken about it in my books. The child is on the descending path of nonknowledge. For me, what I said today is a preface to what I intend to say.

L. ABEL: Is not night the last refuge in this despair?

G. BATAILLE: In all these successions, one is unable to escape lying to oneself.

L. ABEL: You limited your enthusiastic attitude in regard to the world to the perspective of nonknowledge. I would oppose this attitude with Tolstoy's . . .

G. BATAILLE: I don't believe that it's necessary to think as I think in order to have an extremely rich life. I have sought to show an easier way. It would have been necessary to find more diverse features.

The Teaching of Death

Thursday, May 8, 1952.

(I explained myself poorly last time. Trouble presenting and listening to my lectures. Good intentions. A violent passion remains.)

Death teaches nothing, since we lose the benefit of the instruction that it might offer us by dying. It's true, we think about the death of the other. We reconcile the impression that the death of the other gives us with ourselves. We often imagine ourselves in the position of those who we see dying, but we can only justifiably do this on the condition of living. Reflection on death is much more seriously derisive than living, it is always scattering our attention, and we speak in vain about exerting ourselves, when death is at stake.

Of course, talking about death is the most profound *practical joke*.

The only out for Gribouille:[1] to throw oneself in the water so as not to be wet.

In fact, it is surely not important to die, or to think about death, or to talk about it, but we can allude to a kind of *correction*, obviously not absolute, though it remains possible to respond with some precision to the given facts of the problem.

Reflection might, for example, set out from the *amok*.[2]

What is notable is that this ends everything.

However, one can say at least that the amok as an individual subject has the merit of attracting the attention *of others* to death.

Now it is hardly [*out?*] of the question to talk about the fact that the anxiety of making the representation of the amok present can be considered to be fundamental, essential. In tragedy, in the end, there is always a movement that arrives at an impasse and at a violent situation. It's a question of making this representation appropriate to the amok.

(deficient nature of tragedy)

If I talk personally, I must above all tell myself: *what will be lacking essentially in my lecture* . . . This is not a joke. No, this is what would count!

Of course, language is there to remedy the situation. But, in the first place, there is a certain interest in attracting attention to the deficient nature of this process, which is in effect my own, to which I will be bound. I am even talking about tragedy. If only I had been able to attract attention to what I am talking about to the same point as if I had produced the effect of a tragedy.

Now in effect tragedy has advantages over the *[true?]* amok.

It is therefore a question of knowing *if my presentation does not have, in turn, an advantage over tragedy.* The *correction* of my presentation will consist in this knowledge.

Of course, I am starting from my powerlessness to present what I would like to talk about. But, though tragedy itself cannot, I can talk about the consequences of the representation of tragedy for each of us. The silence that follows tragedy is proper to it, and without doubt this is still, in my opinion, an advantage of tragedy. It is not explained. Here, meanwhile, in the absence of explanations of tragedy I can offer an advantage in this sense: tragedy that is not explained is still at the mercy of explanations. The tragic author does not explain himself, but he is defenseless against the explanations of others. *In order to suppress explanation it is not sufficient to not give any.* The human mind is made such that tragedy does not take place without instruction, without any consequences. It must have consequences. Or otherwise, it is as if it did not exist. Justifiably, it is a question of knowing if tragedy has no effect on the nontragic world, where one acts usefully or stupidly. If it is at the mercy of explanations given on the level of this world, or if it is something sovereign.

Here I believe I can introduce a fundamental proposition. Given tragedy and the emotion that results from it, not only is tragedy presented as sovereign in relation to this world (this is a question on which I will not insist for the moment), but what it introduces is precisely the inadequacy of every word. Now this inadequacy, at least, must be spoken. In other words, beyond the amok or beyond tragedy, I can go further in saying that the amok and tragedy put an end to all discourse.

At this particular moment, I must resist the fact that I am superfluous and that even tragedy can express itself. When, at the end of tragedy, the hero submerged in crime, in violence, succumbs to violence, can himself say: the rest is silence. A story spoken by an idiot, signifying nothing. The rest is silence. However, these words are essentially lacking a universal character that *philosophy* alone can give them.

I must interrupt myself here to observe that my proposition is still in suspension. In fact, philosophy cannot grant this universal meaning inasmuch as this is essentially and, *completely, what the words "The rest is silence" oppose*. If I commit myself to the field of philosophy, I therefore betray my intuition in the most painful way. In fact, my situation is no less difficult than previously; nevertheless, I can still defend myself. I believe it is no more difficult. Tragedy also strayed painfully away from what we were looking for there, because we justifiably sought it without hurling ourselves into death. It is on this point that I can intervene in specifying a demand. The amok fails if I die. Tragedy also fails insofar as it fails to attract the attention of the living strongly enough. The living are the spectators of the fact that tragedy invokes in them if not death, which takes them out of the game, at least the death of thought. In other words, what tragedy teaches is silence, and *silence is nothing if it does not put an end to thought at least for a little while*. Evidently, there is nothing to say about death.

Meanwhile, philosophy recovers its rights in the sense that it alone can raise these problems. From my point of view, philosophy intervenes as a demand for rigor. Philosophy can be a barrier against every possible philosophy. Philosophy alone can be. Otherwise it is occultism, mythology, and so on. Science, which continues to believe in the possibility of responding. No: one must, I believe, make a resolution one day. It is a question of pushing things to the end, of not holding on to the first subterfuge that comes along and, on the contrary, of grasping completely that if anything merits going to the end, it is this: *this is no longer even a philosophy*. I said that philosophy was a job, therefore a confidence, it always assumes the initially anticipated result, even if there is doubt. And especially, philosophy initially assumes at least that philosophy is possible. But we must go further.

Distancing myself from the preceding remarks, I say:

There is a possibility of negatively accounting for mythology, religion, occultism, and naive confidence in oneself.

Let's put the following principle forward as a hypothesis: tradition and spontaneity bring us nothing, absolutely nothing.

We must reject them, act as if they did not exist.

Then one single certainty remains: the dull facts of science. What a worker or a peasant knows outside of every religious presupposition or otherwise.

This is added in the meantime: these dull achievements oppose only a subterfuge to death, they by no means allow us to bring death into the field of vision, to freeze death; on the contrary, they abandon us to the anticipated result.

There aren't even any presuppositions, religious or otherwise. One can even consider these achievements as a means of facing death, of making human life a synthesis of its presence and its absence.

But if I return to what I said earlier, there is obviously a slippage. This is the passage from distracted reflection on death to any subterfuge whatsoever. This is in relation to what I wanted to envision, a movement contrary to sense.

Philosophy alone can accomplish the rigorous movement that leaves one mute in a consequential way, which dismisses derivatives.

But if we attempted this, we quickly perceive that philosophy cannot accomplish this movement while remaining on its own terrain.

It only intervenes negatively, not in order to be fulfilled, but connected subsidiarily to the effort of the mind, which suffers from being unable to experience death. It can only dismiss presuppositions and denounce masks, and so on, in scientific responses. But this experience that approaches death dismisses death in the meantime. Insofar as it is reflection and work, it distances itself from death. Therefore, it cannot go further than a clearing away. Finally, it remains essential not to lose sight of the point of departure and to return insofar as it is possible to the intensity of the amok, and of tragedy, to violence. In other words to the REBELLION that philosophy has consciously turned into rebellion against the world of work and against the world of presuppositions.

The search for the most perfect silence, the search that actually takes place, the search for what approaches the maximum silence. Rebellion contesting every possibility and only holding on to the impossible.

I set out from experience and I had recourse to philosophical reflection only negatively. Philosophy sought to disengage this experience. It has perhaps attenuated it, but its intensity (its violence) seemed to be that which it was necessary to hold on to, against the winds and floods, on account of a refusal to yield to what prevents us from experiencing being.

At this moment, the indifference of nonknowledge is a fact, the most distant indifference that we were able to tempt, insofar as it ruins our usual position, our servitude to the anticipated result—as much as I might see, since in indifference [nothing] is anticipated any longer, anguish but also the suppression of anguish are essentially present at the same time in nonknowledge. From that moment on, it becomes possible to furtively create the furtive experience that I call the experience of the instant.

Founded on the abandonment of knowledge, from that moment on, an ordered reflection on the experience of non-nonknowledge becomes possible.

Friday, May 9, 1952.

Yesterday I presented an imperfect experience, driven, however, with a kind of stubbornness into a countercurrent, setting out from a consideration of the amok and of tragedy—in other words, a moment of extreme violence. In my way, I presented something fundamental that death can teach us nothing because we have no experience of it, if not mediated by another person. In the resulting situation, there is a kind of interest brought to bear on death that never goes further than a kind of practical joke, an element of rebellion. We live with an obsession with a moment when life would be at the height of death. There is an experimental truth there: not only must we die, not only are we frightened and anguished by this, not only do we turn away from death, but an incessant movement brings us back to it. And we are always looking to death for what life does not give us. I hope to show the purpose of this bizarre attitude in what follows. I take it as a fact for now, contenting myself with saying that it testifies to the nonacceptance of the possible life, like a rebellion. But this rebellion makes us participate in lies. One could see it as a practical joke. I have pursued its movement through the representation of the amok—a rough, purely pretentious representation, from the position of someone who does not fling himself onto his neighbors in order to be finished with them, so as to kill as many of them as possible and to die at the hands of the survivors. I offered tragedy, inasmuch as it is an institution, as an attempt to satisfy itself and to satisfy its spectators, to help this representation of an amok who results in some fatalities from the movement of life and the play of passions. I wanted to show that the silence of thought, that the death of thought responded to the movement of representation that is tragedy.

But only this silence or this death of thought was able to be maintained and to leave room for the transaction of religious thought, for all the more or less gratuitous mythological representations that make us return, in an indirect way, to the world of facility and of the project.

Following my presentation, Jean Wahl very justifiably showed me that it was necessary to distinguish between death and the death of thought, and it is true that I seem to confuse them entirely. I am speaking in accordance with the title of my two conferences on the teachings of death, and, to my mind, it is in fact not only a question of the so-called teachings of death, but of the teaching of the death of thought. I am wrong (I say "I am" because I persist) in passing through a sort of dialectic from the first, simple physical death, to the second, where it is thought that founders. Truthfully speaking, thought also founders in the first, but in the second the thought that founders accomplishes its shipwreck, if one may say so, within thought, in other words, in a thought where the consciousness of foundering persists. Now it is completely evident that the first teaches nothing, whereas, in the second, a possibility of consequences subsists. The second can in the meantime be considered as a substitute for the first. In the second, thought makes use of representations of the death of the other in order to arrive at dying itself. This is not necessary, the dead point of thought can be produced without being connected to the representation of physical death; nevertheless, what can be true of one particular case is not so in general of what one may call the death of thought, which proceeds humanely, generally, from the movement of the representation of physical death. The simple death of thought offers itself to itself as equal to the physical death of thought, at least equal to it if possible.

Whatever it might be, what cannot be brought out by physical death, the death of thought brings about. If the death of thought is pushed to the point where it is sufficiently *dead thought* in order to no longer be either desperate, or anguished, there is no longer any difference between the death of thought and ecstasy. The former can occur or not occur. But it is a fact, a fact of experience; ecstasy differs little from the death of thought. Therefore, a new domain opens to consciousness from the death of thought, from nonknowledge a new knowledge is possible.

From the very beginning, I should insist on what generally taints this new sphere as it did the preceding. Neither the death of thought nor ecstasy is any less imprinted with trickery or with profound powerlessness than the simple consciousness of the death of the other. The death of thought always fails. It is in fact only an *impotent movement*. Likewise, ecstasy is impotent. In ecstasy, a sort of constant conscious-ness of ecstasy persists, placing ecstasy on the same undue level that the head of cattle is on for the cattle breeder, on the level of things des-ignated as property. Besides, in the end, taking it as an appropriated thing in order to make it the object of a teaching, as I intended to, is inevitable.

I won't insist on this difficulty. It is the same difficulty that I encoun-tered at the very beginning and I can even say that the failures that re-sulted from it will confound themselves with the resulting successes on the level of the knowledge before which I am heading on account of my powerlessness. Besides, this is of little importance. The kind of study to which I aspire, compared to science, will be nonetheless something very different. Science envisions subordinated things—only things sub-ordinated in time to their results. There are also things, in a sense, that the study will envision; now I'm coming to the principles of the study, but the subordinated nature of these things will not be the object of my research. I will not, in fact, envision an object of thought as identical to the thought into which I could change it, insofar as it contains such and such a possibility of change or reduction. On the contrary, I will envision the moments of this thing (represented as a thing due to in-ability) as sovereign moments, in other words, as moments having their end in themselves and not as middle terms. In this way, not pre-cisely a science, but what I might call a study of sovereign moments follows from the death of thought. A study also in the sense that the word *study* means an application toward a possibility. Such a study is characterized by the fact that we could not enter into it without a prac-tice. It is insofar as we tend—in fact, if not necessarily in intention, in our project—toward the moments or the states that it questions that we can have an understanding of it. In these conditions, let's take one example among others, not necessarily the principal example, but the example that I set out from, from which I necessarily had to set out. There already is a science of mystical states. For example, Janet, in the magisterial work that he had published under the title *De L'Angoisse à l'extase,*[3] studies these states like other objects without the slightest anxiety about reaching them. But, from that moment on, these are no longer sovereign moments in the sense that there is a difference be-tween placing them within the field of attention and wanting them. If these states are envisioned as sovereign states, necessarily, envisioning them and aspiring to them is, on the contrary, the same. We have just as many extremely different tableaux in both cases. For Saint John of the Cross, the study of the mystical moment is in fact a study of the sovereign moment. For Janet, it is a question of entering this moment into a series of causes and effects as such, if it is possible, in which the crises are reabsorbed and in which the normal state recovers itself once the factors of disorder are eliminated. The therapeutic aspect to which the pathological classification is bound is obviously unnecessary. Nevertheless, it is not by chance that the data offered to scientific research is here as elsewhere engaged in a project of change. This is, in sum, the condition of science. The study I envision is, on the contrary, dominated by an end; it has no meaning except in relation to this end, which, in relation to this research, has a sovereign value. It is no doubt also a study in the sense of scientific research, but in that case this research appears as contradictory to the sovereign moment itself. At this point we encounter the prolongation of this constant difficulty, present from the very beginning, which distances thought from its object when this object is a sovereign moment. The sovereign is in the domain of silence, and if we talk about it we incriminate the silence that constitutes it. It is always a comedy, a practical joke. We can certainly execute the study, but only in the worst, the most painful conditions. On the level of the sovereign moment, language troubles everything it touches, it spoils it, it corrupts it, it stains it through a process that is only appropriate for everyday operations, such as planing down a board or plowing a field. And it does not even suffice to say: we cannot speak about the sovereign moment without spoiling it as truly sovereign. Even, as far as talking about it, it is contradictory to *search for* these movements. Insofar as we seek something, whatever this might be, we do not live sovereignly, we subordinate the present moment to a future moment, which will follow it. Perhaps we will attain the sovereign moment as a result of our effort, and it is possible in fact that an effort is necessary, but between the time of our effort and sovereign time, there is obligatorily a fissure, and we can even say an abyss. This fissure is itself found in other cases. For example, if someone prepares a meal, a roast or grilled meat, there is a fissure, even an abyss, between the moment when the meat is cooked and the moment when it is eaten at the table. There is a disparity between eating and cooking. I must say that this disparity is something very important, essential. It is what differentiates animal and man. The animal eats immediately, animals eat voraciously; in other words, the animal postpones nothing and can in principle postpone nothing for later. It cannot subordinate one moment to another. If the animal wants food and if the animal is hungry, the animal searches for food; there is no difference between being hungry and being in search of food. The time in which an animal searches for food is not subordinated to its result, for the simple reason that food would be eaten as soon as it is present. The properly human attitude is regained as much as in questions of mystical experience as in matters of cuisine. Such an experience is necessarily prepared, but it is not as easy to introduce an abyss, or rather, the introduction of the abyss is a rupture at once voluntary and tolerated in spite of oneself.

In sum, now when we come to found this knowledge, which is beyond nonknowledge, this teaching which is that of the death of thought, we cannot be surprised, and if we always encounter this stagnation, this way of advancing against the grain and against meaning is simultaneously poison and cure since this resistance by counter-meaning is itself against meaning.

But, in any case, there is an important domain opened to study in this way, in these exhausting conditions, and what is remarkable is that in this domain the same elements are found:

rebellion amok's whimsy

representation similar to tragedy

maintenance of a profound ruin

destruction and dead point

the method's [weapons?]

1. eroticism:

opposition to animal sexuality

where we grasp even the principle of dividing into two

in the act of following the movement

there is something that is threatened with foundering

difference from the rebellion seized in the amok

but also profound proximity

anguish

the moment when anguish abates, which is also sensuality's point
    of departure

multiplicity of erotic possibilities

diverse objects

Beneficial alibi birth marriage orgy prostitution

the search for the totality and for sovereignty

divinity and its profound connection with eroticism

The beneficial side like the alibi always hiding the tragic side, the inaccessible amok side, the divine side as perfect destruction.

This could permit the construction of a general representation if one wants a philosophy similar to theology

But the criticism was made while this presentation advanced.

We cannot reject it, but we remain suspended, awake.

Nonknowledge and Rebellion

Monday, November 24, 1952.

In the several presentations I have given in this room, I have struggled to communicate my experience of nonknowledge. This experience is in certain respects personal for me, but is, I believe, communicable in the sense that it seems to differ only a priori from the experience of others by a sort of defect that is my own, the consciousness that this experience is the experience of nonknowledge. Obviously, I can never talk about nonknowledge without recapturing the same difficulty. For this reason, I must recall it each time. But I pass on and I recognize it without hesitation; I will develop this paradox before you as I did the other times, the consciousness of nonknowledge, a consciousness of the absence of consciousness.

As the announcement for my lecture warned you, I intend to talk about rebellion. I think that knowledge enslaves us, that at the base of all knowledge there is a servility, the acceptation of a way of life wherein each moment has meaning only in relation to another or others that will follow it. To make my thought more clear, I will represent things in this way. Today, like the other times, I am going to attempt to communicate my experience of nonknowledge to you. Of course, like the other times, I will fail. But first I would like to show you the extent of my failure. I can say precisely that if I had succeeded, the tangible contact between you and me would have had the nature not of work but of play.[1] I would have known how to make you perceive what is for me a decisive fact; the only object of my thought is play, and in play my thought, the work of my thought, is annihilated.

Those who have followed the presentation of my thought have been able to grasp that it was, in a fundamental way, a perpetual rebellion against itself. Today, I will try to give an example of this rebellion on a point that exercises a dominant interest from the point of view of philosophical anxiety, a point of view from which I will begin. I will begin, in sum, with the articulation of a general philosophy, which I could offer as my own philosophy. I have to say it in order to begin. It is a question of a very common philosophy, of a philosophy that must make one think that it truly is far too simple, that a philosopher capable of affirming such vulgarities has nothing to do with the subtle person who deserves the name of philosopher today because, ultimately, anyone could have an idea like this. I completely understand it, this thought which I find to be common is my thought. I remember a long time ago having met a young medical intern who had a philosophy like this. He never ceased, with an extraordinarily confident self-possession, to return to an explicative thought: in his eyes, everything went back to the conservative instinct. Thirty years ago. It would be more difficult to come across the same antenna today. My way of seeing is no doubt less out-of-date, and perhaps, despite everything, responds better, or less badly, to the idea that one can create oneself out of a philosophy. It consists in saying that everything is play, that being is play, that the universe is play, that the idea of God is unwelcome amid the unbearable surplus, in that God, who can initially only be a game, outside time, is harnessed by human thought to creation and to all the implications of creation, which are contrary to play. Besides, in this respect, there is a heaviness to the most ancient human thought, which hardly exceeds the idea of play when it is a question of what is considered in its totality. But this heaviness belongs by no means uniquely to Christian thought. Plato still considered the act sacred, even though religion places our participation in the essence of things, as a game, before humanity as a possibility. But this heaviness exists elsewhere and Christianity is no doubt not the first religion that no longer had the strength to situate human action within the universal game. This only holds Christianity back; Christian thought is still the screen that separates us from what I will voluntarily call the beatific vision of play. It seems to me that within us, this is the conception of the world and of man in the world proper to Christianity, which, from the beginning, opposes within us the thought that everything is a game.

The possibility of a philosophy of play—it supposes Christianity. — But Christianity is the mouthpiece only for pain and death. —From here one could show that a series of problems arise because the being is in space and duration. I won't talk about it anymore. —There is another question—if one opposes play to the opportunity to act, it is a question of a risk that one might call minor. The difficulty: one cannot make the game the *end* of serious activity if it is minor. Further, one cannot give useful activity any other end than play. Here something isn't right.

To say that one can make something more weighty out of a game. From that moment on, it is no longer a game.

The truth itself appears at the foundation of the philosophy of play, indisputably, base, but unstable in that we suffer and we die.

The other way out: we can think and be the game, make a game of the world and of ourselves on the condition of defying suffering and death. —The major risk—more difficult than one thinks. —The dialectic of the master who defies death. —According to Hegel, the master is wrong, it is the slave who defeats him. But the slave is defeated in spite of everything and after having defeated the master he makes himself be defeated. —He must not act as a master but as a rebel—first of all, the rebel wants to suppress the master, chase him from the world—but at the same time he conducts himself like a master since he defies death. The rebel is, therefore, the most equivocal figure in the situation.

The essential problem of rebellion is in disengaging the man of commitment from the slave.

For the master, the risk was neither minor nor major. But the rebel, rebellious against neither the minor nor the major risk, is obligated to reduce the game to the minor state, yet he must envision the necessity of the major risk, which is essentially rebellion against the minor risk, the limit of the game. —Without this the minor man dominates reason.

Here the rebel is constrained because he had to accept death. He must proceed up to the end of his rebellion, he cannot be a rebel in order to perfect submission. This leads to the consciousness that even the worst is a game, to a negation of the power of suffering and death—

cowardice before such a perspective

But this time I believe I left the first proposition of a philosophy of play in passing to the game itself [*crossed out*: and no one will be surprised if] I set a trap

In this way it appears that we are leaving the philosophy of play, we are at the point when knowledge yields and what appears is that the major game is nonknowledge—the game is the undefinable, what thought cannot conceive

This is a thought that exists in me only in a timid way, a thought that I don't feel able to support. I am really thinking it, it's true, but I must say it, like a coward, like someone who covers their eyes, who hides and who is, at base, delirious with fear. Yet that signifies a rather cowardly reaction.

Nonknowledge, Laughter, and Tears

February 9, 1953.

Knowledge demands a certain stability of things known. In any case, the domain of the known is, in one sense at least, a stable domain, where one recognizes oneself, where one recovers oneself, whereas in the unknown there isn't necessarily any movement, things can even be quite immobile, but there is no guarantee of stability. Stability can exist, but there is not even any guarantee as to the limits of the movements that can occur. The unknown is obviously always unforeseeable.

One of the most remarkable aspects of the domain of the unforeseeable unknown is given in the laughable, in the objects that excite in us this effect of intimate overturning, of suffocating surprise, that we call laughter. This is what is very strange in the laughable. Nothing is easier to study, finally to know, than laughter. We can observe and define the different themes of the laughable precisely enough; it does not at all elude clear and distinct knowledge, methodical consciousness. What's more, once the cause of laughter is revealed in its various aspects, we can reproduce its effects at will. We have veritable recipes handy, we can unleash laughter, through various means, just like all the other *known* effects we have at our disposal. In sum, we can create the laughable. Now, one might say, and we have said, that to understand [*connaître*] is to know [*savoir*] how to do. But because we know how to laugh, can we say that we truly understand the laughable?

It does not appear so, if we refer to the history of philosophical works on laughter. It is, in sum, the story of an insoluble problem. What at first seems so accessible never ceased to escape investigation. The domain of laughter is perhaps even, definitively, or at least so it seems to me, a closed domain, given that the laughable remains unknown and unknowable.

At this time I do not intend to take up all the explanations of laughter that have been given, all the explanations that never knew how to resolve the given enigma in a truly thorough way. No doubt, the most well known is Bergson's, that of the mechanism applied to the living being. It seems that Bergson's theory, very well known, is sometimes the object of a hardly justified discredit.

I was surprised, in particular, to see Francis Jeanson in a recent book on laughter, and one of the most significant works that has been recently published, make something of Marcel Pagnol's theory.[1] Perhaps you know that Marcel Pagnol published, maybe three or four years ago, a little book on laughter.[2] His theory, however, is in fact not very original, and it even seems to me among the most summary. For the author of *Marius,* laughter responds to the laughing person's feeling of superiority.

Fundamentally, in the last place, Pagnol's short book might substantiate the opinion according to which it is one thing to know how to make someone laugh, and something else to understand laughter. Besides, I'm not denying that the philosophical theorists of laughter have ever excelled in the art of having fun and rousing waves of laughter.

It is no less true that Bergson's hypothesis is, from his own point of view, far from being able to be given as the solution of the enigma for which he himself offered it as explanation, not of the laughable in general, but of a particular aspect of the laughable that he names the comic.

Thus, independently of the value of Bergson's attempt, we must confirm that laughters which, all the same, have many meanings, like the laughter of the accidental meeting, the laughter of tickling, the child's immediate laughter, are excluded from it.

In fact, studies have multiplied without our being able to explain laughter fundamentally. Beyond the convictions of the authors of each particular theory, fundamentally, we don't know the meaning of laughter. The laughable always remains unknown, a kind of unknown that invades us suddenly, that overturns our habitual course, and that produces in us this "abrupt broadening of the face," these "explosive noises from the larynx," and these "rhythmic jolts of the thorax and abdomen" that doctors talk about.

Perhaps one final theory remains, which would at least merit application on the most remarkable part, on that which is essential to all the theories that have preceded it, *their failure.*

Suppose that the laughable is not only unknown, but unknowable. We still have to envision a possibility. The laughable could simply be *the unknowable*. In other words, the unknown character of the laughable would not be accidental, but essential. We would laugh, not for a reason that we would not happen to know, for lack of information, or for want of sufficient penetration, but because *the unknown makes us laugh*.

In sum, it makes us laugh to pass very abruptly, all of a sudden, from a world in which each thing is well qualified, in which each thing is given in its stability, generally in a stable order, to a world in which our assurance is suddenly overthrown, in which we perceive that this assurance is deceptive, and where we believed that everything was strictly anticipated, an unforeseeable and upsetting element appeared unexpectedly from the unforeseeable, that reveals to us in sum a final truth: that superficial appearances conceal a perfect lack of response to our anticipation.

We see that finally, given the exercise of knowledge, the world is likewise situated completely out of the reach of this exercise, and even that not only the world, but the being that we are, is out of reach. There is, in us and in the world, something that reveals that knowledge was not given to us, and that situates itself uniquely as being unable to be attained by knowledge. This, it seems to me, is that at which we laugh. And fundamentally, one must to say it immediately, when it is a question of a theory of laughter, this is what illuminates us and what fills us with joy.

Obviously, this theory presents a lot of difficulties from the very beginning, possibly even more difficulties than most.

In fact, I believe that, first, it does not give us the specificity of laughter. This is obviously its principal flaw. It will perhaps be possible for me to show, if necessary, that in every case when we laugh we pass from the sphere of the known, from the anticipated sphere, to the sphere of the unknown and of the unforeseeable. An example of this is a chance meeting in the street, which perhaps does not make us burst out laughing, but which most often makes us laugh. Likewise, another example is laughter from tickling, which overtakes us at the moment when we least expect it. There is also something of this, I think, in the confusion that a very young child can experience when leaving the kind of torpor that we might imagine embryonic existence as being, when it discovers the affection of its mother, when all of a sudden it discovers something disturbing, exciting, and absolutely inconsistent with its already given experience.

Meanwhile, this does not mean that we laugh every time a calm vision consistent with our expectations follows, through an overturning, even the reversal of this vision. And this is easily proven.

Suppose, in fact, that abruptly, as sometimes happens in certain cities, the ground begins to tremble, that the floor shakes beneath our feet. I think that none of us will dream of laughing.

It is true that in spite of this we can say that there is, in the relationship between laughter and the unknown, a relatively measurable element. The causality of laughter given in the unknown can be represented as having an effect that will be proportional to the importance that this diminution of the known nature, or this suppression of the known character of nature, makes us laugh. It is certain that the more that what happens unexpectedly is unknown, the more vigorously we laugh.

And, on the other hand, the abruptness of the appearance of an element unknown to us plays with us. Now, this abruptness has precisely the sense of intensity. The more rapid the change is, the greater the sensation, the more perceptible the experience that we have of it is intense. And the alteration that I mentioned earlier is much more perceptible than this intensity is strong.

But finally, this does not make a sudden catastrophe laughable. I think that it is necessary, in these conditions, to envision the thing in another way.

I profoundly believe that the principal fault, characteristic of those who wanted to talk about laughter on the philosophical level, is of having isolated the laughable. It seems that laughter is part of an ensemble of possible reactions when facing the same fact. This same fact that I was talking about, this suppression of the known, can result in several reactions, each different one from the other.

Laughter, in this respect, can serve to lead us on the path, the consideration of the laughable can introduce us onto the path that will lead us to the comprehension of this fundamental fact. But, we have hardly succeeded in determining this fact when we must immediately add that the sudden invasion of the unknown can, depending on the case, have laughter, tears, and not only laughter or tears, but other reactions for its effect.

Furthermore, laughter and tears—I must mention it because this goes a bit counter to what I'm saying—have not always been studied in isolation. Recently, a philosopher who lives in America, Alfred Stern, studied laughter in connection with tears, in what is, in my opinion, an interesting work. This work is called *La Philosophie du Rire et des Pleurs*.[3]

But, as I was saying, other reactions might still be connected to the same fact. For example, the sudden invasion of the unknown can have as an effect the poetic feeling or the feeling of the sacred. It can also have anguish or ecstasy as an effect, and not only anguish, but of course even terror.

Furthermore, I don't think that this picture is complete. In fact, there are other aspects. But it is perhaps complete insofar as certain other forms are not exactly reducible to a single one of those that I have just enumerated. This is the case with tragedy, for example.

Anyway, it seems that we might recognize the impossibility of talking about laughter in any other way than within the framework of a philosophy that goes beyond laughter alone, as does, for example, what I might call a philosophy of nonknowledge, which I am trying to sketch for you, through a series of conferences that are planned, up to a certain point.

It's necessary to note a reciprocity in this respect: I think it is impossible to talk about nonknowledge other than in the experience that we make of it. This experience is an experience that always has an effect, an effect like, for example, laughter or tears, or the poetic, or anguish, or ecstasy. And I don't think that it is possible to talk seriously about nonknowledge independent of its effects.

Evidently we can speak about these effects, in spite of the primary contradiction that the fact of talking about nonknowledge always represents. Of course, something paradoxical will remain in the act of speaking, when the principle of nonknowledge is articulated. Though in fact I have already expressed myself on this question. It seems that we might admit that, whatever the proposition into which a philosophy of nonknowledge would finally resolve itself, we are not restricted from speaking of the possibility of its effects.

Furthermore, I will now emphasize another aspect of the difficulties posed by the interpretation of laughter. I believe it is fruitless to want to approach laughter as an enigma that the personal philosophy of an author, elaborated independently of the consideration of laughter, would allow him to resolve.

There is always something very interesting in the effort that consists in putting a philosophy to the test of the problem of laughter after the fact. It is always very interesting in the sense that one recognizes in this way that a philosophy must be capable of offering the key to the problem of laughter. But I think this key can open nothing if it is not made expressly for the lock in question.

In trying to resolve the problem of laughter, I think it is necessary to begin with the consideration of laughter, insofar as one is writing a philosophical work. It seems that, in order to resolve the problem, philosophical reflection must *first* focus on laughter.

This might be surprising, given what I have just said a moment ago. But it is obviously a question of a superficial contradiction. I said that it wasn't necessary to isolate the problem of laughter, that it was, on the contrary, necessary to associate it with the problem of tears, with the problem of sacrifice, and so on. But what I mean is essentially that it is necessary to begin with an experience of laughter given in relation to the experience of sacrifice, to the experience of the poetic, and so on. Understood. I don't mean that these experiences must necessarily be given simultaneously, but I believe in the possibility of beginning with the experience of laughter first of all, and not letting go of it when ones passes from this particular experience to the neighboring experiences of the sacred or of the poetic. If you will, this is tantamount to finding, in the given that is laughter, the central given, the primary given, and perhaps even the given behind philosophy.

Now I would like to explain myself further on this point. I would love to make the determined orientation of philosophy tangible, in the most precise way I can, or at least the reflective experience apart from the experience of laughter. And I will set out toward this from my own personal experience.

In fact, I can say that, insofar as I am doing philosophical work, my philosophy is a philosophy of laughter. It is a philosophy founded on the experience of laughter, and it does not even claim to go further. It is a philosophy that doesn't concern itself with problems other than those that have been given to me in this precise experience.

I am emphasizing the fact that I prefer talking about reflective experience. This, in my opinion, has a great advantage. It is that, in the word *experience,* despite its association with the word *reflective,* a precise effect, like that of laughter, or ecstasy, or anguish, is maintained in a continuous fashion.

My philosophical reflection never proceeds independently of this experience. And I must say that this has a double meaning: it is that my philosophical reflection is valuable to the degree that it modifies the effects in question, that it makes these effects conscious. And I believe it is useful to recognize the way in which I attempted to bring my reflection to this point.

From the outset, I must specify that I am not at all a philosopher by profession. I cannot say that I did not study philosophy, but I have not studied philosophy as it is normal to study philosophy, I did not study it as a student. Furthermore, in a rather systematic way, I wanted to study things other than philosophy. And my studies, as it turned out—excuse the anecdotal nature of this explanation—brought me to London, and in London I was received into a home where Bergson was also received.

In spite of everything, I said I had, like everyone else, studied some philosophy, and during this rather elementary study, the kind that one does in order to take an exam, I had indeed read some of Bergson's writings. But I had the very common reaction that one might have to the idea that one is going to meet a great philosopher; one is embarrassed to know nothing, or nearly nothing, about his philosophy. Then, as I have also said in one of my books,[4] though I would like to say it here in a slightly more concise way, I went to the British Museum, and I read *Laughter* by Bergson.[5]

This reading didn't satisfy me much, though it strongly interested me just the same. And I haven't stopped, in my various considerations of laughter, referring to this theory, which, all things considered, seems like one of the most profound theories that anyone has developed.

I have therefore read this little book, which impassioned me for reasons other than the contents that it develops. What impassioned me at that time was the possibility of reflecting on laughter, the possibility of making laughter the object of a reflection. Increasingly, I wanted to deepen this reflection, to distance myself from what I had been able to retain from Bergson's book, but from the very beginning this reflection followed the trend, which I sought to represent to you, of being simultaneously an experience and a reflection.

Furthermore, I must say that, remembering rather precisely the first movements of thought that I developed at that time, its experiential character was truly its sole interest. I lost myself in rather secondary difficulties; I was lacking, I was going to say experience, but I cannot use this word, since I am using it in another way while speaking now; I was lacking sufficient knowledge to bring this reflection to fruition. With the help of these unsteady reflections, I believe I was always able to deliver myself into a kind of dive, which tended to be vertiginous, into the possibility of laughter.

Still, there is something that I can retain from my reflection at that particular time, its principle. This principle was to consider that the major problem was the problem of laughter; and formulating this rather generally, very far from what I am even now presenting, I told myself that if I happened to know what laughter was, I would know everything, I would have resolved the problem of philosophies. It seemed that to resolve the problem of laughter and to resolve the philosophical problem were evidently the same thing. The object that I grasped while laughing, if you will, seemed to me of comparable interest to the object that philosophy poses to itself most of the time.

I don't intend to defend this point of view, at least not in the precise form that I am now presenting. I need to express myself in this way in order to arrive at describing this experience.

Further, I must specify that at the beginning of this experience, I was completely animated by a very precise religious faith, conforming to a dogma, and that this meant a lot to me, so much that I reconciled, as completely as I was able, my behavior to my thought. But it is certain that from the moment I posed the possibility of descending as far as possible into the sphere of laughter, I felt, as the first effect, everything that the dogma brought me as carried away by a type of difluvial flood that decomposed it. I felt that, after all, it was quite possible for me, at this particular moment, to maintain in myself all of the beliefs and all of the behaviors that were connected to these beliefs, but that the flood of laughter I underwent made a game of these beliefs, a game in which I was able to continue to believe, but which was surpassed by the movement of the game that was given to me in laughter. I was no longer able, from that moment on, to adhere to this game other than as to something that laughter had surpassed.

It is hardly useful to say that, in these conditions, beliefs in a dogma cannot persist, and that, little by little, without attributing the least importance to it, I separated myself from every belief.

In this sense, I emphasize that the fundamental idea to which I am clinging is the complete absence of presuppositions. The philosophy that I am advancing would be, at any rate, absolutely deprived of presupposition.

When I speak of nonknowledge now, I mean essentially that I know nothing, and that if I am still talking, it is essentially insofar as I have a knowledge that brings me to *nothing*. This is particularly true in the kind of knowledge that I am developing before you, since it is in order to succeed in placing myself before this *nothing* about which I am speaking, to put myself and my interlocutors, if it is possible, before this *nothing*.

Furthermore, I must say that, from the very beginning, there was another aspect of this conflict between belief and laughter. What very quickly appeared to me is that, in my experience of laughter, there was nothing that was recovered from the religious experience that I once had. In other words, I didn't express myself in a precise enough way when I represented that I maintained my beliefs within the sphere of laughter. I maintained them, but they were so completely submerged that I felt that they were able to be indefinitely transposed in a movement of laughter, and that they were not impoverished by this. I was able to recover in myself all the movements of the religious experience, and to confound them with the experience of laughter, without feeling this religious experience as impoverished.

I can further say that, in an essential way, the movement, I would say more of my life than of my thought, has consisted in maintaining, in unexpected forms and perhaps as little satisfying as possible from the point of view of those who maintain themselves within the limits of dogma, all the religious experience that I had acquired in the limits of the dogma wherein I once contained myself.

Similarly, I believe that when I pass, as I am presently, from the pure and simple consideration of laughter to a more general consideration, such as that of nonknowledge, from the fact that, by nonknowledge, I mean principally an experience that I had once known. Nonknowledge, as I understand it, does not suppress for me the possibility of an experience that I consider as rich as the religious experience offered at the height of the knowledge that is revelation.

It is entirely in the act of posing being as a problem for myself, being as completely unknown, and of throwing myself into this nonunderstanding [*non-connaissance*], that I discover an experience not only as rich as religious experience but, it seems to me, even richer, more profound, if that's possible, because in this experience I separate myself further from communal experience. I separate myself further from the experience of the profane life, wherein we entirely adhere to objects that have only an extremely debatable right over us, a right these objects acquired by the isolated fact that we are hungry, by the isolated fact that we can suffer, by the isolated fact that fear often governs our actions. In the experience of nonknowledge about which I am speaking, if there remains a religious experience, it is entirely detached from our anxiety over the future, it is entirely detached from a possible and threatening suffering that would govern this future, it is no more than a game.

Of course, I am led to emphasize the fact that this experience of laughter is rather far from the common experience of laughter. At first, I must say, because this can seem rather peculiar, that this experience can be as completely detached from the movements described by the doctors as I previously detached it. It is always possible not to enlarge the face, and fundamentally this does not change much. All that I might say in this regard is that of course the enlargement, the opening of the face, and even mad laughter are part of this experience, that one cannot assume that this experience does not know moments of real mad laughter, as they are defined by physiology. But, on the other hand, what seems important to me is to specify that I separate myself from the experience as from laughter on a point that is all the same very important, insofar as, in laughter, I no longer understand only that which is in principle given when one uses the word but something more.

Of course, the joyousness of laughter remains. But in spite of everything, the joy that is given in laughter, and that it is paradoxical to see associated with the objects of laughter, which are not usually joyous, for me, this joy cannot be separated from a tragic feeling.

Furthermore, I believe that this is not quite outside the joy that is commonly granted by laughter, in the sense that, for each of us, for everyone, it is always possible to pass from the movement of common joy to the tragic feeling, without even having that joy diminished. Though one always, in most cases, refrains from this passage.

Here I will further insist on a point on which I have often insisted in my books; it is the fact that this is a question of an experience that is, I believe, rather profoundly in common with that of Nietzsche. I have often had a means of presenting rather bizarre things, I believe, by saying that I felt united with Nietzsche's thought, with Nietzsche himself, also with Nietzsche's experience, through a fundamental connection. And, in principle, one can wonder if this means much; we are all isolated, communication from one being to another is minimal; on the other hand, my interpretation of Nietzsche could be contestable. Meanwhile, I insist on it, and there is a reason, that isn't simply an intellectual reason, for this comparison between what Nietzsche was and what I am. This reason is that there is a kind of very particular experience that seems to me to have been Nietzsche's and to be my own, in the same way that, for example, Saint Teresa's experience was equally proper to Saint John of the Cross as to Saint Teresa herself, if you will, in that they were brought together on the level of a communication given in dogma and by belonging to the same religion. This community can be found between two beings, outside of their belonging to a religious community. This is why I spoke about community while speaking about Nietzsche. I am saying precisely this: I believe that there is a rapport between Nietzsche's thought and experience and my own, analogous to the one that exists in a community.

Furthermore, I don't want to remain vague about this. I think Nietzsche's thought makes this experience very understandable. It is given in particular, naturally, in the importance that Nietzsche attributed to laughter, and this in a very large number of passages, but especially in a rather late text in the posthumous work: "To see tragic characters founder and to be able to laugh . . . this is divine."⁶ I don't think that what I am representing in general when I talk about nonknowledge and about the experience [of] its effects [can] be disassociated from an expression like this one.

If you will, what is important to me when I am talking about laughter is to situate laughter at the point of slippage that leads to this particular experience, laughter that becomes divine insofar as it can be the laughter that one has in seeing a tragic character founder. I don't know if there isn't, in spite of everything, something that bothers me in Nietzsche's phrase. It is perhaps a little, I wouldn't say grandiloquent, but a little too tragic. In fact, from the moment that one clarifies the experience of what is properly tragic, up to the possibility of being able to laugh at it, everything is lightened, everything is simple, and everything could be said without any kind of painful accent, without any call to emotions other than emotions that are already overcome.

In fact, this is, I believe, what characterizes laughter inside of the ensemble of effects that I connect to nonknowledge; it is connected to a dominant position. In tears, for example, one's experience of nonknowledge, of what is given when one cries, is not an experience wherein one is situated in a dominant position. Here one is clearly overcome.

Now, in this regard it is necessary to specify that the overcoming offered in laughter is not very interesting, as long as it isn't the overcoming that Nietzsche's phrase indicates. In general, one laughs on the condition that the dominant situation in which one finds oneself is not at the mercy of laughter, of the object of laughter. In order to laugh, for example, it is necessary that one not risk losing one's dominant situation.

If you will, in order return to the terms that I presented earlier, if laughter is the effect of nonknowledge, in principle, laughter does not have the fact of not knowing as its object, we don't accept the idea that we know nothing by the fact that we laugh. Something unexpected is produced, something contrary, something in contradiction to the knowledge that we have.

Here I will cite a sentence from an article by Charles Eubé that was particularly interesting to me.[7] I am a little chagrined to say it, since I published the article in the last issue of *Critique,* but there is one sentence in particular that I retained, which seems to be very meaningful. This is how he defines laughter at a given moment. This is not a definition of laughter strictly speaking. It is a definition of the position of someone who is laughing. Laughing implies, according to Charles Eubé, "the refusal to *accept* that which most profoundly within us, we *know.*"[8]

In fact, someone who laughs, in principle, does not abandon his science, but he refuses to accept it for a while, a limited time, he lets himself pass beyond it through the movement of laughter, so that what he knows is destroyed, but in his depths he preserves the conviction that, just the same, it isn't destroyed. Someone who laughs preserves, deep within him, what laughter suppresses, but that it only suppressed artificially, if you will; likewise, laughter has the ability to suspend a very closed logic. In fact, when we are in this domain, we are just as able to preserve our beliefs without believing in them, and reciprocally we can know that which we simultaneously destroy as known.

Here I am returning to the theme I developed last time when I spoke about the opposition between the minor risk and the major risk. There is a major laughter beside a minor laughter. Today, I don't want to be limited to speaking about the major laughter, though, nevertheless, I am essentially referring to this laughter.

The strangest mystery to be found in laughter is attached to the fact that we rejoice in something that puts the equilibrium of life in danger. We even rejoice in the strongest way.

Further, I believe that this is the case without ever showing that we cannot consider a question like this in isolation, in the sphere of laughter. In fact, the same thing exists in tears.

There is a profound ambiguity in tears. Everyone knows that it is pleasant to cry, that one finds a kind of consolation in tears that we would often even not like to accept, but that goes beyond us. There is something intoxicating in tears, just as there is something intoxicating in laughter. I think it will not be difficult to show that tears can be considered as linked, as well as laughter, to the invasion of the unknown, to the suppression of one part of the world that we consider as a world known in all its parts, that we consider as an ensemble. If someone dies, for example, the known order is in fact profoundly altered, and we must see something that we don't know substituted in front of us, in spite of ourselves, for something that we know, such as, for example, the presence of a death, or more precisely the absence of the living, the disappearance, the sudden destruction of the known universe to which we belong.

But tears, the same as laughter, present a stranger character. And this strange character, I will have a little difficulty talking about it, because it is not classically the object of study. There are, beyond tears of pain, tears of sadness, tears of death, initially tears of joy. Now, about tears of joy, if necessary, we speak fairly often. But, beyond the tears of joy there are perhaps still more curious tears, which are not the object of a common dread. I believe that tears rise to the eyes for all sorts of complex reasons. Further, I don't believe I'm capable of doing anything here other than offering indications in the direction of what I mean.

There are, I believe, tears of success, which are extremely frequent. Obviously, they are not frequent to the point to which I might not be, for example, curious to know if some of you have not had such a concrete experience, and weren't aware of tears of success. At bottom, I don't know anything about what I call the tears of success; these tears have not been the object of studies corresponding to the studies done, for example, of laughter; at any rate, I am not aware of such studies.

For example, an unhoped-for success or even a quite extraordinary bit of luck can bring tears to the eyes. I will cite an example of this, which even surprises me, like all the things about which one generally does not speak. This surprises me, but I was never capable, without bringing tears to my eyes, to talk or hear talk about a certain act. I knew someone who, during the war was an officer aboard the *Hood*, nearly up to the day of the catastrophe. That particular day, or perhaps the day before, it was a question of a difference of a few hours, he left on a mission in an observation boat; thus, his mother had naturally believed him to be dead. Besides, his death had been announced, and it took days and days before his mother would learn that he was still alive. And well, I think that this unhoped-for character is something, I'm not saying that it necessarily brings tears to your eyes, but that it might bring tears to your eyes. And this is situated, I think, rather far from what one generally, classically says about tears.

I must say that in this regard I was taken aback by one thing; it is not that it is the only example that I have known, but generally I am not good at remembering the examples that my memory should offer me; I almost always forget this one. This experience has happened to me quite often, but I have never taken note of it, so to speak; I am not very methodical, and in general I forget about it. Furthermore, you see that here I am talking about a domain that remains completely open to investigation, which in sum is not at all known.

I don't want to make things more confusing. It is certain that when I am speaking about the unknown, I am not speaking about the genre of the unknown. But there is something quite particular, which in the meantime appears rather clear to me, which is that what makes us cry in this way is essentially the unhoped-for, the unexpected, and this seems to bring us back to the theme that I have developed generally.

I won't prolong this presentation by speaking more generally about the different effects that I enumerated earlier. I have already spoken here, in this series of lectures, about the relations between eroticism and nonknowledge, and between the sacred and nonknowledge. Perhaps, in another lecture, I will be able to talk about the relations between ecstasy, anguish, and nonknowledge, but this evening I will stop with what I have already shown.

Pronouncing the word *ecstasy*, I will limit myself to saying only this. Which is that laughter, considered as I have described it, opens a sort of general experience that, in my opinion, is comparable to what theologians have named "mystical theology" or "negative theology." But I must add that, in this regard, it is necessary to differentiate: this experience, for my part, is not only negative within certain limits, but totally negative. I will willfully give this experience, and the reflection that accompanies it, the name *atheology*, formed with the privitive prefix *a*, and the word *theology*. If you will, this is given in a proposition like the following: *God is an effect of nonknowledge*. Though, as an effect of nonknowledge, God is always knowable, like laughter, like the sacred.

This allows me to show that this experience situates itself in sum in the general line of religions. In speaking as I do, I am conscious not only of assuming a fundamentally religious attitude, but even of representing a kind of constituted religion. It is not a question of the foundation of a religion. No, there is no foundation, because there isn't any possible presupposition, because only one experience is possible. But, after all, all religions have not been founded; religions were simply able to be experiences constituting a more or less coherent dogma, often less coherent than more.

Furthermore, I will conclude in showing that despite this I wouldn't want to underestimate the philosophical character of this whole way of seeing. First of all, I really want to show that this way of seeing, in spite of its negative character, is associated with a kind of necessity toward a positive philosophy, and that all that it can add to this principle, to the principle of negation, is that the positive philosophy is not itself given for the principle that is situated in the experience about which I spoke as a kind of inevitable necessity, but that it is suspended, if you will, as I said that dogma was able to be suspended, within laughter.

I would also like to talk about something that seems to me to be of particular importance. The philosophies I am talking about—Hegel as much as Heidegger—have a theological experience in common. This seems very curious to me. The word *experience* is perhaps out of place, I don't know, but they had knowledge of theology. And even, I think there is every reason to think that negative theology was not unknown to Heidegger or to Hegel, and that in particular the Hegelian dialectic cannot be considered as completely without relation, historical relation at least, to negative theology.

Furthermore, I will add what seems more important to me, that it is truly necessary, when one expresses oneself in this manner, to arrive at saying what one believes possible in the domain, if you will, of morality, of human conduct. I have already indicated certain principles in this regard in the lecture I gave last time. But I'm not sure that this was sufficient; I am furthermore also not even sure that what I will say this evening will be insufficient. But I was rather taken aback seeing that one of the listeners, last time, asked me if I was not able to say something like: in these conditions, what must one do? I think that the question was not as badly posed as I have just posed it, but it amounted to about as much.

What I had said was very simple. I had represented that the risk would demand a certain boldness and that it was in the boldness of the risk that one was able to find the only possibility, in the boldness of the risk wherein nothing is ever given, wherein, after all, one can have no assurance. All this is to make evident in relative coherence in relation to what I said earlier. But I would like to offer a more tangible idea of what I now have to add.

A few days ago, I read a book that a certain number of you have no doubt also read, a book by Hemingway called *The Old Man and the Sea*,[9] and I was taken aback after reading this book, to see for myself that Hemingway's morality is, after all, a well-known one. I say Hemingway's morality, because it is evident that he has moral preoccupations, that it would be an injustice not to see the morality in his work. And fundamentally, it is very simple, it is the morality of the master, the morality of the master according to Hegel, I don't think according to Nietzsche, but this might be stated more precisely.

In sum, Hemingway loves only what men who had adopted the attitude of master were able to love. The master is a man who can hunt, who can fish, who does not work. The master confronts death through risk, and this is always what interests Hemingway. One does not see a working-class hero represented, for example. He always shows men that take a risk, and not a risk wherein anguish enters as a destruction . . . Something is always overcome in Hemingway's characters. Now, it is possible that this means of overcoming is more perceptible in the last book that he wrote: *The Old Man and the Sea*.

For those who have not read it, I will say that this book shows an old man struck by bad luck, who is fishing for a swordfish, a very large fish, and who, each time he disembarks, leaves in vain, and returns continually without anything to bring back. Finally, he leaves once more, but alone, without anyone to help him, because, since he has bad luck, no one wants to follow him anymore or can no longer follow him. He has some good luck, but in conditions that become, in a very short amount of time, the height of misfortune. In other words, he first has the largest misfortune to undergo with the big fish that he has caught and that drags him where he does not want to go, that makes him, to a large extent, endure a veritable torment, because he doesn't have the strength to manage this big fish; and all this in order to end with the fact that upon his return, when he has all the same gotten through it, the sharks begin little by little, and in spite of the old fisherman's desperate efforts, to eat this fish, which could have allowed him to live for a long time; and, despite his efforts to kill the largest number of sharks possible, he returns with nothing.

In my opinion, from my point of view, there is something remarkable here; it is that despite everything there is something in the old man that remains, from beginning to end, essentially *sovereign*. It is not without importance that this man is not a worker in the proper sense of the word, but a fisherman. Fishing is not quite a job. It is, if you will, the job of the primitive man, but it is a job that does not create the alienation that is characteristic of the work of the slave. At the present time even, there is no one who, considering himself a master, cannot fish. Fishing is still a thing for masters.

Well, I think that the possibility that Hemingway represented here is rather remarkable. It is that which consists in knowing how to keep quiet, in knowing how to put up with everything, and, finally, while living in the only possibility offered by luck, of knowing how to be in a state of finding oneself in a dominant position, in spite of every imaginable misfortune.

I must say that I cannot speak about this without any reservations. It was rather pleasant for me to present things in this way; but, in spite of everything, there is something bothersome, it seems to me, in Hemingway's characters. I am bothered perhaps, in particular, since the day that I found out that Hemingway, whom I don't know, converted to Catholicism. Obviously, for many people, this can, on the contrary, be agreeable knowledge. For me, it was profoundly disappointing. And, moreover, I place this in relation to what the character has furthermore that is deceptive. Everyone knows about Hemingway's profound anti-intellectualism, and I think that this anti-intellectualism exposes that which in this affirmation of the morality of the master is fundamentally very limited, and quite anachronistic, which he furthered throughout his work. I am saying that he affirmed the morality of the master, but I think that it is possible to say it.

Nevertheless, I would like to emphasize the rather painful feeling that fills me with the same hate that someone like Hemingway has for the intellectual effort of men; not that I don't perceive and even that I don't share the possibility of feeling a great repugnance in regard to everything that is intellectual, but I think that this repugnance must also be overcome. It is necessary to overcome it. In fact, I don't believe in the possibility of avoiding going to the end of things. The present world poses multiple problems for us, which are connected, for example, to work and to all the questions that it poses. Anyway, I think that, in this world of work, we are like people who submit to its law, we cannot escape it, we cannot play fisherman, hunters, and amateur bullfighters who have nothing else to do, and, reciprocally, we cannot ignore what is represented by the desperate effort of men to go to the end of their intellectual possibilities.

In any case, it seems to me that if what is seductive about Hemingway, which is connected to ignorance, might be attained by us, it can only be attained on one condition, that of having first been to the end of the possibilities of knowing. It is only beyond knowledge, perhaps in the nonknowledge that I have presented, that we could conquer the right to ignorance. But I don't think that this can be done immediately. I don't think that we can disappear before whatever the problem might be, and I think that we must also have the resolute courage that can be demanded of us in every way, in order to bear what is perhaps exhausting, wearisome even, in the work of the ant that is accomplished in our mind.

Part V

Aphorisms for the "System"

(Collected at the end of 1952)

[1. Memories of Bergson and Shestov, prolonging autobiographical elements continuing "Nonknowledge, Laughter, and Tears"][1]

Even before the end of high school, I associated philosophy with the meaning of my life. No doubt the way one can at that age . . . But from the very beginning, this fundamental determination, which should have drawn me toward specialized study, diverted me from it.

By chance, at first from lack of money, then from lack of time, I didn't take the philosophy class in high school. Discharged for medical reasons after having been called up for service, I had to study at home for the *baccalauréat* in philosophy in a short period of time. But I deliberately decided not to be a specialist in philosophy. History classes, which I took at the École des Chartes, where I was, it seems, a brilliant student, appeared to me to be more appropriate to my research. My only contact with accepted philosophy around this time (in 1920) was meeting Henri Bergson in London, where I was doing research at the British Museum. Forewarned, I read *Laughter,* which, like the philosopher in person, disappointed me (as early as this period I had an extreme mind). But the problem of laughter appeared indisputably foundational. I didn't imagine that *laughter* would dispose me toward *thought,* but that *laughter,* being in certain respects antecedent to my thought, would carry me further than thought. *Laughing* and *thinking* at first appeared to complete each other. Thought without laughter seemed mutilated, laughter without thought was reduced to this insignificance that is commonly accorded it, and which Bergson described very poorly. From that moment on, in my mind, *laughter,* no longer being limited to Bergson's seedy comedy, was tantamount to God on the level of lived experience: although raised outside of religion, I then

153

had the Catholic faith, and, I must say, in the most ardent way (I had even envisioned myself becoming a monk), but my entire thought resolved itself in this immense hilarity (this would be incomplete if I didn't add that this experience of laughter and the experience of pleasant sensuality found themselves intermingled).

My fundamental interest in philosophy manifested itself in the most virulent way in this attitude, but at first it was not conveyed with any consequence. I even did no reading. (I limited myself to reflection, all the while perceiving the abyss that separated my embryonic thought from the intended result.) I began reading Nietzsche only in 1923. This reading, furthermore, gave me a decisive feeling: why continue to think, why envision writing, since my thought—all my thought—had been so completely, so admirably expressed? (Perhaps Nietzsche didn't give the experience of laughter a sufficient explanation, but he was the first to locate it.) I foundered, decidedly, in a sort of indolence. In the end, I read Freud with sufficient persistence. But the disorder triumphed within me.

Although I was already a librarian at the Bibliothèque Nationale, I entered the École des Langues Orientales. I began to learn Chinese and Russian; I abandoned these courses quickly enough, but I had the opportunity to meet the Russian philosopher Lev Shestov. Lev Shestov philosophized in the wake of Dostoevsky and Nietzsche, which seduced me. Soon enough I had the impression that I differed from him irrevocably on account of a fundamental violence that affected me. Nevertheless, I respected him; he was scandalized by my extreme aversion to philosophical study, and I listened to him docilely while he guided me smartly in reading Plato. It is to Shestov that I owe the foundation of my philosophical knowledge, which, lacking the character of what is commonly expected under this name, in the long run became no less real. A little later, like the rest of my generation, I had to lean toward Marxism. Shestov was a socialist émigré and I distanced myself from him, but I maintain a great respect for him; what he knew to say to me about Plato was what I needed to hear and I can't see who would have known to tell me these things in this way if I had not met him. From this first step, sloth and sometimes excessiveness often diverted me from the narrow path that he had lead me to enter, but today I am moved remembering what I learned listening to him, that the violence of human thought is nothing if it is not its fulfillment. For me, Lev Shestov's thought distanced me from the final violence, the end of which I had glimpsed from the very beginning in London. Anyway, I had to separate myself from him, but I admire the patience he had with me, though I then knew how to express myself only through a kind of sad delirium.[2]

[2. Plans and notes for "Atheology"]

A. Introduction. The destruction of what I am not.

B. The unknown.

   1. Test of luck (the three failures).

     a) comical approaches

     b) hazardous conscious approaches, the primacy of experience (mixed up aspect even of this book)

     c) circular thought

   2. The irreducible unknown.

     a) the rarity of suffering

     b) impossibility of formulating the question

     c) the minor unknown

     d) the paradoxical wealth of a philosophy of the unknown

C. The effects of the unknown.

   1. The study of effects.

     a) impossibility of setting out from the unknown

     b) enumeration of domains

     c) laughter

     d) criticism of phenomenology: the destruction of the reiterated

     e) criticism of Heidegger

   2. The cause of effects (the so-called consciousness of the unknown).

     a) the unique cause and forms: intensity, rhythm, disordering, and violence

     b) dialectic of sense and nonsense

     c) disordering to excessiveness

D. Return to the point of departure. Definition of atheology.

   1. Primacy of experience.

   2. Irrefutable character except inexperience.

   3. Sartre's refutation-apology.

   4. The criticism of the will to be everything and sovereignty: the philosophy of the exception.

   5. Community and the refusal of the project.

Introduction

I want to speak as a philosopher and without reserve. This means that I commit myself: (1) not to limit the object of my discourse; (2) to empty of meaning or to relate to a meaning that I will give to everything that philosophers have said before me or will say after me.

I will therefore strive to get out of the imprecision and the incompleteness of the thoughts to which I have, almost, limited myself to up till this point.

In the first place, I must be aware of the comic nature of my intention. Philosophers succeeding each other resemble the inveterate gambler who has always lost but is no less sure of winning the next time: the only difference is that a gambler is more judicious . . . Furthermore, whatever my attention and my mistrust might be, I do not want to laugh at myself, or at others. My purpose is as sincere as the gambler's if I say: "this time, all the luck is on my side." I myself am more honest than the gambler in that: when I speak, I recognize that, from the outside, all the luck is apparently against me. This is why I begin my presentation of "my philosophy" with a

Test of Luck

At the point where we are, it is clear that a process of philosophical thought is in principle never but a *hazardous process*. It is even in the essence of this thought to be founded on the *originality* of each person, though this is foreign to the philosophical world, strictly speaking. I hardly see philosophers as having assumed the position of renouncing this quality. At this point, things are such that if I now said that I am renouncing it, I would only seem pretentious. Because every thought is engaged in a struggle for supremacy and to aspire to impersonal thought is to naively betray an unavowable intention to dominate.

It is no less true that this fleeting attitude finally leads to the emasculation of all thought. One even ceased perceiving the responsibility essential not only to these statements but even to the fact of

The question of suffering understood in this way is among the most strange.

Few men feel this pain. One might even say few philosophers. Besides, shouldn't I, personally, admit it in connection with the will to indefinite growth, the will to be everything? Perhaps. Perhaps even, insofar as this will dissolves, suffering is changed into rapture. This rapture is from this suffering in particular as it is generally from anguish. It is possible that suffering might be the consequence of an attraction to the "unknown," that without the attraction toward the unknown this suffering might be missing. Rather, it is the consciousness of a fascinating value beyond the unknown, and it is the impossibility of grasping what is desirable in this way that gives birth to despair. Without doubt, it is possible to live in the progressively known world, not to suffer given that one is waiting patiently for the progressive reduction of the unknown to the known. This is the postulate of science. Suffering only begins if the vanity of a reduction of the unknown to the known is revealed. This is why this circularity is deceptive.

Nevertheless, suffering just hasn't been able to understand the unknown, the inaccessible loved as such. I can tell myself: there are men, and possibly there are also some in other worlds, but where does that come from? Where does it lead? And then: isn't this a stupid way of asking questions? In truth, I see the world and I see myself, all of this exists and it is so enigmatic that I cannot formulate a question for this purpose, this is a pure enigma and a limitless question, this is a question and nothing else. Saying "what is this?" is still an impossible precision. This would be to imply an imaginable response, like: "this is a phantasmagoria." But of course not. The question is so irreducibly such that the thought of words in response, whatever they might be, is an obvious contradiction. This is unexplainable not on account of my not knowing the explanation; looking for the explanation would only show that I lowered the question. In fact, every "what is this?" would be stupid, the possible response to which would only be a part of it. Whether one supposes responses like this is a window, a sponge—whatever word, whatever formula, everything is equivalent. Every possible response makes me a pure suffering, my eyes out of their sockets, in a foundationless obscurity. At this level, light or the object that emerges in the light is in some way a more profound obscurity. The obscurity is what light or the elucidated object conceals: at least the obscurity doesn't lie, blind, I am more advanced than if I see, no appearance separates me from the unknown.

What is nevertheless paradoxical is that I spoke about the unknown, a singular possibility of knowledge begins here. Of course, the unknown cannot be given to me as an object, as a thing, I cannot hypostatize it. In other words, I cannot know the unknown. I have only *really* spoken about myself.

Meanwhile, I can only talk about myself insofar as I am for myself and an object for others, the hypostasis defined by distinct "states." I am a man, not only this man here but a man: supposing that my phrases are not written by me, Bataille, but by Kant, by Hegel, or by someone else, nothing would change. They concern man insofar as man is generally given as an object, as a thing of a definable species. I can contest the possibility of this given, claim that this man and this other man exist, not man in general. But in that case I would go against the possibility even of knowledge. I would say in an approximate and fleeting way, of the known—when I could not speak if there was not any knowledge—that it is the unknown itself. It is comical to speak in order to deny the possibility of knowing: here I only want to put the bearing of knowledge in question or to show its effects, and when I speak of the *unknown,* I know that I couldn't do it if I knew nothing.

Knowledge concerning the unknown cannot have the unknown as its object but man having the experience of the unknown, wanting and not being able to know it.

This can take place in two ways. I am a mailman, I carry a letter to its address, but neither in the designated house nor in the neighboring houses is the recipient known. Or I am a mathematician and I talk about the unknown in a problem. Each time it is a question of an interruption, of minor importance, of an activity of discernment. (Cite Sartre.) In this interruption, knowledge is still not called upon in its principle, but in its application at determinate points. It is a question either of what is still not known but could be a bit later, or of the impossibility of knowing more than the given (I only know through experience or through hearsay). But in that case the impossibility of knowing touches an object. I can talk about the unknown and define it.

(The secret of the richest knowledge, of a bond before knowledge, is to honestly recognize that we know nothing and to talk about the unknown.)

One of the points to specify concerning this domain of knowledge (since it is understood . . .) is that this is not what interests us anymore, it interests us sovereignly.

To substitute the unknown for all the presupposed entities of different philosophies, it had to seem that knowledge was going to become impoverished in two ways, its extent would be restrained, and it would be generally reduced to its most exterior elements. What happens is really different. A lot goes toward offering the apparent reason for this from the very beginning. Insofar as we tried to locate under the light of one distinct knowledge what we must honestly consider as unknown, the categories of the known were introduced into the domain of the unknown. References to the unknown (to which, finally, the meaning of words such as *God* or *matter* are reduced) have been defined as though they were elements of a distinctly known world, articulated within the connections of this world in a similar way to the one that connects those of the best-known elements. It comes from an impoverishment of the *inconceivable* (which is the unknown), to which in principle nothing can be *subordinated,* but which is perceived, in disguise, is called to servile functions. It is really necessary to envision God from this perspective, if proof of his existence is drawn from the need for a first *cause* (if, in order to grant the world a creator, the unknown must enter into the category of the worker).

In this initial impoverishment it seems that the unknown is "richer" than the known. Truthfully speaking, the use of the epithet *rich* in this place is disconcerting, but the meaning appears in the consequences of the limits of knowledge inside the known world—contrary to those of the introduction of the categories of knowledge into the unknown. Life restrained to its intelligible operations is clearly the most impoverished.

• • •

(Impossibility of setting out from the unknown.)

The positive atheology[3] cannot have the unknown as its object. In principle, from the two things one, it had to be established independently of a consideration of the unknown, or not exist. Its authenticity from all points of view demanded this independent origin. There cannot be a science that would offer knowledge of the unknown. Nobody can seek the unknown, it can only be given, in a *passive* experience. The unknown I'm talking about is that which knowledge does not have any means of grasping.

Of course, I can in principle find in the reflection on knowledge, therefore on its limits, the point of departure from negative considerations of the unknown, but reflection engaged in this path without the aid of a discipline constituted like that of the sciences in general cannot go far. It is even inconceivable—at least in principle, and for reasons that cannot even be clear a priori—that in the desire, itself unjustifiable, to take the unknown as its object, someone might have spontaneously intended a search for the effects of the *unknown* in the specific behaviors of human beings. This search was only able to happen in one (or several) domains of science already established toward other ends, where "the effect of the *unknown,*" "the effect of an experience of the limit of knowledge," would be encountered.[4]

(Domains. Laughter.)

These domains must be enumerated from now on. They are:

—laughter

—tears

—sexual excitation

—poetic emotion (envisioned at first in the form of sentiment of the beauty of nature)

—the sentiment of the sacred

—ecstasy

In my personal research, it is true that I was guided by a singular hypothesis. I will express the idea of it, or rather, the initial view, as correctly as I can at present, but in remaining strictly faithful to its intention: when I laugh, there is something incomparable in the object of my laughter. Philosophy cannot have any other object. Besides, in my mind, I made the object of this laughter a substitute for God; here I saw nothing less than a principle of the universe. What was revealed to me, with a *violence* that astounded me, was that in the world and in the inconceivable void that it opens up, there is nothing that is not violently laughable. I was perhaps the only one to laugh in this way, but my experience was no less irrefutable than that of ordinary laughter. No one doubts, in comic laughter, that the object at which one laughs is not laughable, but in ordinary laughter the object of laughter is taken as inferior. What does not make us laugh is dignified, and what makes us laugh is judged. It could go without saying that the feeling of indignity that my immense laughter gave me of its object was not superior to human or divine dignity.

(claiming every place or none—my universality—end of the ath., exhausted by deafness, miserable effort—I must complain about Sartre, who took my sovereign laughter for a sickly smile)

(Criticism of phenomenology. The destruction of the reiterated.)

The pain-rapture cannot be apprehended as a thing in this regard: it is a thing insofar as we apprehend it, but a sovereign thing, or rather, this is *the* sovereign thing, this is the divine or sacred thing, this is the thing in which a destruction of the thing takes place. It is sovereign in that it is not subordinated to rules. Consequently, it is excluded from the will to apprehend it if one is oneself subordinate to rules. It is at first a lost will, the object of which is in itself the destruction of the object. But one is unable to want this object in order to destroy it. The destruction of the object is offered as grace. As in poetry. This grace is perhaps only energy, but one is unable to intend to attain it. Thus a multitude of consequences: language, if not sovereign at least morally posing sovereignty, disengaging itself from the philosophical attitude. Opposition of Heidegger to inner experience: what is missing in H. is sovereignty. Sovereignty is an act of rebellion against every rule, including the logical rule. A negation of every limit, of every *condition,* this is the taste for an experience that can no longer be limited by any of the given conditions, the affirmation of a choice against philosophy.

• • •

Philosophy without any revelation is trickery (to treat what is not an object as an object) or is pain.

In pain, a *sovereign thing* is given, a thing that can be an object of thought, but insofar as among things it destroys the thing in itself.

This is not the beginning of a philosophy of existence because:

a) there is a primacy of experience, of violence, like grace;

b) experience cannot be envisioned in any other way than as a thing *in the minor mode,* subordinated to a consideration of the result.

The minor mode: (1) things given in narratives; (2) reflection on things in narratives.

• • •

The experience of living *against* is indisputably given in the human experience. Subordinated existence postponed until later. Man needs sovereignty more than bread. There is not only joy or suffering: there is living in the present moment and living for the future, in other words, consumption or growth. In the case of growth, there is the being that does not exist yet, subordinated to the being that will be. I grow, therefore I do not exist yet, I expend, therefore I am. Thus the being is insofar as it is against the will to growth. Let's substitute for this naked truth a truth dressed in clothes given in the succession of romantic history: the poet is against the prudent man: the bourgeois, bound to capitalist accumulation. That is to say that the being that is, is given in a rebellion. Naturally, the danger is that the rebellion itself changes into a project, the suppression of the bourgeoisie, having the same subordinations as the bourgeoisie. But let's continue with the search for transpositions of the truth seen this time not on the level of particular and historical existences, but on that of forms of fundamental unity, which substitute themselves for unity and are given in language—this must set out from history.

Nature—on account of man being inscribed in society, there is a natural man against authority, constraint, limit. But what happens if man rebels against constraint in the name of nature? He makes nature an equivalent of constraint

the sovereign operation that is negation destruction remains

in this way redo what I missed about Levinas[5]

Negative philosophy is a discourse on anxiety and rapture, in other words, on the divine. It is an experience connected to the other, the exterior, on which philosophy is constructed as the change into the foolishness of thought determined by objects, at the point which, from knowledge of the object, the mind seeks to pass to knowledge of the nonobject, from what is by no means an object on the level of the knowledge of objects, in other words, on the level of the discourse.

My knowledge of Heidegger is (this time Sartre has seen rightly) insufficient: it is only a development from points of reference

I didn't know that Heidegger refused the label of philosopher, or that he was in a kind of [illegible] in search of sovereignty. Proust, on the contrary, who gave experience the framework of universal stupidity . . . the two greatest minds Marcel Proust and Maurice Blanchot (who made derangement the result of the search for rules)

Here the dialectic of solitude and of loyalty

The essence of sovereignty is the derangement attendant on the execution of the sovereign. The final question is therefore this one: can one make a rule of derangement?

Insofar as man is not God, there is only philosophy subordinated to stupidity. Stupidity, this is consciousness, since consciousness is conscious of limits. Consciousness is completely on the side of the rules. If consciousness is lacking, at this point only philosophy could begin.

However a metaphilosophy is possible for this reason: the moment where consciousness is lacking is one (a) of anguish (from suffering), (b) of rapture

In one sense, making philosophy into an experience of suffering seems to engage in a philosophy of existence (of course, not in existentialism, whose fundamental proposition of the primacy of existence over essence is vertiginous or is nothing—the same thing with homeopathy). My philosophy has none of this, my philosophy is purely negative insofar as it is philosophy. It is a retreat into science.

Some will say to me that it isn't, that I insert givens that are not from science but from the philosophy of existence.

To this I respond:

I threw myself in the water. My thought went in all directions. Not without consciousness of the fragility of this process. But from the very beginning without being worried about purity.

(The question: social facts are not things)

It was only slowly that I began to insist against many of the steps taken: only the reduction of the object of this experience to a thing can be maintained without any stupidity.

But of course the application of thought to the object of my experience as to a thing (about which I won't hesitate to say that it is the only field open to philosophy in the end) poses a certain number of new and serious problems from the very beginning:

a) its scientific rigor is foundationless,

b) and is much more worthy of distrust than can be realized, at least in the present moment, inasmuch as it is a true science.

c) Nevertheless, it presents an interest, it prolongs philosophy in particular in this form: it envisions the metaphysical problem insofar as it has the divine and consequently God as its essential object. However, the heritage of this philosophy is not from metaphysics, but in fact from theology; it is a theology without God, close to negative theology in particular.

d) Its obstacle is drawn from this. This kind of knowledge is continuously drawn toward the metaphysical (if not toward positive theology). In other words, at any instant thought engaged in its chosen objects of knowledge risks making absolutes of them. Sartre represented me as hypostatizing the unknown. This accusation is rather absurd precisely in that Sartre was able to see me as very worried about this failure, but it is not false in the sense that I succumb at every instant and that I give rise to confusion in this way. Naturally, *savage* history, and so on, cannot have the meaning that S. gives it. S. lets himself be taken in a rather evident, reprehensible abuse of language—I really want, from the outside, not for me (but in this matter it's necessary that I reject judgment from the outside, I only reproach Sartre for not having made an effort that he is certainly capable of; my mistake in his eyes certainly being that of addressing myself not only to him, but also to minds that have the right that we spare them such an effort). Whatever it might be, the question posed by Sartre is a question (even more my question than it is his). It results precisely from the fact that the unknown is not just anything and that introducing a modification into consciousness, this modification is situated immediately on the level of objects. Every possibility of "pseudophilosophy" follows from this (and I fear that my thought has most often been confused with this pseudophilosophy and apparently, as surprising as this might be, this is the case with Sartre; once more, he could have, easily, made the effort that would have eluded him. But I believe he didn't consider it to be worthwhile. This can be interpreted in two ways: general malevolence, or, to the contrary, this twofold benevolence demanding my interest and that of readers that all this no longer be equivocal)

I will now specify the problem raised by the objective givens concerning the *suffering* owed to the impossibility of knowledge. In sum, the experience of suffering from knowing nothing, from the moment when, in pure suffering, it becomes conscious above all of the object of reflection which is suffering, inevitably proposes a secondary response to the desire for knowledge. This secondary response can be formulated as follows: I know nothing, but the suffering that I have from knowing nothing, becoming an object of knowledge, gives me the response at the very instant that I despaired of finding it.

It is difficult to challenge this formula.

No doubt I will say: from the moment I extract knowledge from my suffering from knowing nothing, my thought is a derangement of thought.

But this judgment is still only a *general* proposition, of negative value. It incites distrust, it cannot suppress the positive meaning of thought proceeding from a derangement of thought.

In fact, continuing in a similar direction, I arrive at a new formula that apparently offers an acceptable response (and perhaps impervious to the desire for knowledge): no doubt no thought remaining within the rules of thought was able to offer any response to the desire for knowledge, no object of thought, remaining within the regular limits of thought, was able to do anything more than offer this desire, the limit of which cannot be determined, cannot be envisioned objectively, in that, in regard to the posed object, it would be immediately necessary to confess that, being unable to be determined, it is not the object that cannot be indicated in positive terms but only through negations (an expression like the *universe* is still objective, in other words, not limitless—one might oppose God to the universe, for example, or thought, and if one goes all the way to saying *what is,* the incomplete formula must be specified by a negation like *envisioned without any limitations*). This detour is, furthermore, superfluous; I could content myself with showing that every positive predicate touching on being in general is inconceivable, that the being in general can only be spoken of negatively (see Hegel). Thought, nevertheless, can be adequate to what is not authentically an object of thought by means of the derangement of thought. This proposition is more difficult to dismiss than it seems at first

I underline the fact that in the sense that philosophers mean it, I ignore philosophy, even that I ignore it more and more. It is therefore in bad taste, on my part, to invite philosophers to take me into consideration. I invite them to consider themselves as fools. Nevertheless, my attitude in their respect deserves a modicum of consideration on their part. First, I am also a fool, it is as much my foolishness as it is their own that I am attempting to show. Then, I am unable to engage myself in showing this foolishness without straying from it to some extent.

But between various philosophers and myself there is a certain difference. It is that I have suffered, "in some way physically," not exactly from nonknowledge, but from the nonknowledge of knowledge, if you will, from the foolishness of knowledge.

This suffering having carried knowledge away in every other consideration, insofar as my effort prolongs that of the philosophers, I made philosophy the experience of this suffering. Or: I substituted for philosophy the experience of suffering that philosophers don't have insofar as they fail at philosophy

The problem with philosophy is the passage from the knowledge of limited objects to the knowledge of the entirety of what is.

Is the essence of foolishness in the act of identifying the ensemble with an unlimited sum of limited objects? No. No doubt this is foolishness. Nevertheless, foolishness gets its true character only in the effort to escape from this foolishness, that is, to pass from science to so-called philosophy. No doubt foolishness consists in not seeing that thoughts that go against the scientific point of view are contradictory and sworn to incessant movement, and that it is essentially impossible to be conscious of something without making this something a limit [*crossed out*: without making an object of it], since consciousness is always consciousness of an object and thought is nothing other than the establishment of constant relations between some consciousness of an object and some other consciousness of an object. Consequently, thought can envision the absolute only on one condition, by opposing it to what is not absolute, that is, by making a negation of it. The fact that the absolute is a negation means that the absolute is not given in consciousness.

There is no philosophical given, no revealed theory, but there is a point where thought resolves itself in something other than thought. In this convergent point, two opposed currents:

—the negative effort of thought to go from the consciousness of limited objects to something else

—the activity of thought searching in knowledge of limited objects for that which concerns knowledge of "that which alone matters," which begins with suffering from failure. To pass from this to the effect of derangement.

But the problem posed at the moment of the convergence of currents that can never converge finds its true position only in solitude, sovereignty, the disposition of infinite energy, therefore the instant realized and negation accomplished from the *condition*

(Return to the point of departure. Definition of atheology.)

Define atheology: the science of the death or destruction of God (the science of the thing being destroyed inasmuch as it is a thing).

Reflection on the reflection on the sovereign thing:

Consciousness is consciousness of limited objects, consequently there cannot be consciousness of an object if its limits are denied (or destroyed) by it. Consciousness enters into the night, as soon as the limits of the object, or of the subject insofar as it is an object, are denied (or destroyed). Or rather, consciousness becomes consciousness of objects of which the limit (the definition) is the negation (the destruction) of their limit. In other words, the play of consciousness substitutes a new limit for the absence of a limit, a new kind of object for the object where the destruction of the object takes place, a new meaning for nonsense.

Always reflection on the reflection on the sovereign thing. One might say: the sovereign thing would be grasped on one condition, that consciousness dies in conceiving it—at the limit, there would therefore be a response to the question, I would come close to a response, I would hold on to it if it didn't destroy consciousness.

• • •

(Criticism of the will to be everything and sovereignty: the philosophy of the exception.)

To want to be everything, this is no longer taking everything as an object, to want the objectified subject, that I am, to be in everything as an adequate sovereign, be it at the price of an adequation of the objectified subject, but not at the price of a destruction (as a particular subject, in other words, as an object).

I add that the operation that consists in denying oneself as an objectified subject cannot implicate the will to be everything.

• • •

Propositions

1. Circular thought is the only plausible thought. To be of one's time is quite simply to be a stooge.

2. But circular thought must begin not from a proposition but from the ignorance that precedes it, and it culminates in nonknowledge as well.

3. All mystical positions are shortened circles, therefore the moments of nonknowledge are intellectually short.

4. My position is the one that is opposed to Hegel-Kojève as 2 and to 3 as Hegel.

5. The identification of God, of the sacred, of the erotic, of the laughable, of the poetic, and so on, with the unknown is the key to all philosophical difficulties.

6. It is absolute nonknowledge admitting the wisdom of variable knowledge adequate to variable situations, but substituting absolute dissatisfaction for relative insufficiencies: the passage from subordination to sovereignty.

7. The final nature of dissatisfaction is the truth of awakening (the experience of eroticism, etc.), the sought-after satisfaction in the *Phenomenology,* whether it is a question of *anerkennen,*[6] it doesn't matter, is only a means to postpone it until later.

8. Unformulatable interrogation.

9. The relation between the known and the unknown introduces the most important knowledge into *[the domain of the known?].*

10. Sovereignty, loyalty, and solitude.

• • •

One must not say: suffering prevents man from being indifferent to annihilation. This would be inadequate. Suffering, misfortune, and principally anguish have their meaning in indicating the being's preference for anguish, suffering, and misfortune—in relation to nonexistence on the individual level. There is no anguish in making choices but the choice of anguish that is the adherence of the being to itself, or more precisely of the present to the future. The anguish is the being's anxiety over its future, the temporality of the spatial being is itself anguish. If the being were not leaning over the abyss of anguish and of suffering, if its presence in space and time were not threatened, if the approach of death did not have to be incessantly compensated for by a growth of the spatial field of possibilities comparable to shortening the distance in time

More simply, it is possible to say that spatiotemporal existence is itself a dereliction, an abandonment to cruelty. Just as certain men choose a dangerous life, likewise and independently of every individual orientation, existence pure and simple is the choice of one situation governed by the risk of horror. The mystery of conscious, personal life is given (1) in desire, which is always that of a negation of this evil in destruction, which is a question on the plane of biology or of recognition.

• • •

Revelation and Autonomy

The first phase of autonomy is trickery (before the feeling of annoyance). The second phase, annoyance and stupefying moments, is linked to the consciousness of a sovereignty where one cannot cheat.

Useful activity is the condition of thought (a durable thing, capable of changes), therefore sovereign thought must come out of the movement of growth and of the will, on the part of the subject-object, to be everything.

Thought measuring the beyond of things where it has no access is necessarily negative and it cannot take something that it denies for a thing. Thought should address suffering, anguish, ecstasy.

• • •

That philosophy is foolishness is the most tangible truth, and the least defensible. No one can say it if he is not a philosopher. But a philosopher admitting it, calling himself a fool, would not know how to prove that others are fools if he hadn't offered the philosophical proof of it. The consequences of this difficulty are severe. I know them, I must admit, but cannot reach the end of other consequences: they demand proof, and I cannot deny it or offer it. I drafted out the response, boredom came, the trouble that I have following my ideas gave me the taste to do something else, to eat, to laugh, or even . . . to escape anxiety through trickery.

Sadly, I tell myself that no matter what I do, the idiocy of philosophy engages me. I must take my part: if I submit to it, I live in the sovereignty of foolishness; if I deny it, I must have some basis for this denial. I think that most people deny but that their reasons are no less foolish than the philosophers. I am a man, and human intelligence compromises me: nobody can leave it in suspense, if it is subordinated to the judgment of others. One often does it in a very cowardly way; the most subordinated make an evil genie through the most miserable idiocies, and nothing is more common.

From the very beginning, one must admit that the matter has begun badly, that nobody extricates himself, that humankind received intelligence in part only to be infinitely sworn to idiocy. The most intelligent humans have only succeeded in demonstrating some intelligence: a little later, their efforts were judged just as they themselves judged the efforts of their predecessors. Finally, it was only a question of having a name on the list of honors, at the most funereal distribution of prizes.

We still hardly perceive what happened when Christianity lost an uncontested monopoly in the sphere of thought. Christian faith was not nonsense, but a resignation of the mind, which received its determinations from the outside. In a series of coincidences that responded to each other, from one sphere to the other, proceeded an assemblage of myths, of authentic story narratives, of judgments and of values from which the extreme [novelty? movement?] assumed the meaning of a miraculously received solution. To receive this solution, in a kind of anguished shock, which was communicated from one to another, was to show weakness. But the weakness in this case was in the failure of a newborn rational effort, which only the blind were able to deny. True foolishness is offered in the pretension of the one who extracts from himself a response to the enigma "we are here—on the slope where we slide." If you will, foolishness is autonomy, it is the sovereignty of the mind. It is the glory and the disaster of man: in the final analysis, no one can dream of our destined communion without seeing it connected to some I don't know what that is disappointed, shameful, unavowable, that pains us to hear a fool saying what he doesn't know.

Nevertheless . . .

It is touching, it is sweet—madly—to no longer see, from all sides, anything but the deserted expanse of folly. It is like going away into the night, into the snow, going away without knowing where: the silence of the snow carries the footsteps into the silence of the universe.

In this way, therefore, the adventure of autonomy led thought to the death of thought! The divinity of silence proceeds from an unlimited folly, and from the feeling of annoyance that follows from it.

I think of a shipwrecked person; he exhausts his strength and, suddenly, perceiving the vanity of his effort, he has a feeling of annoyance. Sadly, he tells himself: it would have been better not to swim, but if, for lack of knowing, I hadn't swum, at the moment of . . . , I would not have been capable of being disappointed.

It is necessary to say that in the final moments of intellectual games, the short spans of time that open themselves up and steal away pose problems to the mind that would empty it—and would further degrade it—if it held itself to some solid position. To distance itself from ordinary perspectives, the mind discovers a mad mobility of an aspect of a singular subject of reflection. In this way a demonstration of the nonsense of thought is first, fatally, given in discomfort, if necessary in the raptures, of anyone who readies himself to follow truly stupefying movements. There isn't, initially, a philosophy that *would establish* the foolishness of every philosophy, but (in fact) a mobile way of thinking disappearing within every solidification of thought—as its object it had the idea that all solidified thought is folly—or even—that a principle of mobility always escapes folly.

But from the real mobility of thought up to me, I can grasp this mobility empirically in a connection with a will to the autonomy of those who think, who do not want their thought to depend on an authority given from without (Descartes was subordinated to this authority, but he denied that his thought was). But the disturbed Christian authority, thought, in its search for a true framework, nevertheless followed the most humble paths, always acknowledging a principle given to the being that we are from without, and to the laws we have to conform to. In other words, sovereignty still belonged, in these contradictory pursuits, to some reality whose fundamental importance, summing up the universe, everything that is, whatever that might be, blocked it into a knowable system. In these exercises, man always derived from these various elements, the unity of which was given in a system wherein, practically, man had the right to be situated, if not at the center, at least *within* the totality wherein he loses himself

[3. Other notes and aphorisms (1950–53?)]

I have the burden, against a modern—existentialist—philosophy, of defending poetry, consequently Surrealism. More precisely perhaps, a possibility for a religious attitude (independent of religions), against the ethical attitude. I am saying it, I am insisting on it: Sartre's existential choice is bizarrely suspended between action *(ethics)* and poetry (which is less *aesthetic* than *religious*: Julien Gracq has very rightly spoken about this hardly indecisive orientation of the Surrealists in the religious sense). I denounce a position that is that of an ass out of Buridan.

Contradictorily, I see that action must [*engage itself? crossed out*: be accomplished] anyway (ethics that founds action would not know how to limit it). But action is the means and the end is poetry. Action has the future in mind and the end is necessarily given only in the moment, which is *sovereign* and which poetry restores. I know that it is conventional to see in action only a means of maintenance, of growth, or of improvement. And it is possible to abandon to pleasure or to immaterial principles the final reason, in the instant, for its undertakings. But if one demands, at the same time, the strength, the moral wealth, and the (immanent) human nature of purpose, it is time to go as far as poetry.

I would like one to regain, in this declaration, the tone that detonated in the first moments of Surrealism. Since then, after many mistakes, confusions, and irreducible humor, the possible was clarified.

Even today we know that it is the *impossible*. But for all that nobody can disarm it. It is possible that the *impossibility* of poetry is itself the condition of poetry: is not satisfied desire (possession) the death of desire? With regard to the *instant,* all that enters into duration must misunderstand the instant. Pitilessly, the instant demands what can in no way *be*. It demands the community, but the community is *[derisive?]*. It wants the poetry that it hates and, like a tragic character, it can scream out nothing that doesn't strangle the scream in the throat.

But, *impossible,* it is, in what it defiles, though joyously, like a lover.

• • •

Laughter, after all, is only a feeling that in principle motivates a particular situation. I cannot claim while laughing *to know*: *to know* insofar as it is a linguistic term is given to me in the discursive articulation of my thought, not in some revelation exterior to language.

Nevertheless, I can say (no doubt taking advantage of the preposterous gratuitousness of language): as long as I think discursively, I align my thought parallel to the object of my thought: I establish rather stable correspondences from this object to my thought, but I don't have the genre of knowledge of this object—questionable or not—that I have of myself, for example.

I envision this: I don't know *myself,* what I am, for me; I can see it just as easily as unknowable.

Who am I? And *what* am I?

Every response from my thought leaves behind a feeling of derision. Not that I have trouble recognizing myself as this man that I am, occupying this situation on this date, like recognizing a man . . . But it doesn't matter (the last thing I would know how to make myself guilty of would be of demanding to be more—I willfully see myself, rather, as nothing).

1. The philosophy before which I am

2. Thus subject-object identity, but it doesn't matter much. This here, which is, myself, everything that is, I find this laughable—it is obviously exterior to knowledge but in laughing I can introduce a judgment—evidently pure knowledge being what it is can enclose laughter, but laughter too can enclose knowledge.

3. If I say that my laughter encloses knowledge, it is an intellectual position, it's true, but in this way I realize a sovereign operation in that my judgment is related to an element that is no longer intellectual.

On another level, I can say that I have no less abandoned knowledge than I have ethics. Knowledge and ethics are related to practice, but each like the other allows an aesthetic element that is subordinate to them to intervene.

The ethical sphere is opposed to that of the aesthetic. And above the aesthetic there is the religious, which seems to differ absolutely from the aesthetic, which nevertheless is only a compromise with the aesthetic, in which the aesthetic is no longer purely and simply subordinated to the ethical but in which an aesthetico-ethical hybrid element rises above the ethical.

But if on the subject of laughter I say (and this could be another aesthetic reaction) that my laughter encloses the ethical as it enclosed knowledge, if I emit a value judgment on laughter, in posing sovereignty, instead of the sovereignty of an aesthetico-ethical God it is the sovereignty of the aesthetic that I pose, but the sovereign aesthetic is not the sovereign that Kierkegaard rejected, it is something else:

1. it is naked and abandoned, it is that of the death of God (N.)

2. it is beyond the religious and is imaginable only when the faithful have been denied all the way to the end (citation from N.)

3. it implicates the rigor of an absence of choice and the . . . to almighty luck.

4. it is in a sense misfortune itself, it is the subordination to the instant, and if one wants to have an idea of the difficulties encountered in this case, one must say this: nothing more than hope remains, that of freezing the instant, which literature attempts—for example, Proust (literature is the greatest valorization of the instant)—but culmination is also denial, this already inclining toward the ethical. There is from that moment on a semi-impossibility. Simultaneously with the vulgarity of Proust's ethical judgment on the literary work, one arrives at a substitute for knowledge instead of a loss of knowledge and of the consciousness of the thorough "impossibility" of thought

the greatest tension is linked to the consciousness of impossibility

What is in some way dispersed in these conditions is traditional philosophy. The sovereignty (sovereign authority) of the aesthetic (previously I spoke of experience) subordinates philosophy, as Christians subordinated it to theology, but this time it is no longer subordinated to the object intellectually and dogmatically defined by the experience, but directly to the experience that is taking place, no longer accepting any limit and always going to the extreme of the possible.

In other words, in these conditions, ethics and knowledge disengage themselves from every transcendent element.

• • •

[. . .]⁷

• • •

Preface of *To Die Laughing*

I said what impatience forced me to say. I didn't say it according to the rules. This was clear enough, and Sartre envisioning the *contents* of my book had to take this into account. I was unable to offer the form befitting my thought. Sartre, who praised my style, understood this, but he nonetheless attempted to look for the contents as if he was in the presence of a definitive form. And furthermore, he did it badly.

My horror of polemics is as great as always, but in the end I can't let go

Theme of the introduction: impatience initially. Protest against a philosopher who didn't recognize the right to impatience, who developed nothing himself—but in the end the maturation that primary impatience guaranteed.

The lectures from the Collège Philosophique. My articles. This is the mature—or nearly—oeuvre that I offer the critics. The contents were given in *Inner Experience* to those who should have looked for them.

(Some time or another I should add a short note on the lacuna in *Being and Nothingness* in regard to animal life—first part, chap. 1, §3.)

• • •

I was unable to postpone
I would have been able to die, it's true, without having explained
But I believe in the conclusion no more now than yesterday
First of all, what I undertake today is not completed, will perhaps never be, and will hardly be more when, from lectures already given, I will have made the expression of my thought less incomplete.

• • •

(look for an epigraph in Blanchot)

In *Inner Experience,* I didn't fulfill the rules. I wrote what a philosopher never writes, a book without rigor, more an expression, a debauchery of thought. Honestly speaking, I didn't do it unconsciously. I also didn't have the feeling of my impotence. Or rather, I saw myself as in some way bound by my principles, which were not to let the *project* enslave me (to subordinate my life and to reach the end of a *majesty* at which I no doubt laughed, but with a sovereign laughter, that was no less than death the same thing as myself). Without feeling extremely incapable, I had to tell myself that my thought, which from the very beginning granted precedence to the experience of thought, would itself be denied insofar as it would subordinate the intensity of the experience—the inner violence and the deregulated course of life (a contempt for the *project* analogous to that of the wolf for the collar).

But it is one thing to write, to publish a book, the book might be something else. In the long run, I had to suffer through the powerlessness of these pages that any title might assemble. I had left them at the mercy not only of a common and peremptory criticism, but of an admiration that I abhorred, that of confused minds, easy and weak. In a word, when I was treated as a "new *mystic*,"[8] I was able to sense myself the victim of a truly mad error, but whatever the frivolity of the one who committed it, I honestly knew that fundamentally "I hadn't stolen it."

Added to the fact of being disarmed in front of others, and the object of a comical confusion, was the feeling of a fundamental problem. What my lack of rigor sacrificed was nothing less than consciousness—in the first sense of the word. This problem, I admit, had from the very beginning been my book's problem. I knew it, no one can at the same moment be conscious and have the experience I'm talking about. My experience, essentially, is that of a negation of consciousness, it is the annihilated consciousness, deprived of an object. All of modern philosophy created minds from the idea that consciousness is always conscious *of* something. Husserl wants it to be *intentional*: it is as if one were saying that it is a *project*. This *thing*, in fact, of which I am conscious, is conscious only insofar as it is the announcement of a possible project. It is a book, a road, a suffering: I can read the book, pass over the road, endure or not the suffering. No doubt, my suffering is given to me—and conscious—in a sense before being envisioned in the plan of the future. Nevertheless, "pure pain as the simple 'lived' can not be reached; it belongs to the category of indefinables and indescribables which are what they are. But pain-consciousness is a project toward a further consciousness which would be empty of all pain; that is, to a consciousness whose contexture, whose being-there would not be painful" (Sartre, *Being and Nothingness*).[9]

Inner Experience
New edition
preceded by
Power and powerlessness of my thought—and of thought
and followed by
Reflections on "Inner Experience"

Speaking of *Inner Experience* and *Guilty*, someone whose thought I had never found fault with told me that he didn't like these books. They seemed to him to be dangerous, he said. On this point as—except for only one—on all the others (on the condition that they matter), I am truly in agreement with L. I had proof that these books easily engaged those who read them. They most often agree with empty and impotent minds who want to escape and sleep, and are *fulfilled* by the literary evasion. It is even certain that to write them, writing them with rigor, in consideration of an *awakening* that obligated me to it, I myself slipped into sleep. I wrote in disorder, having to respond to a *moral* demand, but the fatigue and *unhappy* immorality that resulted from the awakening engaged a slipping into the powerlessness of thought that turns into literature. I didn't really surrender, I didn't translate my fatigue into presuppositions founded on a sentimental facility, but I expressed myself in the mode of those who surrender. I didn't indicate horror any more than I had their weakness; I seemed to say to them: love me, I am one of you, and like them I prostituted thought to literary success. I am not writing now in order to disavow myself: I assume responsibility for mistakes the danger of which appeared to me from the very beginning.

Whoever would follow my thought to the end would recognize this: coherent thought necessarily makes room for the necessity of sleep, and it is arbitrary to throw this necessity to others and never to welcome it. Similarly, nothing seems more important to me than never to separate the coherence of this continual incoherence without which coherence would leave its object on the outside. But in the end it appears essential to me to distinguish the greatest effort from fatigue depriving one of the possibility of effort. The greatest effort of thought necessarily rises to the *general* condemnation of effort—in which accomplished thought closes the circle, it is in the end only a condition of the absence of thought—but this completion has nothing to do with whims that have no meaning other than an absence of imperfect effort, other than an absence of effort translating an aleatory absence of strength. For this reason, my friend's opinion condemning my books pleases me, and their usual reception would be odious to me . . . if the coherence of thought generally didn't have what it hates for its object, which for many ceases to be purely detestable.

The same L., having read Sartre's article on *Inner Experience,* tells me—with a coarseness that seems misplaced to me even today, but coarseness, apparently, eases conversation—that it was a piece of shit. If, as I believe, my books give way to confusion, it is difficult to condemn Sartre so quickly. Was Sartre not right to rise up against a book that was preceded by a miserable interpretation? It is nevertheless necessary to recognize that, a philosopher by profession, Sartre was ill endowed to see, in order to denounce it, the misery that empty minds saw favorably in it. It is good that he denounced this misery, but it was his duty to see that it was not there. Unfortunately, Sartre works quickly.

• • •

All that I can do today: propose reading my book the way I would have ruins visited. I am not the man in my book. I don't disown him, but I especially cannot deny the immense expanse of haze in which the entirety of human thought is lost. I no longer have the heart to express my thought but the truth about the haze in which thought universally errs. But as the river mixed with the sea cannot go down, so thought that errs knowing it cannot err any further.

But this manner of thought would by no means know how to justify an errance that had not been preceded by the exhaustion of the thought's resources.

Horror of ceasing to be personally.

Horror of knowing existence and of being solicited by a fundamental question: how and why, the whole teleological question, which wants teleology in the night that annihilates it as an effect of a more perfect teleology: an absence of all teleology, the abandonment (the death of God) that is gentler, more sure, and more tolerable than a guarantee. If the truth is a woman, it is necessary to plunge her into debauchery, to dishonor her, to soil her, to deny her up to the moment of a scream, of negation, of joy, wherein nothing remains in repose, wherein nothing remains that assures, wherein in the excessive awakening, meaning is nothing more than the means to fall asleep

• • •

[. . .]¹⁰

• • •

(introduction to the second part)¹¹

I feel foreign to the world. This does not mean that I am. But the reflection that I pursue—which is not only logical, in that my logically elaborated representations are never indifferent to the sensibility—slowly makes me a stranger to the world, which is fine with me, it's artificial, but I will willfully call my impotent freedom this awakening through which I break my connections with my equals, who draw me out with the agonizing and sensitive narrowness of a clear and discordant world, which projects me into a beyond where *my eternal silence* occurs.

But this beyond, to which I belong, which distances me from the world formed by the coordinated reflections, really poorly coordinated, of humanity as a whole, does not distance me from what escapes this failed coordination (from one important part at least of that which escapes it). I subsist among men, in a sense with suspended breath, awaiting the moment when the deceit of the figures of coordinated action will be revealed, during the kind of night that, falling in me, will carry my presence to the extreme degree of intensity. The moment always comes, in fact, when these figures lose their virtue and we can even provoke it, only a great strength is necessary to do so. But in far-off times, those who held power didn't forget to provoke it. We must wait for it, and since patience is our lot (sovereign power also falls to us), we would no longer agree to hasten the coming at the expense of others, even if, slyly and freely, the opportunity were offered.

Existence demanding the duration of a body is a continuous sinking from which each being tries to free itself through a violent effort. Difficulty helps in this by offering everyone enough violent suffering and uneasiness to assure the intensity of the effort.

In a sense, sovereignty is the absence of effort, but, in suffering, it can be maintained only through an effort—and the effort destroys it.

There is, in fact, never an absence of effort. What resembles the absence of effort is ambiguous, it is a collapse without suffering, *Inner Experience* asserts itself against this.

• • •

§1. Nonknowledge begins in the very instant that absolute knowledge is achieved.

Nonknowledge, inevitably, springs from anxiety over attaining not only the most expansive but the most profound knowledge. First of all, if I was unable to satisfy my curiosity in regard to a sphere that is still unknown to me, I must strive to reduce this unknown portion to what I already know. Only if I knew everything that can be known could I say that my knowledge does not differ from nonknowledge. If an insufficiency persists in my knowledge, I must begin by ending this insufficiency. Only about *absolute knowledge* could I say: it is the same thing in me as if I knew nothing, absolutely nothing. I know I will never really dispose of accomplished knowledge. I can, however, imagine myself, as Hegel did, disposing of this *absolute knowledge* that absolves me from every new operation of science (from every movement that risks my *active* faculty of knowing). It is perhaps sufficient, toward this end, that knowledge has closed the circle within me, and that, meanwhile, I no longer truly support an automatic curiosity, which still troubles me but henceforth can no longer bring me anything that might open in me, the way a sword opens a wound, the circle wherein my thought becomes inert. It is difficult to grasp what I now want to specify. It is an experience: let's suppose that, right or wrong, I no longer want to know anything more, thought dies in me. What I already know is nothing, as it is absolved of the effort necessary for knowledge to be produced, but meanwhile what is no longer anything deprives me of the possibility of the effort in the course of which every knowledge appeared to me as a response to my insufficiency. Insofar as my knowledge set the stage for new questions leading to new knowledge, knowledge was produced within me, but at the moment when the circle closes, knowledge entered into the night wherein the absence of the desire to know made me founder.

§2. —

This is not entirely true. Insofar as I was able to produce the experience about which I am in fact speaking, I can also say that my desire to know has never been greater. But I knew that I was unable to know anything more: my desire to know henceforth no longer hinged on a possibility that I might have seized, on a hope that an imaginable effort would justify. I remained tormented in this dissolution. It was, in a sense, comparable to the nightmare or to the kind of indefinable dream that sometimes accompanies a serious illness, wherein nothing happens except that the absence of every event, even of every thing, responds to an impotent attempt, to a desperate attempt wherein terrible cries are smothered.

In *Inner Experience,* I attempted to describe this state of mind: I am sure I did it poorly. My excuse is perhaps the lack of familiarity most minds have with an experience different from the experiences that thought ordinarily presents. Jean-Paul Sartre didn't expressly deny this suffering clinging to the final impossibility of knowing, but when he wrote a review of *Inner Experience,* he spoke about it to one of his friends: he didn't understand that someone could be so unhappy not knowing: this seemed far-fetched to him. In his review of the same work, Gabriel Marcel reproached me for having made "a troublesome misuse" of the word *torture*.[12] Truthfully, the word is rare in my book, the exception made in the running titles of the part that I in fact called "The Torture." Gabriel Marcel would have liked *torment* better: how could he have confessed that he didn't understand me? The *torture* in fact begins in the conditions that I have just defined. Otherwise it is inexplicable: who would experience more than torment for the lack of a response to the question that it raised?

Even less can I complain about this incomprehension in that I found that I had myself left things in ambiguity. In *Inner Experience,* did I not attempt to ask a decisive question? Heidegger had

What eludes Wahl in Hegel. It is that the movement of his philosophy—which necessarily has an oscillation, double aspects following that . . . (Wahl perceives this duality of possible interpretations)—is also, and, for us, no doubt mostly the report of the various aspects of human reality, of historical reality producing itself everywhere, of multiplicity, successive or not, of facets of the human being. A philosophy neglecting this multiple pulverization of being—entirely in oppositions—this sinking of the mind in the various necessities of the particularity, the fact that the mind itself, as a so-called structure of being, appears as the result of the play of these necessities—up to the unity of a clear conscience, is fundamental. But the question remains open on certain, general aspects whose duality is not reducible: is this a question of a result or of a realized goal (of a given goal)? As if it were impossible for thought to remain in ambiguity? Would it not be, rather, impossible to get out of this? If we want to grasp the meaning of what I call the "destruction of the subject," we must place ourselves—in the imagination—before *nature*. Nature *in itself* is nothing, but *for us* it is the abolition of work; each time that we lose ourselves in it, it suppresses the sense of exhausting effort linked to work, the effort that gives us a view of factory towns, of rows of factories. The finished products of work, like monuments or ships, also abolish this feeling.

• • •

[. . .][13]

• • •

Global nonknowledge is introduced into the phenomenology of human knowledge as the ultimate moment, but previously in the relations between knowledge and sovereignty, implied every time that knowledge is not contented in serving practical (servile) ends. The domain of global nonknowledge, if not nonknowledge itself, is given each time that philosophy develops its interrogation without limiting it. Only Newtonian science, or rather, science in general, avoids this empty interrogation. God's position maintains the interrogation of global nonknowledge between two connected affirmations. There is a fault, a rupture in the tissue of knowledge. And it is justifiably in the faults in the linkages between thought and servile reflection that sovereignty is maintained. Sovereignty is interior, every time. Insofar as nonknowledge, that is, the refusal of servile knowledge, composes sovereignty, the question of passing from this nonknowledge embraced by the sacred (and more closely surrounded by God, etc.) to a nonknowledge that is sovereign as such, without the procrastination and the coercive explanations, is posed. From here, the principle of an embracing nonknowledge is therefore (and finally, in numerous cases) the recognition of all the behaviors in which nonknowledge is embraced, intellectual behaviors, emotive, moral, active . . . Such recognition always has a negative, intellectual aspect in the sense that nonknowledge is here revealed in its purity. And a positive aspect as well, in the sense that the otherwise unintelligible behaviors appear clear. This second aspect supposes the—provisional—reduction given the maintenance of the first aspect as absolutely sovereign. Of course, if it is a question of intellectual behavior, philosophical reflection is led to moments of decision that at first leave a subsidiary aspect to moments of nonknowledge offered in moral and affective behaviors (pure, active behaviors being, on the contrary, turned from the side of knowledge). But it quickly appears that all of these questions are interdependent. Consciousness of global nonknowledge is, in fact, not total (it leaves questions to which it is possible to respond) insofar as it is purely intellectual. On the one hand, the fact that this consciousness is not indifferent, on the other hand, the fact that global nonknowledge appears, in the lucidity of this consciousness, implicated *in its unconscious form* in desire (for example, being lucid, I understand that laughing is the passage from knowledge to nonknowledge, from the known to the unknown, which interests me, which delights me). These facts pose the strangest question, in any case, the final question of philosophy: why does the search for knowledge only interest me up to a certain point? Why, beyond this point, is it "global nonknowledge" that becomes the object of my desire? I propose a simple response: the moment comes (perhaps it came before, perhaps now, it doesn't matter) when knowledge seems contrary to sovereignty in that even "disinterested" knowledge has the same form as interested knowledge: similar to useful work, but employed beyond its use, in order to enliven, and if it is apparently in a sovereign manner, it is simply that there is a confusion between the sovereign attitude and the servile play used as a hobby by those who have the habit of servile behaviors. Nonknowledge therefore seems to respond to the demand for sovereignty (in the strongest sense). In fact, what is then contestable is that the value of nonknowledge is one value among many, but without this value, among others

In other words, if we envision the formula: the absence of a concept (or the disappearance of the concept) is the absence of this time (negative eternity) like a corollary of the Hegelian formula (the concept is time), I can refuse various aspects of it:

—sacrifice

—the death of God

—laughter

and so on, that is, the various effects being produced in restricted domains: the disappearance of given concepts provokes specific physiological changes and it is necessary to envision:

1. the sum of these effects, these effects aside, then their total as a given effect

2. the total effect as a recognition of the limited effects, explaining the limited effects

3. the necessity of a contestation of the new concept being formed through the course of these analyses, then of a contestation of a concept born from the first contestation, and in this way consecutively,

so that the eternal instant is resolved in nonsense, in the absence of every concept, or rather, in the absence *of the* Concept

What is decisive in the return of the global effect to the limited effects, then of the limited effects to the global effect, is that the vanishing global Concept cannot be envisioned independently of its effect any more than a similarly vanishing concept can have a burst of laughter or an erection as an effect. Not that the global effect can be the *meaning* of the absence of the Concept

Part VI

The Sovereign

Nothing is more necessary or stronger in us than rebellion. We are no longer able to love anything, to respect anything, that bears the mark of subordination. Nevertheless, as a whole, the world from which we come, from which we become what we are, lives in interminable prostration: this origin forewarns us, if we allow ourselves to be led without distrust by our most assured feelings, we might slip from autonomous and capricious moods to fleeting judgments, the verbalism of which subordinates the minds of those that form them. A mechanism of words in the name of the principle of insubordination, this is no less contrary to rebellion against *subordination* than naively yielding before a sovereign power. Could the entirety of the past have been enslaved? And would history be proud of the hate or envy that covers our refusals?

The most burdensome misery inherent in our condition requires that we never be limitlessly disinterested—or without trickery—and that, lastly, rigor, bitterly required of us, is still insufficient. The human mind has too many deep folds in which it would be useless to linger: because the truths that are discovered there mislead us no less than honest appearances do.

In these difficult conditions, we can only laugh or cower, but an *insidious* laugh is more sincere than trembling: at least it means that we haven't any asylum and that we gaily refuse to be at risk.

I had to say that first. In fact, I can only make the "claim" to rebellion that is connected, from near or afar, to that which conceals the folds of a human soul from the unavowable, but *I laugh* and I think that the rebellious mind laughs with me; it was a day of trembling from this interminable weight: I am laughing, as I said, a happy laugh, but

185

my ardor sovereignly wants to be *"insidious."* The proper sense of rebellion is not to allow oneself to submit easily. I can put myself in question, doubt my good faith. But I cannot let the *subordinated mind* recall the authority that inclines it toward me. Here I take up the claim to rebellion rather weakly, recognizing nothing sovereign above me (as my solitude measures the obscurity of the universe to the vanishing point) and no longer waiting for a response from the uninterrupted silence.

A desire for accuracy in the instant guides me, according relief only under conditions of nudity, abandonment, nonsense; I would find myself prostrated before a comforting power. A state of passion forbids me not to allow the sob to rise freely, the sob that sometimes leaves me stranded, feeling alone, having only ever found my shadow around me. I know that in me humanity is alone in the solitude created by death, if it strikes someone we loved; and my appeal is a deceptive silence: I know only this naked, immensely gay, and trembling *instant,* that even a sob can't *restrain.*

II

First of all, I wanted to oppose the rebellious beings that we are essentially to this otherwise undisputed world, ordered by submission. But we are not *everything* and we are not *equally* rebellious in the same way. And as rebellion binds itself to the human condition, given in history, I could not attribute a meaning to the position of *my* rebellion—to our happy, clumsy, and often uncertain rebellion—without situating it in history *from the very beginning.*

I think that *being* vanishes in submission, but the fatigue, the desire to vanish, and the decay that follows it force their way through just as much when we assert, not without gravity, our rebellion: inversely, by ruse or by offering ourselves without reservation, rebellion often forces its way through under the allure of submission. We must therefore be careful not to see it in the malice that speaks in its name, and also not to mistake it in those terrible flashes that illuminated the past. Encountering those who link awareness to obedience, we must also assume that being does not have a real or sovereign presence in us, only a rebellious one; that its full magnitude—which cannot, *like the sun or death, be looked at fixedly*—demands extreme relinquishment to rebellion. In this way, the astonishing glare or the furtive joy of ecstasy, apparently linked to a startled attitude, are given only *despite* the submission that fright seems to occasion. In the same way, neutral and bland tempers, matter-of-fact neediness, or the flat lyricism of the rebel deceive us: it isn't from the side of a humble or formal belief, but in the initial spark of a refusal, that a burning experience opens up, which lets us err limitlessly in the end. It would be a deception to definitively link being, along its most errant paths, to *correct* truths, made from concessions to the docile mind: the leap that uproots us with gravity has the naïveté of rebellion, it has it, *in fact, in the experience,* and if it's true that it leaves us speechless, we nonetheless cannot remain silent before having said it.

It is true that a limitless opening—neglecting those calculations that connect us to an existence articulated in time—abandons us to bizarre difficulties, which those who followed (or thought they followed) the pathways of obedience didn't know. If it excites us rather boldly, rebellion condemns us to overturn its object. This final and mischievous solitude of the *instant,* which I am and just as assuredly I will be, and which, finally, I will, in a way, be completed in the sudden trick rigorously staked on my death,[1] nothing in my rebellion evokes it, but nothing separates me from it just the same. If I envision the *instant* in isolation from a thought that entangles the past and the future of manageable things, the instant that is closed in one sense but that, in another, much more acute sense, opens itself up while denying that which limits separate beings, the instant alone is the sovereign being. Through rebellion, I refuse to grant a sovereign share, although it might have seemed irreducible in me, ceasing to be a being subordinated to other powers that treat this being and use it as a thing, that enchain this thing with the intentions of efficient thought. If I grant consequences to this rebellious movement, I must strive and struggle to deny the power of that which alienates me, which treats me like a thing, and confines that which wanted to burn *for nothing* to utility: in this way I escape the prison of servitude only to enter into the chains of a rebellion that entails consequences; these differ from the prison that this rebellion intended to open only *in degree of force.*

III

Returning to the topic at hand, as I delimited it, through the historical course of rebellion, I cannot therefore doubt that the rebel loses a lot—perhaps everything—if he enters the narrow path of consequences: from that moment on, he must lead, without any clear limit, a struggle wherein he will have to subordinate the present to distant ends, and sink into obedience.

But I can reinterpret the course of history: in the past, at least in periods preceding "subordination," a wide path opened before someone who refused to immediately enslave life in his person. He wanted the *being,* of which he is the repository, to remain unruly, never subordinating it to anything. This being could not be the servile means to an end more important than the being itself; it had to be there, sovereign, limitless and never-ending, for no future goal, to reject whatever enslaved it. If it engages life, this attitude is without retort: between slavery and death, everyone is free to choose death.

But this audacious resolution could only postpone; gravity took over and solidified humanity: the way an unfamiliar gait numbs the legs, imposed and unpleasant work marked *the others*. Humanity isn't the grand inspiration of poetry, exhausting me in vain: it is a type of greed engulfed in the December mud of a farm, in a country of frost, of jealousy, of harsh disease. Even a human being's face tells me that it's better to live with a little calculation and to subordinate every gesture to profit. The stigma linked to this behavior isn't prejudicial to the human being, and the limit here is the enslavement of being. Every man is still, potentially, a sovereign being, but on the condition of loving death more than slavery. I can, from this moment on, want nothing more than my caprices and, in accordance with my luck, I will make it, or I will die. Because of this I can say, without lying and without even stretching the truth, that every man is sovereign if he puts his life in the hands of his caprice. And if the caprice of princes, once, disposed of everything in the world, this was insofar as they gambled even with their lives. The vicissitudes of men are so variable that other, apparently contradictory, principles oppose this view. But first this truth: *that there were princes,* although, most often, their meaning escapes us, and we have obstinately resolved not to see *that this first principle dominates us,* reminding us no less clearly that a sovereign path, more accessible and more simple than rebellion, was, from the first, open to the unyielding will.

At some point in the movement within me that refuses the servitude the human condition imposes on the multitudes, I can always stop concerning myself with other men, limiting an always precarious solidarity to my family and friends. That a small number of men put themselves in this way *above* servitude is even less worthy of astonishment when one considers that, taken in its entirety and from the very beginning, humanity tended spontaneously to put itself a little *under* servitude. If one historical moment seems hardly debatable, it is truly that which touches on work, in which men, unlike animals, at least most of them, are reduced to slavery by their own accord. Work is on the same level with the prohibitions to which the first men seem to have been just as subordinate without being bound to them by others. Apparently, these beings at once so near and so far from us distinguished themselves from the animals through a willful supplication to laws like those prohibiting free sexual commerce and murder. Despite preceding history in the narrow sense. And even if we doubt, presuming some ancient imposition of constraint, we must believe that humanity has subordinated itself in its entirety, almost simultaneously, to the law of work and the major prohibitions. It has subordinated itself, it has renounced the natural sovereignty of the animals.

But this act of subordination must justifiably have involved the necessity of compensation, in conditions without constraint. A willful servitude necessarily had an end beyond the activity itself, adequate for subsistence and common to animals and men. Humanity allowed the period of license to prevail, the tedious design of work no longer functioned—and the prohibitions faltered—among the enslaved. The sovereign act of the festival, where nothing matters but the instant, the present, compensates for the contrary action, which had engaged subordinated attitudes, and of which it is, through deafness to what it isn't, the resolution and the end.

What the whims of the festival are, in time, to the subordination of work, the sovereign is, in space, to the subject who works in his service. Not that the sovereign is himself subordinate to laws. But these particular laws reign over each sovereign's relations with other sovereigns, and the precautions that they must take in the presence of this irreducible force, a force that cannot be subordinated to anything. These laws place limits, from the outside, on the ruinous effects that unfold from the one who nothing limits of his own accord. But in the kingdom of the instant, the sovereign not only puts other men in the grip of dangerous and capricious acts, he remains there himself; the sovereign is in this way one who can in no way bring himself to safety, being unable to live beneath the burden of design.[2]

Cruelty isn't at risk, but sovereignty without servitude has something to offer . . . While servitude was imposed on the conquered so that death alone would have permitted insubordination. The working slave is nothing more than the effect of a constraint. Those who don't bow on their own accord before the sovereign, subordinate—by force—men who, otherwise, would refuse work. Thus the slave hasn't willfully placed the master over him. In the end, the sovereign, who wanted to protect *being,* in himself, from subordination sets *being,* the essence of which seemed irreducible to subordination, free, when this *being* is that of the defeated or of a stranger. The refusal that the capricious oppose to servitude remains seemingly unchanged. But the excuse that they had in this secret arrangement disappeared if the involuntary slave, not the subject, is held in servitude. Or rather, the sovereign acquires the power to use work toward ends other than the dangerous sovereignty of being: under these conditions, the sovereign might want to retire from the game, to seek shelter, and, far from living in the instant, to deprive himself of the sacred force that he had risked, in order to substitute the duration of the instant for this desire, which justifiably offers the gift of blowing out the flame.

In the end, the failure of the sovereign in ancient times, whose actions may have seemed less aberrant than those of the modern rebel, is therefore no less complete than the general discredit suggests. If we are worried about leaving a sovereign movement of being intact within ourselves, we can no more reduce it in others than leave it to ourselves; this movement, provisionally, subordinates itself to the expectation of a final emancipation.

IV

An immeasurable act of submission apparently avoids this dilemma. In the eyes of the subordinate man, the sovereign state wasn't accessible to the *creature* that he was. Or, if you will, in a human estimation, the sovereign state—wherein there is no recognized limit or tolerable submission—is sin. And we should have, if possible, eliminated sin from the earth, even from the universe more generally, but we couldn't—besides, we don't want to—harm that which is sovereign at the heart of being, that which dominates us and dominates that which humanly elevates itself most powerfully. Sovereignty in submission becomes an affair of the otherworld: in a sense, the subordinate, pious, and religious man doesn't *delay* the restoration of sovereign being, but puts it into the beyond, which doesn't come later if we envision the totality of what is *at once.* The beyond, for us, is not only ulterior but is separated from us in space—or, if you will, in the order of space, outside space.

This arrangement isn't arbitrary. In comparison with that which defined a sovereign *in this world*, it opened a field of renewed possibilities to the being. It simultaneously denounced, although prudently, the light show that abused human simplicity most crudely. But there's a necessity in this, the consequence of which is *mortal*, in that it maintains the distance between the sovereign being and the subordinate man only with difficulty. This God that nothing definite manifests, and that depends in the final analysis on these men, whose spirit he—formally—represents, tends, in himself, to answer, in turn, the demands of submission to which these men bow. God is sovereign but human anguish—the strongest measure of that which nothing limits or subordinates—tends to charge this lightness with its weight, to make the irrational reasonable, and to give laws to caprice. The God of the philosophers, a good God in the image of Good and Reason, was introduced by servility, exchanging the present for concern about the future, annihilating the instant and making calculation an empty figure opposed to immensity—like that which is separated, fixed in the refusal of every limit.

I don't mean that "religion," which submission defines, is limited to this movement of the burden within it: its initial impetus carries religion in the opposite direction, but "religion" is this body ceaselessly overcome by numbness and sleep, this body that lives only on the condition of its return to life. There isn't anything "religious" that doesn't incessantly demand that a kind of limited *rebellion* deny it, reform it, or begin it again: submission always distances itself imperceptibly from the sovereignty that is its goal. Even an impetus lessened by nothing, that no anguish turned silently from the sovereign object that I said, entangles itself immediately in the plans that are, from the start, essential to the docile mind.

Piety should forget these plans. Indeed, piety does. Sometimes the fear of hell (or of renewed incarnation) and the desire for salvation lose, in the emotions of the enraptured soul, the meaning they have for the docile being. But for a leap into divinity, in which, through breathing exercises and weighty meditations, access to sovereignty is anticipated as a voyage!

That said, the methods of religious meditation, which tend to offer us, if not sovereignty, a vision of the sovereign sphere, cannot be envisioned in a unilateral way. For humanity, there is never a simple action: there is never a careless state in which calculation has no part to play; inversely, the most indiscreet plans are often followed by naive actions.

In search of salvation, we enter a world of slips, of equivocations, of clever misunderstandings and tricks screaming with sincerity. At first, salvation appears to be the preeminent operation. Opposed to a naive and sovereign enjoyment, no plan is more servile than that of the believer, who, in the spirit of submission, refuses the appeal that the instant offers him and condemns immediate life in favor of the infinitely greater good that will be given to him *later*. But *later* isn't exactly it. It's true for the tempted devotee, in the moment of temptation. Other times, the appeal of the sovereign good is *felt* without waiting. The power of seduction with which this good offers itself to us is not always weaker than that of other objects of desire: but it can be given to us independently of exterior reality, in such a way that luck, audacity, or the abuse of power procure it. It isn't the same in those attractions to which we are commonly unable to yield without sin, such as love or murder. We can only love or destroy beings placed by fate at our mercy; and we must, in most cases, do so at their expense. Meanwhile, of necessity, attaining the sovereign good depends on us and on our efforts.

Without any doubt, the divine was often given to men in the same way as the object of sensuality or of murder: it was revealed to them from the outside. Similarly, we must imagine that the divine was at first objectively perceptible, and that rites revealed it in places that were consecrated to it. This didn't happen without the destruction that is sacrifice, and the God of the church was himself given to us only on the cross. But from this it was possible to evoke in our memory that which had the virtue of ecstasy. This is possible in other spheres, but only these manifestations of the divine were from the start evocations enriched by solitude rather than impoverished by it. In this way, meditation on the divine sphere was the crucible wherein the human being slowly became undone, then consumed itself in the instant, to the point of attaining, in contempt of the world of flesh and blood, the most careless sovereign state.

If men, focusing their attention entirely on the instant, were tempted to search for a sovereign moment, in the ordinary mode of knowledge, the powerlessness of their attention alone would have been at stake.[3] But religious meditation, setting itself a goal of incomparable value, salvation, in reality only delayed consciousness through an already perceptible attraction. Methodical meditation orchestrated a theme— already given—or developed variations on this theme, stripped it to the point of reducing it to its elementary terms, which shock the sensibility so intensely that there is no longer any conceivable point of interest beyond this. At this point, the soul, which had initially claimed *to die from not dying,* welcomes simplicity in silence, empty of meaning, of death. But the operation, so clearly subordinate, that attains this *result* didn't find what it sought and didn't seek what it found, it never became what it wanted to be and the mystic never received a response in regard to his undertaking, other than that of the mockingbird that he himself had become, the mockingbird who whistled without listeners. No doubt this is why the practitioners of Zen, being facetious "masters" and seeing their followers as victims designated by a *sovereign* farce, were the most capable guides of all; they didn't ruin the notions of project and path through discourse but through their behavior. Further, it is possible to see that, as mystics, speaking of their experiences, lead those who listen to them astray, because they are speaking of something their listeners know nothing about, they chance upon luck, not the difficulties of their proclaimed search. I cannot in fact claim that there is such a search insofar as we never find anything except on the condition of not searching for it. Not that the immense effort that led the religious world through the centuries and various civilizations meant nothing. But if it had a meaning, it is *in spite of* the principle of subordination and of the enterprise of salvation, about which, however, I still have the following reason not speak too simply: wasn't it in fact, in another sense, really a *rebellion* against a general submission to the real world, the world that limited the power of seduction to luck, and made sovereign moments depend on force?

V

Thus the world of submission ceased being overrun by unexpected, sovereign flashes, but this was insofar as it refused those burdens that were linked to submission. The exodus from the real world—the conquest of a sovereign sphere located in the beyond—certainly had the sense of the Almighty's refusal of this world on its side. But in this way submission maintained the sovereignty of the burden and the deception at the limits of reality: the sovereign affirmation of whatever was wasted by pride (the proudest being henceforth the most comically subordinate). Thus, the principle of submission wagered on the scale of humanity could only place life in the sovereign power of comedy.

Can one imagine a more tangled misunderstanding? It brings nearly cynical brutality to an end . . . but we only escape through risk—wanting to resolve it today, and we are able to, but only in the fever of rebellion—tangling it much more . . .

There can be no question of disentangling it entirely! In order to try, one must, of necessity, be unaware of the fact that a world of resolved contradictions would no longer have a sovereign end—that a world having a sovereign end shares a fundamental contradiction, opposing reason (that which is sensible, rational, but being only a *means* cannot be an *end*) to the *end*, which is always *useless*, and is always *senseless*. (The useful is useful for a given end that, by definition, is not useful. In the same way, nothing, properly speaking, can have any meaning other than in relation to some other thing. That in relation to which the meaning is given cannot but be indefinitely postponed: this is a sovereign moment lost in the inconsequence of the instant.) A senseless background, sometimes a composition of the imagination, sometimes of disorder, occasionally the extreme tension of life, clearly escapes every conceivable rationalization; otherwise we would cease being in the world *in the present*: we would be completely *at the service* of moments to come. Of course, we wouldn't know how to think of any way of gaining entrance into the sovereign sphere unless it should be by rational or premeditated means. Humanity, oriented by prohibitions and the law of work since the beginning, is unable to be at once human, in the sense of being opposed to the animal, and authentically sovereign: for humanity, sovereignty has been forever reserved, as a measure of savagery (of absurdity, of childishness, or of brutality, even more rarely of extreme love, of striking beauty, of an enraptured plunge into the night). How can we astonish ourselves if rebellion, in our day, in refusing to alienate this irreducible share that belongs to each of us, cannot at the same time take it on? In fact, one must limit it, at least in the sense that without contradiction we wouldn't know how to reduce the other's share without reducing our own share. The adjustment of rights, however, is difficult, and rebellion is overwhelmed, yoked to the task it had to give itself: rebellion is so completely lost in interminable work that nothing is presently further from the rebel's thought than the sovereign end of being (this end perhaps recovers itself, but, fearing scandal, sovereignty then offers itself up for that which it isn't, for usefulness). Thus the dilemma of sovereignty is posed in no less derisive a fashion for the modern rebel than for the divine king or the monk. If he has the desire to escape the conditions that condemn him, the rebel has, like them, recourse only to luck and persistence of refusal. The only incidental change is attached to the clarity that reveals itself in this situation, a situation so stripped that no one until our time could conceive of something more harshly revealed: humanity entirely blocked, here in the archaic contradictions of religions or kings, there in the impasse of a rebellion that reverts to submission when successful, though more perfect and lacking a beyond.

It would be difficult to show, without having thought out their precise antecedents, the conditions in which a man reaches his sovereign—
immediate—end at the present time. Rebellion has ruined and scattered that which in the depths of the ages possessed the capricious tone
of authority, and nothing remains, outwardly, of the sovereign who
might offer us the *violent desire* to bow. How might these tired voices
still have a power to shatter us? It is hardly possible to imagine a refuge, a comforting sojourn in these ruins: they are majestic, and sometimes they welcome those who can no longer confront a world that
seems completely hostile to them. Nothing really remains and nothing
in the universe appears that might comfort or guide the uncertain existence of humanity. We can only offer ourselves the glory of being in
our own eyes this senseless, laughable, and agonizing vision. Thus, on
the last night, as we sink, the possibility is left to us to know ourselves
as blind and to draw from refusal that which we will oppose to these
scraps of knowledge that we grant one virtue: that of waking us immeasurably to the night and standing us up, vacillating or laughing,
anguished, lost in an unbearable joy!
But without doubt we should avoid speaking narrowly about an experience that is still to come. At most one might say that the *sovereign
rebel* apparently situates himself as much in a continuation of the ecstasies of saints as of the liberties of the festival . . . But the anxiety of
self-effacement, of passing discreetly away into the obscurity of the
sovereign domain, returns to him. If the poetic outburst is linked to the
rebel, if discourse prolongs in him its final and precise splendors, his life
nevertheless gives way to a contradictory outpouring wherein it seems
that silence and death are definitively established. Unquestionably, in
the full negation that follows the ruin of every authority, we have no
more truth than in the instant.[4] But the instant, of which only its truth
touches us and cannot meanwhile be denied, will never be a better instant than when it is the last (except when it is that of the last man . . .).
Once more, before drifting into silence, I will divert the possibility of a
typical misunderstanding: there is no room in this picture for anything
stupid or arrogant, death's reputation is overrated, the silence I'm talking about is gay. Rebellion is pleasure itself, and it's also—*what is at
stake in every thought.*

Nonknowledge

I

Living in order to be able to die, suffering to enjoy, enjoying to suffer, speaking to say nothing. *No* is the middle term of a consciousness that has as its end point—or as the negation of its end—the passion for not knowing.

There is a point after which there is nothing to say. We reach this point more or less quickly, but definitively, if we've reached it, we are no longer able to allow ourselves to be caught up in the game.

I have nothing to say against gambling. But to take it seriously? Speaking seriously about freedom or about God? We don't know anything about it, and if we talk about it, it's a gamble. Everything that goes beyond common truth is a gamble. But we know that it's a gamble and, finding ourselves engaged in this gamble as in a serious act, we can do nothing but follow it through a little more seriously than the others, so as to disengage it from seriousness.

As for the sphere of thought, it is horror. Yes, it is horror itself.
It is led to be, by an aberration that is nothing more than an unbearable desire, led to the moment of death. To think is to slip in the night on the slope of a roof without parapets, in a wind that nothing appeases. The more rigorous the thought, the more the threat is intensified.

Rigorous thought, the firm resolution to think, is already exhaustion.

The possibility, on the roof, of an anguished equilibrium is itself conditioned by a vocation: that of responding to the call of the wind, responding to the call of death.

But if death calls, although the noise of the call fills the night, the call is a kind of profound silence. The response itself is silence stripped of every possible meaning. This is gripping: the greatest voluptuousness that the heart endures, a morose, crushing voluptuousness, a boundless heaviness.

To this feeling of perfect vice responds the phrase: "Deus sum, nil a me divini alienum puto."[1] But, like a black hole wherein every move, every irony, every thought empties itself; a condition as flat, as hollow as a headache. In the middle of the night, I lit the light in the room, to write. Even with the light, the room is black; the light comes on in the perfect darkness, no less superficially than my vanity in writing that death absorbs life, the way the night strips the light from my lamp. This is *slight* if I write, this is very slight if I open my eyes. What I see: death and the necessity of burying oneself deep in vice to be sure of being, in this way, in the depth of voluptuousness.

A stupid and cruel feeling of insomnia, a monstrous, amoral feeling, in accord with the unregulated cruelty of the universe, the cruelty of famine, of a hopeless sadism: God's unfathomable taste for the extreme suffering of his creatures, suffocating and dishonoring them. In this equality with limitless error, wherein I myself am led astray, have I ever felt more plainly human?

A reading abandons me to this voluptuous terror: this sentence Husserl wrote to Sister Adelgundis, during his last serious illness: "I didn't know that it was so hard to die. And yet I strove throughout my life to eliminate all futility . . . ! Just when I am so completely penetrated with the feeling of being responsible for a task . . . Precisely now I'm coming to the end and everything is finished for me, yet I know that I must begin everything again from the beginning . . . ."[2] This same happy fear, this same feeling of voluptuous powerlessness, persists. Husserl's futility to the second degree doesn't seem discouraging to me.

If I hadn't noted this feeling at once in the night, I would have forgotten it. Such states suppose a kind of withdrawal from the reality of the world: I woke up from a point at which I was certain that I was going to enter into the bed's inertia, I was this drifting life that took hold of nothing, and that was no longer taken hold of by anything. Insofar as they are entirely outside the world, we neglect such moments: their indifference, their solitude, their silence are not objects for our attention; they remain as if they didn't exist (it's the same as with an expanse of deserted mountains). We take such moments as insignificant, though only their daylight meaning has disappeared, like getting dressed, going out, tidying up: herein resides their insignificance. They don't have the meaning of a dream either, but these final moments are those of a day become absurd; their absurdity captures our attention, their absurdity prevents our finally perceiving their *nudity*: this immense silent object, which slips away, resists itself and, escaping, reveals that everything else lied.

In spite of the feverish aspect of these few pages, could there be a more positive, colder mind than mine?

I want to specify what I mean by sovereignty. It is the absence of sin, but this is still ambiguous. This reciprocally defines sin as lacking the attitude of the sovereign.

But sovereignty is nonetheless . . . sin.

No, it's the power to sin, without having the feeling of a missing purpose, or it is this lack that has become a purpose.

I'll offer a paradoxical example. If one of my friends is beyond my reach, he treats me badly, consciousness of my own lack becomes hard to bear: I condemn it as being irremediable. But sovereignty is at stake in friendship, my sovereignty, which is to say the impossibility my friend would have had of reaching me through his own lack—if I had not myself been beyond his reach. It is being beyond his reach that taints my sovereignty. But my friend didn't know that I was beyond his reach. If he had known it, his lack would not have tainted his own sovereignty, he could have sustained it lucidly.

Bergson saw in mysticism a possibility for speech wherein reason no longer had any rights. It's difficult for philosophers to resist the temptation to play, like children. However, if philosophy poses the questions that science avoids, that religion claims to resolve, how can they forget these rare moments in which the religious man *silences himself*?

We continuously move further away, in the examination of thought, from the decisive moment (of resolution) when thought fails, not as an awkward gesture, but, on the contrary, as a conclusion, which cannot be surpassed; because thought gauged the awkwardness involved in the act of accepting the exercise: it's a *servility*! Common men were right to despise those who stoop to thought; those who believed they could escape the truth of this contempt through an effective superiority, which they allowed themselves to the degree that humanity as a whole is engaged in the exercise of thought: but this superiority cannot be reduced to greater or lesser excellence in a servile occupation. But established excellence shows that, so long as the final search for man and thought is sovereignty, resolved thought reveals the servility of all thought: this operation by which, exhausted, thought is itself the annihilation of thought. Even this phrase is uttered in order to establish the silence that is its own suppression.

It is the meaning, or better, the absence of meaning of that which I noted the other night.

In order to perceive the meaning of a novel, it is necessary to go to the window and watch *strangers* go by. Letting go of our profound indifference for everyone we don't know is the most complete protest against the face adopted by humanity as a species of anonymous passersby. The stranger is negligible and, in a character from a novel, the opposing affirmation is implied, that this stranger has the world to himself. That he is sacred, as soon as I lift the profane mask that conceals him.

I imagine the heavens without me, without God, without anything general or particular—this isn't nothingness. In my eyes, nothingness is something else. It is the negation—of myself or of God—God and myself having never been, nothing ever having been (unless nothingness is only a facility for the philosophical game). I'm talking on the contrary about a slipping of my mind wherein I propose the possibility of a total disappearance of the general or the particular to it (the general being only a common aspect of particular things): what remains is not what existentialism calls a foundation from which . . . detaches itself, but if necessary what would appear to the ant if it were outside itself, which it cannot be but which my imagination can represent to me. In the unlimited oblivion, which, through my phrase, in myself, is the moment in transparency, there is, effectively, nothing that can give a *meaning* to my phrase, but my indifference (my indifferent being) rests in a kind of resolution of being: nonknowledge, nonquestion, although, on the level of discourse, it is essentially a question (in this sense it is perfectly intelligible), but, by this even, essentially a return, an annihilation of the question. Everything that happens unexpectedly is indifferent—through the repetition of complexity, we are only a pretext to happiness, to the onanistic anguish of which I have spoken, to the anguish of irony, at stake. But fundamentally, if nothing happens unexpectedly, there isn't even a risk. There is only the negation of meaning, complete enough to allow the persistence of the interest—through habit—that all the objects of my thought have for me.

I'm not alone. If I were, I could have thought that in knowing myself I knew humanity, but, in the multiplicity of irreconcilable thoughts, I admitted that, without a barrier to protect me from the continuous stimulation, my own thought would be lost. But for all of us, not through fault of method, but through the powerlessness of the multitude, which is the great strength of man, about which we know nothing. I, however, add this simple affirmation to the tempestuous noise of discordant minds—similar in battle to the fall of the wounded soldier to the ground, already expiring: "We had limited truths, the meaning, the structure of which was valuable in a given sphere. But from there, we always wanted to go further, being unable to bear the idea of the night into which I am now entering; the night alone is desirable, in comparison to the night, day is as petty avarice to the overture of thought."

The unappeased multitude *that I am* (will nothing permit my withdrawal? Am I not in every way similar to it?) is generous, violent, blind. It is a laugh, a sob, a silence that has nothing, which hopes for and retains nothing. Because the mania of possession made intelligence the opposite of laughter, a poverty at which those who are enriched by their mad generosity laugh endlessly.

I *might* have said, "God is love, only love," "God is not," "God is dead," "I am God." The rigorous condition—rigorous as are birth and death—was to efface in advance, to flee into a *sovereign* silence (in relation to my phrase, comparable to what the celestial universe is to earth) what I said was senseless. A misfortune for whoever would efface it halfway or would leave the door half open: the silence of the glorious, victorious, exalted man, such a transfigured sun is death, in that every will to resolve the universe into a single creation equal to our efforts resolves itself, dissolves itself.

I cannot say what the silence that I enter into possesses of the sovereign, the immensely generous, and the absent. I can't even say: it's delectable, or loathsome. It would always be too much and not enough.

My phrase wanted to make silence from words, but in the same way that knowledge loses itself in nonknowledge, in proportion to the extension of knowledge. The true sage, in the Greek sense, uses science the way it can be used, in view of the moment wherein every notion will be brought to the point at which *its limit* will appear—the beyond of any notion.

My contribution. The honesty of nonknowledge, the reduction of knowledge to what it is. But it will augment itself, through consciousness of the night, through awakening in the night of nonknowledge; I changed a knowledge that dishonestly transgressed its possibilities through dangerous connections, fundamentally unjustified, into a continuously renewed awakening, every time that reflection could no longer be pursued (since on waking, being pursued, it would substitute acts of discernment grounded on falsifications for nonknowledge). Awakening, on the contrary, restores the *sovereign* element, the impenetrable (inserting the moment of nonknowledge into the operation of knowledge; I restore what was missing to knowledge, a recognition, in the anguished awakening, of what it is necessary for me, being human, to resolve whereas the objects of knowledge are subordinated).

Always at the limit, while we think discursively, in the instant, wherein the object of our thought is no longer reducible to discourse, and wherein we have no more than to feel a point in our heart—or to close ourselves to that which exceeds our discourse. It is not about ineffable states: it is possible to speak about all the states we go through. But there remains a point that always has the meaning—rather, the absence of meaning—of totality. Thus a description, from the point of view of discursive knowledge, is imperfect, if through the description, at the desired moment, thought does not open onto the very point wherein totality, the annihilation of this description, is revealed.

Would I talk about God?
I specifically refuse to say a word about the instant in which my breath fails. To talk about God would be—dishonestly—to link that

about which I can speak only through negation to the impossible explanation of what is.

My writing is always a mixture of the aspiration to silence and that which speaks in me, even complaining about money; at least these appropriations enrich me in some way and cannot *all* be the negation of myself, the negation of my interests. Besides, isn't it sad to link proper interest to the negation of proper interest!

II

From two things one, or I've said everything; from that moment on, I only have to live without thinking (I often imagine that in this way transparency wouldn't know how to be more limpid, that I am living in the instant the way noise dissipates in the air . . .). Or I must repeat what I said poorly: it is instantly the torment and the certainty not only of never saying it better but of betraying it once more. But no doubt I'm justified in not surrendering to the temptation of a silence wherein I would have verified my inability to express myself ambiguously, and in the innocence that conveys a feeling of perfect limpidity. Today I could say that the slightest thought granted to my projects, which exist despite me, surpasses me and overwhelms me. But the instant! It is always infinite delirium . . .

But this supposes an open field. Exactly, if I live an instant without the slightest care about what might happen unexpectedly, I am well aware that this absence of anxiety engulfs me. I *should* act, parry threats that take shape. If I attain the impalpable crystal of the instant, I fail in my duty with regard to other instants, which will follow if I survive.

Most difficult: I'm thinking about things like these in a book that demands exhausting effort from me. From the perspective of this book, my thought immediately seems incompatible with this sickening effort. It makes a connection to the "apathy" that Sade talks about and to the theopathic state, associated in my memory with the name Saint John of the Cross. I disengage its true aspect only on the condition of disengaging it from a strict connection (perhaps not enough, because I was *sick* in the end, the order of the thoughts and their ordered expression demanded a power that eluded me). It is not that one such link is in itself an error, but I reject the enchained form of thought from the moment its object fills me.

The principle of morality. There exist two phases in time, the first is necessarily dominated by the rules of morality and certain ends are given to it that can only be attributed to the second.

Hegel's thought *rebelled* at one point along its course. It hardly matters that thought *woke up* at this point (the renunciation of individuality, I think). Apparently, this wasn't the *desired moment*: the scandal isn't the loss of individuality, it is *absolute knowledge*. Not for its imperfections but, on the contrary, in the presupposition of its character as absolute. The contents reveal its equivalence to nonknowledge. If we should arrive at knowledge beyond the search for knowledge, at the result, we must turn ourselves away from it: this isn't what we were looking for. The only nonderisive response is *there is God,* this is unthinkable, a word, a means of forgetting the eternal absence of rest, of satisfaction implied in the search that *we are.* Thought that offers itself the temporary stop that is the word *God* is incorrect in seeing its defeat as a resolution of the difficulties it encountered. The defeat of thought is ecstasy (in power). This is, in effect, the meaning of what I'm saying, but ecstasy has only one meaning for thought: it is the defeat of thought. There is a real temptation to give ecstasy a value for thought: if the dissolution of thought puts me in ecstasy, I will extract a lesson from ecstasy. I will say, what ecstasy revealed to me counts more than the contents of my thought, which seem to me to be the most meaningful. But this only means: nonsense has more meaning than sense.

If laughter degrades man, sovereignty or the sacred also degrades him. Besides, this has a poignant meaning: a woman's vulva is sovereign, it is sacred, but it is also laughable, and anyone who lets it be seen is degraded.

A project demands an effort, possible only under one condition: that vanity be satisfied only in default of the satisfaction of desire. Vanity exists at the level of the project, which it exposes and of which it is, morally, the report. Pride is to vanity what the instant is to the project.

I should have mentioned that the flight from death is essentially something of a gamble, not only in its rapidity, but also "well played," as if it were a question of such a perfect sleight of hand that the entire room melts into clamor and applause: I dream of this applause wherein the exaltation—because the *beauty* of the sleight of hand is unexpected, and because it so greatly surpasses the foreseeable—is so great that it provokes tears at its limit. (It isn't recognized, but it is no less true that one might cry as a result of that which makes a room lacking applause stamp its feet.) Of course, if I die, I am at once the gambler and the gambled. This has no understandable meaning in that nothing in the instant is knowable. In the instant, there is no longer any ego possessing consciousness because the ego that is conscious of himself kills the instant by dressing it in a false costume, that of the future that this ego is. But imagine that the ego doesn't kill the instant! It is the instant that immediately kills the ego! For this reason, there is no more perfect instant than that of death. For this reason, in death alone, the instant offers a crowd of anguished, but provisionally reassured, living beings, its apotheosis, taking their breath away.

III

On entering into nonknowledge, I know I erase the figures from the blackboard. But the obscurity that falls in this way isn't that of annihilation, it is not even the "night when all the cows are black." It is the enjoyment *[jouissance]* of the night. It is only slow death, death that it is possible to enjoy. And I am *learning,* slowly, that the death at work in me wasn't missing only from my knowledge, but also from the depths of my joy. I learn this only in order to die. I know that without this annihilation already within my thought, my thought would be servile babble, and I will not know my ultimate thought as it is the death of thought. I would not delight in my deliverance and I won't ever have dominated anything: I will delight in the moment of my freedom. And I will never know it! In order to know it, it would have been necessary for this joy, the fulguration of joy, not to be the death of my joy and of my thought. But one cannot conceive of the filth wherein I founder, the divine and voluptuous filth, *behind* all thought and everything of this world that raises thought, so that all representable horror is heavy with the possibility of my joy. The death of thought is the voluptuous orgy that prepares death, the festival held in the house of death.

A question without response? Perhaps. But the absence of a response is the death of the question. If there was nothing to know? And if the violation of the law, being the origin of all that we love, after the law, more than the law, destroyed the foundation of thought no less than it put an end to the power of the law? In the instant of expiring reflection, at nightfall, watching death overtake us, how would we maintain this principle, that there was something to know that we didn't know? If I had not rebelled against the law, I would have continued to *know—what I do not know*. I don't even know if there was anything to know, but how could the rebellious laugh that overtakes me not proceed to this point of rebellion, where there is no longer any attachment that might bring me back to the world of law and knowledge? If this is in order to delight in the law and the knowledge that I delight in *when I am leaving it*.

Wouldn't it be laughable to see a philosophy in these expiring propositions? I arranged them so as to bring them to the point where they dissolve and perhaps I haven't done it any worse than the philosophers close themselves off by arranging their propositions. But what I am saying is resolved in a narrative of those instants wherein horror exists and thought doesn't: horror, ecstasy, voluptuous vice, laughter . . . ? In the end, the unforeseeable, as always it is a question of losing one's footing.

How could I be depressed in refusing to take the world and what I myself am for an unavoidable measure and a law? I accept nothing and am satisfied by nothing. I am going into the unknowable future. There is nothing that I could have *recognized* in myself. My gaiety is founded on my ignorance. I am what I am: being is at stake in me, as if it wasn't, it is never what it *was*. Or, if I am what I was, what I was is not what I had been. *Being* never meant *being given*. I might never apperceive the locatable and definite *this* in myself, but only this that surges in the heart of the universe, which is never any more justifiable than the universe. It is nothing if not depressing. I am insofar as I refuse to be *that* which one might define. I am insofar as my ignorance is excessive: in depression, I would fall into the classification of the world and would take myself for the element that freezes its definition. But what does this strength that refuses announce in me? It announces *nothing*.

Post-Scriptum 1953

I am uncomfortable with this book[1] wherein I wanted to exhaust the possibility of being. It doesn't really displease me. But I hate its slowness and obscurity. I would like to say the same thing in fewer words. I would like to free it from the movement, save it from what engulfs it. To do so would be neither easy nor satisfying.

In the manner of thought that I introduce, what counts is never the affirmation. What I say, I believe without doubt, but I know that I carry within me the movement that, later on, will want this affirmation to disappear. If one had to grant me a place in the history of thought, I believe it would be that of having discerned the effects, in our human life, of the "disappearance of the discursive real," and of having drawn a senseless light from the description of these effects:[2] this light is blinding, perhaps, but it announces the opacity of *the night*; it announces the night alone.

Lately, it often seems to me that I was wrong to play such a crepuscular game with a kind of levity, advancing hypotheses candidly, without being in a state to pursue the works that they implied. Nevertheless, my old-fashioned pride pleases me more than it pains me. Now, I strive clumsily—in a slow pursuit—and nevertheless, I am unable to doubt the fact that this informality responds only to the undue situation that necessity leaves to the mind.

This game of the "discursive real" and its disappearance exists *in fact*. It demands honesty, loyalty, and generosity from the player (there is no generosity without loyalty). But when I exceed the "discursive real," the game is over and the honesty about which I spoke isn't the honesty of the law. The law is the foundation of the real, it creates absolute value from it, but it wouldn't be able to if it wasn't the blackmail of a mysticism drawn from death and suffering. Death and suffering being the principle of servitude (no slaves without the fear of death and suffering) are also the mystical foundations of the law.

Only *violent thought* coincides with the disappearance of thought. But it demands a meticulous relentlessness and it yields to violence—its contradiction—only in the end and insofar as, becoming itself, against itself, violence releases itself from the indolence wherein it endured. But the annihilation of thought—letting only the servile coherence of thought subsist, as denounced, spectral, and its multiple failings, gay or tragic—is unable to turn the violence that is its foundation toward the other. Violence bound to the movement of thought leaves no loophole.

• • •

I will stop myself on a point that, it seems to me, has little to do with the movement of *Inner Experience*. I would like to situate my thought in its narrow perspectives, far from the world of facility where one might easily appreciate it.

At the origin of baseness, I perceive the emphatic value granted to the human species. Without any doubt, the difference between animal and man is grounded on the opposition of man to nature. But man barely surmounts the advantage that he has achieved. Man says of himself: "I am divine, immortal, free . . ." (or he solemnly says "the person"). But that is not all. Each of us naively concedes, without control, principles taken as unassailable: we consider killing inhuman, cannibalism still more inhuman . . . We ordinarily add that it is no less odious to exploit other humans. I oppose nothing to these principles; and I even hate those who observe them poorly (besides, as a rule, such people revere these principles in the degree to which they violate them). But this is mysticism, and it is hypocrisy. Exploitation of man by man, as hateful as it is, is given *in humanity*. Even anthropophagy, when this is the convention, coexists with the prohibition of which it is the ritual violation.

Once again, I approve of neither exploitation nor murder (and for cannibals, it goes without saying . . .); and I admit without having to think about it that we exploited, slaughtered, and ate animals.[3] But I am unable to doubt that these reactions are arbitrary. They are convenient; without them humanity would be still more base than it is. It is nevertheless despicable to see more than an effective and traditional attitude. Thought that does not limit this arbitrariness to what it is is mystical thought.

What makes mystical humanism a platitude is the misunderstanding of the human specificity that it implies. It is proper to man to oppose himself to the beast in a movement of nausea. But the nausea that grounds us in this way does not cease: it is even the principle of a game animating our lives from one end to the other. Never are we more human than when impugning one another in horror. The propensity for nausea is stronger if entire peoples are in question: from that moment on, it plays itself out blindly! But it is a question of individuals or classes; it has precise objects. The opposition of one man to another in whom he perceives a foul attitude is still the opposition that initially opposes human to beast. It does not have the same clarity: henceforth it is attackable, and often founded on error. When it is contested, a new mode of opposition, and of disparagement, begins: now opposition has the principle of opposition between these different types of human for its object! If I make a final effort, going to the end of human possibility, I reject in the night those who, with a cowardice that doesn't acknowledge itself, stopped themselves en route.

In this, I distance myself from mysticism more deeply than the mass of my contemporaries do. I even feel myself awakening, on the contrary, on the level of the thought's demand in the state of the hunted animal. In the end, rigor is the point on which I agree with the avowed judgments of men. The tension and drying up of the mind, rigor, the desire to force weakness into its last entrenchment . . . , I feel something like grace, a sort of rage that opposes me to facility. But often nonchalance is the naked aspect, the obscene aspect, of rigor.

These weaknesses and these unintentional ambiguities in my book, these joys and these anguishes that found nothing, never have any meaning beyond themselves, are only an appendage of the game. The tone often linked to my—too weighty—sentences exposes an unlimited opening that the game, if it is no longer inferior, tolerated, serious, arranges with the idle [désœuvré] mind (with the sovereign mind, which is never comical nor tragic, but at once one and the other infinitely). Seriousness has only *one meaning*: the game, that is no longer a game, is serious only insofar as "the absence of meaning is also meaning," but always lost in the night of indifferent nonsense. Seriousness, death, and suffering found their obtuse truth. But taking death and suffering seriously is the servility of thought.

Aphorisms

I summon everything unforeseen and the indistinguishable tumult of life, I summon the laughter that the brusque arrival of intruders stops, but never profoundly stops . . . I was going to talk about my powerlessness—about this desire that fills me with anguish—now . . . I no longer feel this powerlessness . . . Now I am calm, indifferent, the childish simplicity of anguish no longer at play, I am no longer in distress, in the distress that the thought of all this time had thrown me, the thought that still separates me from the instant wherein my desire will be satisfied. I have trouble overcoming the inertia that invades me, this gloomy, static happiness . . . Trouble? Perhaps a little trouble? But the instant? How will I slip from profound indifference into a moment of happiness "that is sung," that will go beyond me, that will suffocate me? From my soft dignity, eyes empty of intention, how will I pass into the feeling of this night filled with riches and with the nudity that summons the desire to die? How will I welcome once again the joyous nightmare of ardent intoxication to the point of looking beaten to death? Although I know it, the pathetic movements of the arts remind me, ceaselessly, the object of my wait is not peace, but the immense delirium of the universe, in which the beating of my heart is mingled—demanding that I be a part of it.

If it wasn't the threshold of death and this tidal surf that a horror of the unlimited apparently dresses in the agonies of refusal, if it weren't for my terror at the idea of taking this step, I would resemble the swell, playing, falling to ruin in the liquid depth. But death frightens me and I remain seated when thinking about it, seated as are those who oppose the drab precision of words to the blinding beauty of this world. The table, the paper, the sinister dam of death align the syllables of my

name. This table and this paper—which promise me disappearance—
make me sick (specifically, I am nauseous), and yet the words I am able
to write here summon that which, making me sicker, would bring me
the subtle violence of the wind, forever taking away this paper and the
words that I write on it.

Beyond Seriousness

I am talking about happiness. But this is, for the moment, only a desire, and the imagined desire separates me from its object. I am writing and I can hardly stand the difference between that which I will be, the finished work, and the me who now wants to do it! I write wanting to be read: but time separates me from a moment wherein I will be read! Endless chain: if I were read as I want to be read and if the desire to read my work were in response to what I have to write, to what degree would the reader suffer from the difference between his condition after reading my work and that which animates an obscure premonition? On the contrary, we read certain books with a little fear of the moment when, coming to the end, we have to let them go . . .

But, in the book that leaves us and from which we are regretfully separated, nothing is said about happiness, but only of the hope for happiness. Or rather, of hope alone (hope is always a fear of not attaining, hope is desire but open to fear), hope alone makes happiness tangible.

I wanted to say my powerlessness, linked to desire, which disturbs me, or is translated, if I don't move, into a little anguish. But, already, I no longer have this feeling of powerlessness. I'm indifferent, the childish simplicity of desire is no longer at play. I have come out of the distress that made me enter the thought of all this time that distances me from the moment when my desire will be fulfilled.

I know that before this date I wasn't born, but I was born a long time ago! I am and am not, and if I stop seeing, around me, the paper, the table, if I see the cloud ripped to pieces in the wind, these words are only a measure of the clouds if I write: "The clouds and the wind deny me"; or: "In the movement that dissolves me, I am from now on what I was previously (before being born) or what I will be (after my death)." Nothing remains of this game, not even a negation of myself that the wind carries far away. I see the world through the window of my death; this is why I can't confuse it with the chair on which I am seated. Otherwise, I wouldn't know that it knocks me over in the moment that it lifts me up, I would scream without knowing that nothing ever crosses this wall of silence.

As an excuse, we have the inequality of men among men, the very diverse meanings of one or another, and the tender attachments that correspond to them. It is no less strange to see the complete difference between people and flies, which makes a mockery of all thought. From two things one: or, the death of one man has the same importance as that of another and, in this case, it has no more importance than that of a fly; or *this* man, if he dies, is irreplaceable for those who love him: so it is the *particular* consequences that matter, not simply the death of a man, in the end, the likeness of those who remain. In truth, men slip from one tableau to another so as to give their death this shameless magnificence that is only the magnificence of their fear.

If I allow unhappiness to speak within me, it strips the festival defined by the light from me to infinity. But happiness, which strips the agonies of hope from me, admits me to the delights of fear. In other words, luck—and luck alone—makes me what I am: it grants all the seriousness of the law through my worries, and it is luck, if it is on my side, that lives my happy disorders with me.

In professorial solemnity and even more simply in profound thought, bad luck always has the most weight: that of something paltry or boring. Life is subordinate to the alternation of luck and bad luck, but it is characteristic of luck not to be able *to be taken over by seriousness*. A pretty young woman seduces, but what she is has no meaning in profound philosophy . . . The intensity of desire is always the effect of the exception, sensuality is luxury, luck, and luck never has depth: no doubt this is why philosophers ignore it. Their authentic domain is unhappiness, the antithesis of the universe, which is a perfect absence of unhappiness.

Insofar as he designates the totality of experience, Hegel escapes reduction to unhappiness. *The Phenomenology of Spirit* takes enjoyment [*jouissance*]*(Genuß)* into account. But, illogically, the *Phenomenology* grants the final value to the seriousness of unhappiness and the absence of play. I don't think that Hegel was fully the atheist that Alexandre Kojève took him to be.[1] Hegel makes the universe a *thing*, a human thing, he makes it God (in the sense that, in God, the immanence or the sacred character of the universe gives way to the transcendence of an object, of a useful object). Hegel hasn't grasped a singular inhumanity in our completion, the absence of all seriousness in the man finally liberated from the *consequences* of servile tasks, no longer having to take these tasks seriously, no longer having to take *anything* seriously.

But, just as the seriousness of our intentions linked human thought to unhappiness and opposed it to luck, so the absence of seriousness presumes the gambler's luck. The absence of seriousness painfully demands luck because someone who is unhappy is unable to gamble, unhappiness being inescapably the serious.

I didn't see it at first, but, specifically, in the indifference to unhappiness, unhappiness attains a perfect happiness from which ordinary happiness still separates us: it attains it at the summit of the inconceivable in death, and the most precise image of it is the naive smile, the sign of happiness. In one respect, thought differs no less from articulated thought than inertia, in life, differs from the slaughterhouse, wherein there is no longer anything that might be cut up, there is no longer anything that might be contrary to what is. *What happens,* then, whatever the outcome, no longer differs from *what doesn't happen,* what is, what was, what will be, without anything happening.

But, in Hegel's thought, this disorder is an order that hides itself, this night is the mask of the day!

The disorder of my thought, which is irreducible to a clear vision, conceals *nothing. I know nothing.* It is true that the lacerated scream that announces it is also silence, if I want it to be. But I protest in the end, anticipating the will to reduce this screaming silence or this inaudible scream that robs me of every conceivable possibility, to some state of intellection: that's it, that's all that my writing masks. I dream of the exhaustion that orders the meanderings of thought, I'm listening to a *call to attention!* that nothing justifies, that demands a courage of me that will only resolve itself in sleep on the condition of having a raw moment, which makes sleep impossible—forever!

I invoke *what doesn't happen,* which is, which was, which will be, without anything happening. I name it, but I am made of this tissue, of these multiplied *noes,* opposed to *what happens,* from these *noes* woven with some *yeses.* If I invoke *what doesn't happen,* if I ask to be neglected by *what happens,* so that I would have nothing to say, neither *yes* nor *no,* then if I have the strength to write, it's only just barely.

If I write, it is my weak, powerless protest against the fact that in writing I can't envision anything, except *what happens,* what needs to happen in order to be happening.

Could I ever say something about *what doesn't happen*, what, miserably, in my mind, would resemble death, if some *non-death* was imaginable on this level? But words refuse their development as words by a jumping around through which they cling to every negation possible from the fatalities inherent in affirmation, with the suicide of every possibility that they designate; mightn't they, words, at the summit, reveal that which words themselves plunge into the night?

Yes, if in the breach wherein my weariness of words leaves me, I denounce the breach no less than the fact that I am left there.

I really wanted to communicate the state in which an indifference to communication leaves me, which prolongs a desire to communicate that nothing would know how to satisfy.

From the perspective wherein my thought is no more to me than the sadness in which it founders, wherein there is nothing that an obsession to strip the back side of thought bare doesn't consume, I remember games that amazed me: beauty and religion, vice, desperate love, ecstasy, laughter . . .

Wasn't this already the same eagerness to deny and to annihilate that which separates me from *that*, which is *nothing*, which is negation, which is the flip side of the seriousness of thought?

Who will dare to articulate the voluptuousness of inverting things?

Silence alone is more voluptuous—more perverse—than the screaming voluptuousness is able to announce. Complete silence, oblivion in the end.

Whatever we envisioned of *what happens*, everything *that happens* is united, it is difficult to appreciate one element of it and to negate the rest. But that's what we do, what we cannot avoid doing.

If each thing that happens is united to the rest, everything *that happens* is stuck. We are in animal blindness from the beginning. *What happens* is, for example, the elephant, anger, the disastrous onslaught of a large number of elephants, an inextricable encumbrance. What happens is never in agreement with the universe. The universe considered as a totality does not happen. The universe is *what does not happen*. Hegel wanted to pass from *what happens* to *what does not happen*, from the particular to the universal. This presupposes recovering the relations of the interdependence of all things among themselves, which happen and, in happening, are detached from other things that happen.

The universe, which does not happen, cannot be destroyed. But the galaxies, the stars, the planets, which do happen, can be destroyed.

What does not happen is not space. *What happens* is "something" and can be determined; space can still be determined. *What does not happen* is "nothing" in that this is not "something." This is not God either. God is *what does not happen,* if you will, but is well determined, as if *what does not happen* had happened. (In one sense, this incommensurable blockage, this solemn desire for justice, had to happen, it is the stickiest aspect of *what happens.*)

About *what does not happen,* we cannot say a word, except that the *totality* of what is does not happen. We are not before *what does not happen* as before God. We only happen before *what does not happen,* inasmuch as *we* happen, only through the most complete negation, pulling the ground from beneath our feet: in the end, we must sink ourselves carefully, slip as into sleep, imperceptibly, into the depths of negation (in negation up to our neck, to the dregs). To represent *what does not happen* is to imagine ourselves dead, in other words, essentially, to represent nothing more.

What does not happen cannot exist like an object, as opposed to a subject. But why grant *what does not happen* subjective existence? It would be a question of an affirmation and we can affirm nothing. We can no longer talk about the nonsubjective, whereas we can talk about nonobjectivity.

We talk about nonobjectivity insofar as the object transcends what it isn't, whereas the subject does not necessarily transcend the rest of the world. We can represent the immanence of the subject for ourselves with regard to *what does not happen.*

What happens happens objectively.

In *what happens,* the possible subjectivity is always objectively limited. It is personal, linked to some determined object. *What happens* is a wolf in regard to *what happens.* *What happens* means the devouring of what is not this thing that happens. The limit is only given insofar as communication, from one subject to the other, is personal: where some immanence is opposed to the propensity of *what happens* to report each thing (that happens) back to itself, to its interest in the thing that happens. In fact, communication supposes a destroyed—or reduced—particularity, the reserve of the particular being, as when you pull up a girl's dress.

What happens never escapes *what happens* except through fulfillment, through the success of the will to happen. If we don't love *to succeed,* up to the extreme limit, we are enclosed, like animals, by *what happens.* We are animally enclosed, in a very limited way, the way brutes are enclosed, like soldiers, who never have the desire to go further, and even further and further. Otherwise, we enclose ourselves like Christians, denying *what happens* within ourselves before having realized it. It is only if we affirm *what happens* within us to the end that we have the strength to bring it to the level of *what does not happen.* (Nietzsche is, according to his own expression, a "hyper-Christian,"[2] and not, as has been said, an animal placing himself above man.)

Humanity, spattered with blood and sweat from drawn-out tortures, is the slow passage of *what happens,* which is animally disengaged from mineral passivity from the very beginning, to *what does not happen.*

The animal is the image of an impossibility, of the hopeless devouring implied in *what happens.*

Man maintains the animal impossibility within himself, ambiguously. He is opposed to the animality within himself, but can then be fulfilled only on condition of liberating this animality. Because the animality repressed in him is no longer *what happens.* *What happens* is man repressing these animal impulses within himself in the guise of his own impossibility. These animal impulses were *what happens* initially, but they became, in opposition to *what happens* in humanity, *what does not happen,* the negation of *what happens* once again.

Knowledge limits itself to *what happens* and all knowledge is extinguished if we envision *what does not happen.* We know only objects, or objectified (personal) subjects. If I now speak about *what does not happen,* I introduce the *unknown,* the unknowable, into the discourse, the meaning of which was to substitute the known for the unknown.

All that I can know about the unknown is that I pass from the known to the unknown. That is the margin abandoned to discourse. I am talking about the instant, and I *know* that the instant brings about in me the passage from the known to the unknown. Insofar as I envision the instant, obscurely, the unknown touches me, the known dissipates within me. *What happens* implies the duration (but not the immutability) of *what happens.* And, in the instant, nothing happens anymore. Eroticism is the substitution of the instant or of the unknown for what we thought we knew. We don't know the erotic, we only recognize this passage from the known to the unknown in it; this passage raises us beyond our abilities, inasmuch as it is true that man aspires toward *what does not happen* from the beginning! Inasmuch as it is true that *what happens* is the insatiable desire for *what does not happen!*

As if the language of philosophy had to, I am not saying always, or from the very beginning, but finally, become mad. Not a madness open to the arbitrary, but mad in that it is fundamentally lacking in seriousness, in that it breathes good sense and lightly climbs those heights where thought seeks nothing more than the vertiginous fall of thought. Never more rigorous than in the flight that carries it *beyond seriousness.*

It doesn't matter to me that clubfooted thinkers don't follow me, and if the facilities of poetry occasionally offer the illusion of impeccable somersaults, that's too bad. Philosophy's last word is the domain of those who, *wisely,* lose their heads. This vertiginous fall is not death, but *satisfaction.*

What happens is always unsatisfied, otherwise what happens would be emblematic of *what does not happen. What happens* is always a search—in sweat—for satisfaction. Satisfaction is, on the contrary, possible through the hatred of satisfaction.

What happens aspires *to what does not happen* . . . This is true, but, in the first place, *what happens* desires to happen . . . , wants satisfaction on the level of platitudes, instead of wanting it the way one wants to die, so that *satisfied* implies the quenched thirst for death, not for success. Unless succeeding at the summit means: at the point of dying from it . . .

If these words were not supported by the movement of an incoercible laughter, I would say what a reasonable man would say about them: that I hardly understand them.

Nietzsche's greatness is in not having left his thought to the misfortune that overwhelmed it. If he didn't yield, this was nevertheless his luck, but his happiness was reduced to not having let the unhappiness within him speak.

Beyond seriousness? Unhappiness doesn't reach it!

Suffering completes it, but let us suppose that it yields to suffering? There is nothing but *seriousness.*

No one can talk himself beyond seriousness if he imagines that unhappiness would make him serious.

What is beyond seriousness differs as much from the here and now as seriousness does from the pleasant. It is much more serious, much more comical—this seriousness being mitigated by nothing pleasant, this comedy by nothing serious. One single instant, the serious man or the jokester could not even breathe here. This said without the least bit of seriousness, but directly, without bias.

Part VII

The Congested Planet

The planet congested by death and wealth, a scream pierces the clouds. Wealth and death close in. No one hears this scream of a miserable waiting.

Knowing that there is no response, I would have wanted to tremble in my imploring:

—Oh God! Relieve them of death and wealth! Deliver them, oh God, from the hope that the feeling of their imminent death and of your nothingness feeds in them! Enclose them in *your* solitude! Enclose them in your *despair*!

Writing, I'm certain I won't reach the end of my project as outlined.

No one ever reaches the end. But how, if I see everything in this excessive light, could I attain happiness?

The agitation and vivaciousness of phrases take hold of everything.

The multitude of words surrounds me and I listen to their clamorous flood.

I savor the sadness of the subsiding waters in advance.

How can one not look forward to the waters' withdrawal before writing?

This knowledge that situates the human being in the world in the first place is that of the animal.

The animal, in the play of this unintelligible world—unintelligible, at least, for the animal—discerns that which fulfills its needs. In principle, human knowledge is nothing more than this elementary knowledge giving form to cohesion through language. Knowledge is the agreement of the organism and the environment from which it emerges. Without knowledge, without the identity of the organism, and without this agreement, life could not be imagined. What therefore is the organism in the world, if not the unconsidered flight of a possible into the heart of the impossible that surrounds it? Developing this idea, knowledge strives to restore the impossible (the unforeseeable) to the possible (the foreseeable). Through knowledge, this hazardous flight is changed into a wise calculation: calculation is itself only possible by giving its possibility a fundamental value.

The wager of knowledge opens two paths.

The first is the implicit affirmation that knowledge *in fact* exists.

Knowledge that strengthens the feeling that knowledge is "possible" perceives all things in the perspective of the "possible." Sometimes, the "possible," as possibility, hypostatizes, sometimes not. But always, on this first path, the world confounds itself with the possible and the possible with the world. Animal knowledge, the first knowledge, was the product of a hazardous search conducted by the organism for a possible worthy of it (the organism being defined by this search); essentially, human knowledge becomes the calculation of possibility when it orders the totality of things for itself, the calculation of possibility seized as a foundation.

An initially intoxicated reaction suspends doubt and, in this certainty, created in sum by foolishness, man has the impression of being at home on the earth. Knowledge, in principle even, is nothing less than the questioning of knowledge itself. If I deepen the pathways of knowledge, I am similar to the ant, conscious of the impending threat that something might overturn the anthill, and of the final truth of this threat. Language sets up an order, it creates the foundation of what is in this order, but it is nothing that exists *in the last place*: everything is in suspense, over the abyss, the ground itself is the illusion of an assurance; *if I know,* I have vertigo in the middle of a field; even in bed, I sense the disappearance of the world and the universe.

The insignificant, provisional nature of the data of even the most certain knowledge is revealed to me in this way. But, in this region where nothing is tragic, or terrifying or sacred, the appearance ordering this illusory certainty does not exile me from it any less each day. Though nothing, in this region, is *poetic.*

Poetic language once again opens me to the abyss.

But poetry cannot effectively deny the affirmation of coherent discourse, it cannot dissipate the lie of this discourse for long. Poetry never establishes what it makes visible. Denying the order in which I am enclosed by a coherent discourse, the coherence of the discourse that denies it is still within me. In an instant, discourse orders within me that which undoes the order wherein I am enclosed, it orders that which—tragically—brings me to death, to the delirium of poetry.

Attaining the possible, endless repose, I would be granted the certainty of living before the truth, *eternally,* I would groan. What I want and what human being wants in me: one moment, I want to exceed my limit, and, another moment, I want to be gripped by nothing.

A disorder of affirmations, in the past, finally abandoning reflection for panic. Would we come out of this abandonment no longer risking anything and no longer affirming anything that does not rest on an often repeated experience? Practically, the certainty that founds such a durable experience is sufficient, but it leaves us at the mercy of intolerable suffering and mortal torment, *in the end.* Does the final truth resemble the most painful death? Or is this prosaic world, ordered by knowledge founded on a lasting experience, its limit? Delivered from ridiculous beliefs, are we happy before death and torture? Is this pure happiness? At the basis of a world from which the only escape is failure?

Pure Happiness

Suicide

Pure happiness is in the moment, but pain chased me from the present moment into waiting for a moment to come, when my pain will be relieved. If pain didn't separate me from the present moment, "pure happiness" would be within me. But presently, I'm talking. In me, language is the effect of pain, of the need that yokes me to work.

I want to, I must, talk about my happiness: from this fact an imperceptible misfortune enters me: this language—that I speak—is in search of the future, it struggles against pain—be it minuscule—which is the need within me to talk about happiness. Language never has pure happiness for its subject matter. Language has action for its subject matter, action whose goal is to *recover* lost happiness, but action cannot attain this goal by itself. If I were happy, I would no longer act.

Pure happiness is the negation of pain, of all pain, even of the apprehension of pain; it is the negation of language.

This is, in the most *senseless sense,* poetry. Language, stubborn in refusal, is poetry, turns back on itself (against itself): this is the analogue of a suicide.

This suicide does not reach the body: it ruins effective activity, it substitutes vision for it.

The vision of the present moment subsists here, detaching the being from the anxiety of what will follow. As if the succession of moments that ordain the perspective of work (actions that waiting changes by subordinating the sovereign being, which the sun of the "present moment" illuminates) were dead.

The suicide of language is a wager. If I talk, I obey the need to escape the present moment. But my suicide announces the leap into which the being liberated from its needs is thrown. The wager demanded the leap: the leap that the wager prolongs in a nonexistent language, in the language of the dead, of those ravaged by happiness, annihilated by happiness.

Insomnia

Work in order to live! I exhaust myself in the effort and thirst for rest. Then there is no longer any time to say: life is rest. Then I am troubled by a deceptive truth: would living be thinkable other than in the guise of work? Even poetry is work. I cannot consume myself like a lamp, which shines and never calculates. I need to produce and I can only rest while granting myself the feeling of increasing in production. For this, I must repair my strengths, accumulating new strengths. Erotic disorder is itself a movement of acquisition. Telling myself that the end of activity is free consumption (the consumption without reserve of the lamp), on the contrary, gives me the feeling of an unbearable abandonment, of a resignation.

Nevertheless, if I want to live, I must first deny myself, forget myself . . .

I remain there, distraught, like a loyal horse, whose master emptied the saddlebags.

Evening, breathless, I long to relax, and I must be deluded by some tempting possibilities! Reading a book, what do I know? I cannot delight in my life (in the visible sequence, the sight of which exhausted me) without giving myself a new goal, which again exhausts me.

Writing: even, in the moment, that I preferred to resign . . . Rather than to respond to the necessities of my life . . . Writing—in order to resign myself—is still another form of work! Writing, thinking are never the opposite of work. To live without acting is unthinkable. In the same way, I can *only* represent myself as *sleeping,* I can *only* represent myself as *dead.*

• • •

I wanted to think at the extreme limit about a kind of difficulty from which I never escape, from which I will never escape.

For a long time, if an exhausting effort imposed itself on me, when at the end of a long wait I succeeded—and as I enjoyed the results—nothing, to my surprise, was offered to me, which gave me the anticipated satisfaction. Repose presaged boredom, reading was an effort. I didn't want to distract myself, I wanted what I *was waiting for,* which, the effort completed, should have justified it.

Then do what, when I was delivered?

Die? Of course not.

Death must have happened unexpectedly. If death was already within me, without my having to work at introducing it. Everything escaped me and opened me up to insignificance.

To write what precedes . . . ?

To cry . . . ?

Forgetting incrementally as a sob mounted . . . Forgetting everything, up to this mounting sob.

Being another at the end, someone other than me. Not the one who, now, reads me, to whom I give a painful feeling. Rather the first to arrive of those who don't know me, if you wish, the mailman who advances, who rings, who makes the violence of the bell resonate in my heart.

It is sometimes so difficult to sleep! I tell myself: I am finally falling asleep. The feeling of falling asleep escapes me. If it escapes me, I am, in effect, falling asleep. But if it subsists . . . ? I cannot fall asleep and I must tell myself: the feeling that I had deceived me.

No difference between the authenticity of being and *nothing*. But *nothing*? The experience of it is possible from something, that I suppress through thought. In the same way, I cannot arrive at the experience of "what does not happen," except through "what happens." One must, in order to access "what does not happen," happen, like an isolated being, separated, like a being "that happens."

Nevertheless, only "what does not happen" is the meaning—or the absence of meaning—of my happening. I feel it if I want to stop, rest, and enjoy the sought-after results. *Incipit comoedia!* An entire ministry of recreation articulates through its work—and its public activities—a feeling of death, a feeling that disarms me. But a ministry of recreation, with its corridors, is only a detour so as to avoid the simplicity of red wine, which is, it seems, redoubtable. Red wine, I am told, destroys us. As if, in any way, it was not a question of *killing* time.

But red wine is the poorest, it is the least expensive of poisons. Its horror is attached precisely to its misery: it is the garbage can of the marvelous.

And yet?

Always at the limit of betraying its inanity (it suffices through a displacement of perspectives), what I'm talking about is marvelous, no lie.

What I'm talking about is *nothing,* it is the immensity of *what is,* it is *nothing,* about which it is possible to speak.

Language only designates things; only the negation of language opens up to the absence of a limit of *what is,* which is *nothing.*

The only limit of the marvelous is a result of this: the marvelous, made of the transparency of "what does not happen" in "what happens," dissolves when death, the essence of which is given in "what does not happen," takes on the meaning of "what happens."

The same anguish every night. As inert in my bed as a fish is on the sand, telling myself that time, which descends on me, which brings me nothing, is useless. I don't know where I'm from. Reduced to saying, to feeling the uselessness of life, the utility of which has disappointed me.

Strange burden insomnia: I lost, if not the order, the reason, which maybe I didn't have, to write these phrases. Would my reason be a literary search? Meanwhile, I cannot conceive of the possibility of not having written them. I have the feeling of writing above all in order to know, to discover, at the heart of my insomnia, what I can, and what I must do. I drift off waiting for the sleeping pill to take effect.

Violence Exceeding Reason

I have always been bothered by the elaboration of my thought. At any time, I worked with regularity only when the work demanded it of me. I read only a small part of what I should have, and I never regulated my acquisition of knowledge. Consequently, I should have renounced speech. I should have recognized my powerlessness and kept my mouth shut.

But I never wanted to resign myself: I told myself that this difficulty held me back, but that in exchange, it determined me. In calm moments, I thought myself no less capable than others. I knew rather few minds who impressed me through their power for coherent thought. Still, I had the possibility of gauging their inferiority on a given point. Today, I can admit that I was able to compete with them, even though I had less of an aptitude for analytical thought. Like my irregular work habits, this very weakness was linked to the violence that, in some way, never ceased unnerving me, making me lose my footing at any moment.

I realized it only belatedly. This violence, which exceeded me, gave me this advantage, which I didn't have to renounce. Now I no longer doubt that while it diminished me, this violence gave me something that was lacking in others, that made me perceive the impasse in which paralyzed thought is limited and, being limited, is unable to embrace the full extent of what moves it. Being that which paralyzes violence within us, thought cannot entirely reflect what is, since violence is in principle that which is opposed to the development of thought. I mean that violence corresponds to animality, in which consciousness, in some way bound up with it, cannot have any autonomy. But unbound because of the fact that it is excluded, and because of the taboo on violence, in counterpart, it forbids itself from grasping the meaning of what it excluded. The most telling result is its inaccuracy, essentially, the incomplete character of self-knowledge. This is evident in the distortion, in Freud's thought, of the notion of libido. The suppression of an excitation, Freud says, defines sensual pleasure. To this negative definition I can directly oppose the role played by violence, a role that cannot be resolved in thought. But, by chance, it might have happened that violence imposed itself without entirely disrupting the flow of methodical thought: thus the distortion given in common conditions is brought to light; in animals, pleasure is connected to the excessive expenditure of energy—or of violence; in man, to the transgression of the law—which is opposed to violence and imposes some barriers on him. But this doesn't reach the summit of thought, where even violence becomes the object (forbidden, seized despite the prohibition) of thought, and finally offers itself as the only answer to the fundamental interrogation implied in the development of thought: the answer can only come from the outside, from that which thought had to exclude *in order to exist.*

The solution isn't new. Is not God an expression of violence offered as a solution? But, offered as a solution, the divinity was transposed on the level of thought: divine violence, as reduced by theological discourse, limited its virtual paralysis through morality. (Returning to the subject of the animal god, we discover its incomparable purity, its violence above laws.)

Hegel, implicating violence in the dialectic, attempts to gain access to the equivalence of thought and violence subtly, but he opens the last chapter in this way: nothing can happen, if, history completed, thought arrives at the dead end where, before the immutable response that it offers itself, drawing this answer from itself, thought grasps the equivalence of this answer with the final silence, the silence proper to violence.

At this point, Hegel lacked the strength without which the implication of his thought failed, clearly, the development that it summoned.

Silence is the unlimited violation of the prohibition that human reason opposes to violence: it is divinity without stops, which thought alone disengaged from the contingency of myths.

I am not the only one to whom the necessity of ruining the effects of work was revealed, but I am the only one who, on perceiving it, *cried out*. The silence without screams, which never diminishes the endless scrutiny of language, is not the equivalent of poetry. Poetry itself diminishes nothing, but it *has access*.

It has access to the summit. From the height of the summit, so many things disappear and no one sees. There is no longer anything.

The "Measure," without Which the "Measureless" Would Not Be, or the "Measureless" End of "Measure"

I am saying that the domain of violence is that of religion (not of the religious organization, but—let's suppose things are cut off—of the intense vision that responds, or can respond, in the name of religion); I might add that the domain of Reason embraces the necessary organization in view of its common effectiveness: I believe I am capable of being understood. No doubt, the equivocation between religious violence and political action is continual, but in two ways, the political, to which I aspire, before which I live, is always an end. Being an end, it is excluded from calculation, which is proper to the means. Full *violence* can be the means to no end. It would be subordinate to no goal.[1] At the same time, this formula limits the power of Reason. Unless condescending, Violence is an end, and can never be a means. Reason is never anything other than a means, but Reason determines the end and the means. Reason can be given as an end arbitrarily: then it refuses the truth that it defines. It is Reason insofar as it is an exclusion, when it is the limit of Violence (which it distinguishes by definition from the reasoned use of violence).

Before blind Violence, which the lucidity of Reason limits, Reason alone knows that it has the power to deify that which it limits. Reason alone can define Violence as its end. The limit that Reason opposes to Violence reserves—provisionally—the precariousness of discontinuous beings, but, in the interior governed by its law, it designates, beyond this precariousness, the *continuity of being* where the absence of limits is sovereign: the absence of limits, excessive Violence, whatever the imaginable limit might be.

Whatever was not initially defined or limited by Reason limited Reason. Violence was unable to define or limit itself. But Reason, in its rational attitude toward Violence, perfects it: it carries the rectitude of definition and of limits to the height of Violence. Thus Reason alone has, *humanely,* the power to designate measureless violence, or the Unmeasureable, which, without measure, would not exist.

Reason liberates Violence from the servitude imposed on it by those who, in opposition to Reason, subjugate it to the calculations of their rational ambition. Men can go, must go, to the end of Violence and of Reason, the coexistence of which defines them. They must renounce themselves to equivocal, unavowable accords, which have randomly assured the servitude of the multitudes, and even the servitude of so-called sovereigns.

Reason, facing violence, master of its domain, leaving Violence the inconsequence of what is. Not the possible, which it organizes, but that which is set free at the end of every possibility: death in human life and in the universe, the totality.

Reason reveals, in the series of possibilities that respond to it, an opening to what it is not: in the array of living beings, (sexual or asexual) reproduction calling on death, and in death, Reason is doubly betrayed, since it is Reason that dies, and since it embraces a totality that calls on its exhaustion, that wants the defeat of Reason.

The frozen confidence of Reason: —I was only a gamble.

But Reason whispers in me: —What, in Reason, survives unreasonableness cannot be a gamble. I am necessary!

I answer for it:

—Is not necessity itself, globally, lost in the immensity of a *gamble?*

—I designate God, Reason tells me, recovering its resolution. I alone was able to designate him, but on the condition of resigning myself, on the condition of dying.

Together we climb the steps of a scaffold . . .

REASON: attaining eternal truth . . .
ME: as well as the eternal absence of truth.

God? If you will. Would I fail to designate him? What, above all, is more designated by *my piety.* On the already bloody scaffold, I designate him. Beforehand, my blood cries out to him, not as vengeance. Beforehand, my blood is known as laughable. My absence also appeals. It appeals to God: it is the joke of jokes, the only one who has the strength to invoke a corpse pissing blood, the corpse of a torture victim.

Keeping quiet by laughing . . . This is not keeping quiet, this is laughing. I know that my piety alone laughs for a rather long time, that it alone laughs to the end.

Would I laugh without Reason? Would I laugh at God without Reason, at God who believes himself to be sovereign? But the domain of laughter opens itself to death, God haunts it! Reason, however, is the key without which we would not laugh (though laughter disparages Reason).

This brings me to the "laughter of Reason."

If it laughs, Reason maintains the absence of respect owed it by others as reasonable at the summit.

The laughter of Reason sees itself in the mirror: it sees itself as death. What opposes Reason to God eludes Reason.

God looks at himself in the mirror: he takes himself for the laughter of Reason.

But only the incommensurable, the *unnamable*, is complete; it is more terrible, more distant than the laughter of Reason!

Nevertheless, could I in the end stop laughing at this laughter of Reason?

Because God . . .

Would God exist in proportion to the accident that opens bodies, which drowns them in blood? In proportion to these pains which are the possibility of each of our vital organs?

God is the mind of a man envisioned in the excess which annihilates him. But excess itself is a given of the mind of man. This given is conceived by this mind, it is conceived in its limits. Would the sum of the pains withheld by the human body exceed the excess that the mind conceives? I believe so. In theory, the mind conceives unlimited excess. But how so? I remind it of an excess that it is not quite capable of conceiving.

Even Madness would not know how to shatter the laughter of Reason. The madman is rational, he is rational at the wrong time, but if he were absolutely irrational, he would still be rational. His reason has foundered, lost amid the remains of *Reason*. Reason alone attains this dizzying height, which would slip away if it was intangible in us.

God's self-reflection can only be translated into theology by imagining God deprived of a part of Reason. I am not saying that Christian theology is open to criticism (maybe it isn't in its furthest intentions).

But the dialogue of a diminished Reason and diminished Violence was inscribed within it.

If the relationship between Violence and Reason leads to the agreement that best conforms to the interests of a diminished violence, as Reason conceives them (I dream of the calculation of so-called sovereign ambitions, indentured to the acquisition of power), the full Violence remains irreducible, *it keeps quiet.* If the parts are not represented by degenerate forms, by hybrids, the dialogue does not take place.

I myself had to feign a dialogue and in order to do it I imagined falsehoods.

[I imagine two kinds of Violence.

The victim of the first kind is led astray.

It is the Violence of a rapid train at the moment of the death of the despairing person who willfully threw himself on the tracks.

The second kind is that of the serpent or the spider, that of an element which is irreconcilable to the order wherein the possibility of being is given, which turns you to stone. It does not confound but slips; it dispossesses, it paralyzes, it fascinates before you might oppose anything to it.

This kind of Violence, the second kind, is in itself imaginary. It is nevertheless the faithful image of a violence, this measureless violence—without form, without method—that at any moment I can equate with God.

I am not saying that the image of God is reducible to that of the serpent or of the spider. But I set out from the fear that these negligible beings inspire in me, that they could inspire in me.

The feeling of horrible power that defeats the defense from within freezes me: to the strongest degree, it touches on paralysis up to the point of murder. I imagine the terror that strikes the sensibility before the unintelligible approach of a specter. Each one represents what it did not know.

I cannot describe what I am talking about in any other words. Its meaning is sacred terror, which nothing intelligible motivates.]

I spoke as much as I trembled! But my trembling concealed me. What I am able to say if it is true that, without terror, I would have known nothing and that, once terrified, everything escaped me. Anyway, that which motivated my state exceeded me: this is why I can laugh at it, with this laughter that is, without doubt, trembling.

[At the far limit of being, a being is nothing more than what it seems to be in conditions of peaceful effacement, connected to the regularity of sentences.

But if one day the sentences invoked the tempest and the unsensed derangement of masses of water? If sentences invoked the violence of waves?]

• • •

Whoever does not want to follow me will have no trouble letting go. On the contrary, whoever wants to follow me still needs rage, the insinuating rage that grows into a trembling.

Strangest: in this voyage to the limits of being, I don't abandon reason.

I know that instead of becoming in me, in its plenitude, the night of violence—at this moment, I would no longer see anything—this world to which, with the agreement of reason, I am devoted, is perhaps closed to me.

But it would be so in the same way if I renounced reason, or if reason let me go.

What would I know about it in the night?

I know even this: I am not trembling, I *could* tremble.

I gauge the possibilities of a man and I misunderstand therein the received limits.

The domain of violence is limitless, or its limits are arbitrary. The infractions at least, through which I reach this domain, are infinite.

Joy, Death

If someone asked me "who I am," I would respond: I looked at Christianity beyond its effects on the political order, and I saw in its transparency, through it, humanity first seized by a horror before death that animals had not attained, drawing out marvelous screams and gestures, expressing an agreement in trembling. Punishment and reward made Christianity opaque. But in the transparency, on the condition of trembling, I recovered the desire, in spite of this trembling, to confront the impossible while trembling to the end. *The first desire . . .*

In reproduction, in the violence of convulsions issued from reproduction, life is not only the accomplice of death: it is the unique and duplicate will of reproduction and of death, of death and of pain. Life only wanted itself in laceration; like floodwaters, the lost screams of horror sink into the river of joy.

Joy and death are mixed, in the limitlessness of violence.

Pure Happiness (Notes)

Multiplicity as the only reference of being for us is opposed to the principle of the individual isolated as a sovereign value. Multiplicity cannot find its end in the individual, the individual being only the exhibitor of multiplicity. This does not mean, however, that we are without relief thrown toward the unicity of a socialization or toward any omega point whatsoever. Doubtless we must see that the granulation, the corpusculation of being, is necessarily dialectical, that the success of a corpuscular shape of being contends with its power to express unity. But how would this power play if the individual did not recognize it at first in its limit, meaning in the inevitable transgression of laws that preside over the socialization of separate beings, that is, in individual death, and consequently in eroticism, which alone gives a meaning to the consequence of unity? It is the strength of Christianity to establish not only this fusion within God, but God himself on death and on sin, the death of the individual situated at the point of the movement of success of the individual being separated, sin of the same individual. But Christianity, in its haste to pass from death to God, from sin to the renunciation of the individual—in its haste to stress a result that legitimates it, and not the scandalous passage—separates the success of the individual, Christ, from those who carry it to the contradiction of death or from those who would have designated it at first as a negation of the unicity, the lust, and the joy of the sovereign's prerogatives. This error is no more monstrous than the contrary error, and, in this sense, it is certain that, without Christianity, the ancient religions would not be legible. Christianity alone makes them legible by accentuating the inevitable negation of the individual, but it does it too quickly. So much so that Christianity alone is itself illegible. It is grandiose only on the condition that we perceive the phantasmagoria of the past through it.

In the end, I am most moved by the feeling of *insignificance*: it is related to writing (to the word), which alone is capable of bringing us to the level of *signification*. Without it, everything is incrementally lost in equivalence. The insistence of the phrase . . . , of rivers, streams of phrases is required. But writing is also capable of calling us into torrents so rapid that *nothing* is recovered. It abandons us to the vertigo of oblivion, where the will of the phrase to impose time is limited to the gentleness of an indifferent laughter, of happy laughter.

At least the literary phrase is closer than the political one to the moment when it will resolve itself, becoming silence.

Notebook for "Pure Happiness"

Explanation of My Writings

Every human is connected to other humans, is only the expression of others. Whatever his ambition might be, a writer is never more than an expression of the human past, present, and future.

Thus he has meaning only on the condition of assuming the past in all its richness, and there might have been a negation in this assumption.

Cutting ourselves off from the Christian past is the equivalent of the abandonment of the millenarian edifice. Much more, Christianity directs itself toward the entirety of human possibility and even if we must perceive a more profound past through Christianity, we can only perceive this past through it. So it is through Christianity that we make the human experience entirely our own and signify its most advanced development in its richest form.

What does Christianity mean? It is the negation of human sovereignty for the benefit of a transcendent sovereignty founded on personal superiority. God himself invites us to humility and to death so as to share his sovereignty.

But God abandons transgression, the sovereign being the transgressor; he maintains it only in the paradox of the cross when he rejects sin.

Essentially, we must reflect on the crucifixion and place ourselves in the situation of personal assumption, abandoning respect in the name of transgression.

It is therefore a question of an experience: the experience is first, but it does not avoid the objective test.

The history of humanity begins with work and prohibition. Work reveals death as violence, and the rejection of violence is implied in the attitude of work. This rejection calls us individually for immediate satisfaction and condemns every recourse to violence.

• • •

[. . .]¹

• • •

Coryphea

Unhappiness! Blood runs from my breasts, my gullet opens itself up to death with a wretched gurgling . . . I give my life to cunning smiles of pleasure, to the intoxicating odor of money.

Let one final embrace grant your loins a dress sticky with death.

• • •

Notes and Aphorisms

(various aphorisms for "Pure Happiness")

[. . .] Hegel's philosophy and Heidegger's are one as well as the other those of the ancient theologians. (I cannot say that I myself have not been a student of theology, that my atheism is also that of a theologian.) I am inserting these few remarks in this book because I want to specify in this way the position that theology has in the development of thought. It is truly a misinterpretation, still made, to connect my philosophy to existentialism. Completely in opposition to Sartre's concepts, my hostility to this movement is great enough for me to have always wanted to avoid its vocabulary, to the point of never having used the word *existential* (if only for the needs of dispute). But I have purposely inscribed myself within the essentially *atheist* current of thought that has not renounced the wealth, meaning the expanse of the visual field, of *theology*. An *atheologism,* in other words, a thought nourished by the experience of God—it became exclusively that of the absence of God—this is the philosophy upon which this little book is founded. It goes without saying that Nietzsche's attitude is decisive in this field and that Russian atheism is its direct opposite: this is the theme of this little book. [. . .]

If the master is sacred, the slave profane, everything is falsified in this way: *(a)* the sacred of the master is servile to dominating the slave; *(b)* the slave's profanity maintains within him, in an hidden state, something that cannot be profaned. But from the beginning, the slave confuses this hidden thing (at least not clearly revealed) with the servile sacred of the master. The slave must therefore completely deny the master, but at first the slave only denies the master in this servile sanctity. He thus denies the true sovereign in order to deny the utility within it. [. . .]

To begin, I must say that this book is not addressed to men whose life is not internally violent.[2] But I must specify the internal violence I'm talking about. It supposes the totality of interest or of passion destined for the consciousness of oneself and of the world. By the world, I mean not the sum of these separate and subordinated objects of thought envisioned by "clear and distinct" knowledge, but the intangible world, the presence of which escapes my acts, addresses my terror.

I feel very distant from an anxiety to know that isn't dominated by a feeling of expectation: in this sense, every particular understanding seems hidden from the violent understanding without which man is the trick card in a game that deceives him. I didn't say that actions or particular understandings were worthy of contempt (I will say the contrary later), but in my eyes they are worthy of interest only insofar as they are taken for what they are, subordinate to the sovereign moment when impatience and understanding confound themselves. For man, there is a moment of unconditional grandeur when silence occurs, when the head that doesn't turn is stronger than the pain, when thought has the purity of vice. [. . .]

Finally, to be able to know nothing or rather to know that if I know nothing, no question has been asked.

One cannot infringe on every prohibition. But only the infraction counts. This is sovereignty. Thought is a useful prohibition.

Notes for Happiness

(from a notebook on the Sanctity of Evil)

Fundamental debate to delineate between work and play. Laughter is the exposition of play, that is, of sovereignty, of violence. But the total affirmation of violence is its very negation.

Eroticism communicates what language refuses to communicate. This is a question of two different kinds of communication. This is the foundation. This is also the profound meaning of nonknowledge. One must cease knowing (speaking) in order to experience. Likewise to laugh.

For me, the question of Being only poses itself in one way: for me, it is a question of knowing if my limited being ceases to differ, not from Being conceived in such and such a way, but from the continuity of Being, in other words from Being envisioned from outside of any way of being.

Language is always a relation of one way of being to another, if necessary from one way of being to the absence of that way. But, in this case, it is that of this way and its death, and consequently in the same movement of the death of language.

This is saying that nothing is conceivable except in our babbling.

Cannot one say: existence: it doesn't matter? How so? We are unable to know it. But it is singular to think that Being might not take place without a condition given in a way of being. This is what the consideration of the continuity of Being urges us to think.

But would Being exist without language? Whatever it is, it seems to me, it would not be *for us*.

• • •

Animality

1. *The animal that eats another animal and its food.*

I envision the animal from a point of view that seems debatable to me, but its meaning will appear following its development. From this point of view, the animal is immanent in the world, animality is its immediateness or the immanence.

The character of the animal's equality with its surroundings is given in a specific situation, the importance of which is fundamental. I will not talk about this very often, but I won't lose sight of it. I will return to this opening point at the end of my discussion: this situation is given when one animal eats another.

There is a superiority in the actions of the carnivore over the prey that it feeds on. Nevertheless, the eaten animal is not the subordinate one, it is not inferior to the animal that eats it. The two animals remain similar; if they are one above the other, it is because their forces differ quantitatively. But no animal looks at another in the same way that a white person looks at a black person or an honest man looks at a common convict. The idea that a white person has of himself transcends the idea that he has of the black person; and likewise, the idea that the honest man has of himself transcends the idea that he has of the convict.

But if an animal eats another animal, the animal introduces no distance between itself and the other, no distance about which it would be possible to speak of transcendence. It eats the other but no affirmation of superiority follows from this difference. If it treats the other as food, it makes a thing of it in effect, but it cannot oppose itself to this thing that it eats. It does not deny the other but it ignores that this thing resembles the being that it is intimately. Likewise, the animal does not know that it made the dead animal into an object. It is only insofar as we are human that the object, the edible prey, is seized as a rather durable thing, having a location in certain appropriate places, and susceptible to our choice.

We might say that this object transcends us at this moment, or, if you will, that we transcend it. But the animal ignores the possibility of opposing what it is not to what it is. The animal is immanent in the world: this means exactly that it flows in this world, and that the world flows in it. The lion is not the king of the animals, he is only a higher wave in the movement of waters, overturning the other, weaker animals. Whether an animal is stronger and eats the other animal hardly modifies a fundamental situation: every animal is in the world like water flowing within water.

2. *The animal's dependence and solitude.*

It is true that this flow doesn't take place. The lion that strives, on the contrary, to endure is even afraid of not enduring, but he admits this situation, he puts up with it because he tolerates it without taking it on. He flows nevertheless insofar as this situation escapes him. The lion is never completely different from the water or the air, which are without ever needing anything else, without needing any other particle flowing in the world in the same way that they themselves are flowing away. Water or air remain in a state of perfect immanence: no necessity imposes itself and, more generally, nothing ever matters in the immanent relation of one particle to one or several others. The immanence of an organism living in the world is truly different: the organism is in search of determined elements with which it must establish immanent connections. Already it is no longer the same thing as flowing water. Or rather, it is that only on the condition of feeding itself. Otherwise the organism wastes away, then dies. The flowing within from outside, from within to without, that is organic life, insofar as it isolates itself from the undifferentiated flow, submits to determined conditions in order to endure in its relative solitude. The organism is striving not so much to endure but to augment for itself, for its own good, the volume or the intensity of what it is, an isolated flowing at the heart of the world, but it constitutes the world in itself exactly as if nothing existed outside of itself. The organism does not seek to endure but it tends toward the possibility of autonomy from the beginning. In this attempt at unlimited development, it doesn't only test the resistance from without. It is difficult for the organism to find and to reduce to itself, through an incessant absorption, everything that is susceptible to acquisition. Nevertheless, the organism cannot cease to flow toward the heart of a world from which it sought to isolate itself. The movement that constitutes the organism is always double, it always opposes itself to itself by dividing itself, as if it wanted to isolate itself and grow only to better squander its acquisitions, to lose them, and finally to lose itself entirely.

I can therefore distinguish, in my first take on this contradictory movement, at once the will to transcendence, denying this flowing that happens only in the most closed-off isolation, and the opposing will to immanence in which the circle reopens itself and isolation is nothing more than a lure. But this contradiction is only truly offered in human existence, in the sense that transcendence must be well defined before inanity appears in it. The animal's isolation is never disengaged to the point of being able to be seized: the temporal pause, which constitutes transcendence, and permits a moment in which to forget the torrent wherein it will founder, isn't offered to the animal. In animality, we can never lose sight of the sovereignty of immanence.

3. *The animal's poetic lie.*

Honestly speaking, nothing is as impenetrable to us as the animal life of which we are a prolongation. Nothing more foreign to the way we see, nothing more inevitable than the earth at the center of the mute universe, lacking both the meaning humans give things and the meaninglessness of things that aren't reflected in some consciousness, that no presence ever limits. In fact, we can represent things to ourselves independently of consciousness only arbitrarily, since *figuring*, since *we*, necessarily imply beings not being things but reflecting them. No doubt these beings die, life might cease to infest the finally bare universe, wherein only things would remain. Truly, this representation of a total absence of representation passes for knowledge without being knowledge: in fact these objects are claiming to make knowledge out of an absence of knowledge, if not from the objects represented. They are given in consciousness; if not, they lack that alone without which they would not be what they are. I'm expressing a common truth, but animal life halfway from our consciousness proposes a more bothersome enigma. If I represent this universe without humans, where the gaze of the animal is all there is to be opened before things, an animal is neither the thing nor the human, and the representation that I create is also an absence of representation. However, a slipping is possible from the animal to things stripped of meaning, if they are alone in a world filled with meaning, a world ordered by man who makes use of this world or compares those things that he uses to those that are of no use to him. Even at the heart of humanity, a lot of men, having known it from childhood, never attain the defined sense without which they would not know how to question our world, which finds its cohesion in the knowledge that represents it. The slipping I'm talking about, which passes from isolated things to known things, would not therefore know how to be rejected in any way, but this is where the animal appeared: I never forget this if I talk about it.

From the beginning, in the difference between the animal and me, the unknowable intermingles with what I know: I know my consciousness, but only insofar as one or more known objects are available to it. This is not to say that there is no consciousness without an object. If this proposition is justified, its bearing is quite narrow: this means that consciousness reveals itself in the first place to itself, as consciousness of an object, or better yet, consciousness only ever reveals objects. In the end, this also means that understanding means understanding objects and that the consciousness that knows would not know itself if it did not first know an object, then itself from outside isolation taken as an object, then this object as other than an object. But the object and nonobject consciousness that I'm talking about is my consciousness inasmuch as humanity determines me. [. . .]

• • •

Consumption [?][3]

We can only "discuss" things, but thought is by no means limited to things; thought can function with the help of thingification, but it is not limited to this manipulation: thought can also destroy within itself the position of the thing that permitted this manipulation, which means that it has the power—one could also correctly say that it has the necessity—to self-destruct. But we should be specific: what is destroyed in this case is not the thing but the intellectual operation, or one of the intellectual operations that permitted thought to place the thing. And on the one hand, this operation thus dissolved can nevertheless recur, though modified by the contestation of which it has been the object. The mind that submitted to its dissolution doesn't stop there but attempts a new operation that takes this position and its negation into consideration at once. Thought develops prodigiously but in every way, and the initial contradiction from which it is born can be found in every successive position, and in the contradictions of these positions among themselves. The only chance for thought hereafter is to construct the ensemble of possibilities caused by the movement of history, and to perceive the necessity, the end, and the unity of this exhausted ensemble. And supposing in effect that at a given moment every possibility of thought had already been produced in some form, these possibilities find themselves as an ensemble having certain accumulated relations in a mind that is able to understand everything through tradition.

The object of the reflection of such a mind will, from this moment on, be to understand this ensemble and its relations as a result. This result, which is its mind, will even be able to appear as such, if it is ordered, as absolute knowledge . . . Whatever it might be absolutely, this is what it was for Hegel.

There is, however, another possibility (which is by no means opposed to the first one), given simply in the development of the sciences envisioning the facts of nature as a whole, in their material objectivity, as things. In one sense this development results in a kind of general volatilization of the objects it studies. But in this it only recovers, by other means, the opposing movement of thought, the movement that initially resulted from a possibility posed immediately by the contesting thought, the thing. But with this completion the situation is no longer the same: in the end, one perceives that the thing ceased to oppose that which it is not, like the known to the unknown. At bottom, the thing is only the unknowable, though consciousness remains no less founded on our relation with things. And if we want to possess some understanding worthy of the name, our only recourse is outside a dialectic that situates this understanding within a completed totality, with the rigor and objectivity of science. All the givens of existentialism represent nothing of the known, but only an object of science: they occur on the level of myth—and as such, by no means negligible from the point of view of an objective understanding analogous to the science of myths (naturally, I mean insofar as they have not let go of existence for philosophy: in this case they represent only one moment in the development of the possibilities of thought, and this moment should be referred to the completed totality). At this point, an unforeseen result occurs.

When we allow observation to bear on the movements of the mind, we generally perceive the material changes that condition these movements. We can envision the physical conditions of anguish, of fatigue, of exertion . . . If we cannot easily determine the particular conditions of a given state, at least we can define the general modifications that are at the origin of these different states. But this leads to a precise development that I have already elaborated elsewhere, though I cannot avoid returning to it here, a development that will initially seem to lead me away from my topic.

One of the most surprising aspects of human nature is given in a consideration of the movements of the energy that we harness, accumulate, and expend. We cannot harness any energy without expending some. This is the principle of work that is inscribed in a rational society in burning letters: WHOEVER DOES NOT WORK DOES NOT EAT. But taking humanity on the whole during a representative average period, humans do not need to expend in order to harness the energy necessary to maintain themselves at an already attained level . . . Humans normally expend larger sums of energy than is necessary for them to continue. There is regularly an excess which must either be accumulated—in this case, there is growth (demographic growth, the augmentation of potential for production)—or *consumed*. This growth is not constant, it cannot be absolutely unlimited: in any case, it is never such that a *consumable* excess cannot almost always be found. It is a fundamental but universal error to think that a sum of expendable energy *should* be put to some use. On the contrary, there is a sum of energy that *must* necessarily have no use. Even the movement of the energy within us, taken as a whole, cannot have any other result than *consumption*. If you will, wealth, accounting for the utilitarian expenditures without which it would not exist, can have no other end than an *unjustifiable* expenditure (about which it would be impossible to make any sense).

From the start, what hinders our discerning the unjustifiable character of this expenditure is precisely related to the importance that man attributes to spending his wealth *without reason*. The act is the source of superficial interpretations, granting an alleged purpose to something that essentially has no purpose.

All mental functioning is connected to the principle of subordination, that is, of giving meaning. It is therefore of the essence of man to divert his attention from that which for him is sovereign, to develop his thought.

Therefore, thought can only be in agreement with the thinker in self-destruction. It is in its negative movements that the general development of thought (the history of philosophy) agreed with the sovereign movements of man. This leads to giving the moment when thought self-destructs, when it recognizes the night, identifies what is unknown as a goal (note: I have never understood why Sartre reproached me for not meaning *nothingness* when I wrote the *unknown*. I would really like it if the proposition that he sets out against me, "Beyond nothing exists because nothing is only what I know," had meaning for him. But setting out to attack from such a hilarious idea is masochistic). In fact, at this point, consciousness deploys that which it has always had for an end: the adequation of the subject to the object, of thought to what it envisions. This adequation is made much earlier because thought not only effects a movement similar to the one it envisioned, but this subjective movement has the same effect as the objective movement. Just as the destruction of wealth (sacrificial, erotic . . .) that is analyzed by thought results in a mental transportation, the destruction of thought as the last phase of analysis, taken in isolation, also results in a transportation (here a passage from Levinas on emotion—vertigo). Thus, at this point, this method is found to be a perfect betrayal of consciousness on behalf of existence. In the end, it illuminates the rigorous opposition of understanding to the sovereign moment, without which we have only a minor existence. [. . .]

• • •

Pure Happiness

The planet Earth is so congested with death, with wealth: a piercing scream is raised: on Earth, wealth and death urge only an enormous scream; it is solitude that screams.

I represent this supplication to myself, I want to carry this representation to the point of trembling.

—Oh God! Relieve them of death and wealth! Oh God! Deliver them from the invocation of your nothingness! Deliver them from *your* solitude! [. . .][4]

The primary knowledge is that which situates the human being in the world; it is also that which prolongs animal knowledge.[5] In the gamble that is the intelligible[6] world, the animal distinguishes for itself what answers its needs. Fundamental human knowledge is nothing more than this elementary knowledge systematized by language. As elementary, it is only an agreement of the organism and the environment without which the organism is inconceivable, in that the organism is that which, in the world, interrogates the environment that surrounds it: from the very beginning, the organism asks its environment what organizes it, what distinguishes it from that which it cannot organize. In other words, the organism is itself the discernment of the possible and of the impossible. The possible is the response to the demand for agreement, the impossible is the absence of a response.

I can envision the organism as blind, groping in search of a possible that clarifies it in the night of the impossible. But I posit, from that moment on, a power that the rudimentary organism would have of knowing negatively. It seems that the rudimentary organism is in fact reducible to a function of the possible agreement. The organism itself simply is this agreement: it is the sum of the responses given by the environment. [. . .]

There are several aspects of nonknowledge:

1. Going into the world of the possible up to the point where the possible agreement fails. To refer to the possible and since the impossible is there saying to itself that the possible is coming to an end, it is as if it weren't coming to an end.

2. Beyond the possible, there is that which does not deceive us, as the possible obviously deceives us, since it comes to an end. Beyond the possible, I can erect what would not have the limit of the possible. But I prepare for this end in projecting into the impossible a false response to my need for an impossible possible. Meanwhile, I can tell myself that this is something that won't deceive me the way something deceives me, I ready myself for self-deception.

3. Within human limits, knowledge is contradicted by numerous and complex movements.

This is because there is a desire for nonknowledge, to be delivered from the bonds of knowledge, even if knowledge is reassuring. The changes of the possible into the impossible, of knowledge into nonknowledge, from the moment when the possible is systematized, and when the impossible is no longer evasive, if the entirety of the possible subsists, do not make themselves known through the ordinary method of knowledge—to the contrary. In fact, if nothing of the possible subsists in us, these changes only make us suffer, but when we are rich enough to love them, without even having isolated them on the level of discursive knowledge, they open pathways within us that are essentially disconcerting, but in which the effect of surprise is the principle of happy reactions. This supposes the passage from necessary organic agreements, in which there is nothing without the possible, to arbitrary human agreements that, for example, want the agreement in the church to be possible, with everybody behaving with dignity or just about, but without a barking dog.

In the forms of nonknowledge that I have described, there is decidedly a progression wherein nonknowledge becomes a greater knowledge, but this new knowledge confronts the same impossibility as did the previous knowledge when it was initially caught in the process of nonknowledge: if you will, knowledge is never anything but a precarious relationship; it is not the eternal relation it seemed to be. Knowledge is only an agreement, and the particular organism that forms this agreement with the environment cannot pass from this agreement to the universal in the sense that the method defined in particular relations no longer merits the universal. It is the same with the relations which are formed between the organism that, for example, laughs and links itself with the normal object of a disagreement (of an impossible agreement) while laughing. Thus, first of all, humans have negative developments that are the inverse of positive developments, like laughter (I'm not talking about sacrifice), but it is already the same with animals. Already in the animal, copulation is a search for agreement against the self through the organism's negativity. This is the principle of communication. [. . .]

Various fundamental possibilities
(from the philosophical formula: *the absence of time responds to the absence of every concept* or *the perfect intelligibility of the moment*; or *Absolute Knowledge dissolves in Absolute Nonknowledge*)

1. There was nothing to know.
2. Everything that we know is true, but on condition of disappearing in us (we know *better* in ceasing to know).
3. Desire having the absence of the object for its object, the absence of the concept, makes the concept the negation of value;

consequently, value is refusal (and in all the apparent accepta-
tions, through a ruse, there was what seemed accepted simply
as the necessity of making the refusal rest on a given); refusal
is the truth of being (God is self-loathing).[7]

4. Everything that is, that is intelligible, but seems better understood at the moment when I cease to understand it, is the
foundation and limit of things.

In this way, I go from *nothing* to *becoming nothing* (passively), then
finally from *becoming nothing* (actively) to *something worse than
nothing*. In the second case, the sacred is the loved object and, in the
third, the sacred is the effect of my violation, of my destruction. The
fourth case is despair.

The four possibilities are *equivalents*; there is no repose in any one
of them and as such they are summarized in their mobility:

Sense = Nonsense

Sense + Nonsense = Profound meaning

Meaning that is too profound = Hatred of all meaning, incessant
rebellion

Narrow unimpeachable meaning = acceptation of an equivalent
of death

The fundamental possibilities being the disappearance of meaning
respond to every disappearance of meaning given in a restrained sphere,
but especially to the disappearance of the richest meaning, given that
the disappearance of global meaning is more dramatic, more terrible,
and lacks the dark nature of that which is global.

The disappearances of the richest meanings are given in Christianity
and eroticism, and essentially in the complex of their perfect opposition-
composition. Almost nothing as violent outside the religious civiliza-
tion of Christians. The theme of the crucifixion demanded the effective
action of the impure, of that which no one, in principle, takes on himself, although, without fulfilled filth, everything is still impoverished
(even in the death of Osiris or in the royal sacrifice of the Mexicans).
What is bizarre is that the priest of Christ lays blame on the other, he
himself cannot commit the fault, he cannot feel the fury of the fault,
though each morning, he gently crucifies his God. Sade, his seductive,
mad, furious, senseless figure, wanting to be this way while reasoning,
wanting to be repugnant amid furious happiness, lacking seriousness

and coherence, drawing all his strength from this lack of seriousness and coherence: in Sade, the passage from unchained violence to apathy is more *direct* than in Christianity, but the ensemble is the ungraspable, torn, Christian world, and, at the same time, drawing a much more resplendent wealth from its laceration than in this world, Hegel's (Franco-Russian) revolutionary world is as lucid and calm as it is violent. It is truly this perfect wealth of meaning, coherent at the summit, from which meaning, all meaning, vanishes, since this possibility of great wealth is that which opens, almost infinitely, the disappearance of meaning. The night does not fall *immediately* with the utter poverty of the sun, but only in the illusory richness of the twilight.

possibility 4 (Sartre): cf. Kojève, p. 338

I represent a variation of the third possibility (there is also another variation along the same line of possibilities 1 and 2 (?), though it is, in any case, less interesting)

add Kojève's preface and talk about Maurice Blanchot

Of course, meaning is never given in the individual but in the whole of humanity, where there is suffocation, communication much more than there is filthy suffocation. [. . .]

Impossible finally to get out of this. The informality of those who read my work (and appreciate it) and their inconsequence condemn me. They chase me back to the weighty thinkers. I will maintain, if I can, the gait of a sylph! . . . But first I must become *a precision instrument*. Perhaps this is difficult, but not too difficult, so much do I hate the sentimental facility, the evasion that offers one's *lack of attention* to one's pride with the meaning of a hidden servility.

Notes for Pure Happiness

Extreme happiness, generally regarded as evil, nevertheless preserves, in principle, a value limited to particular cases.

Insofar as a society has large festivals, extreme happiness is proposed for a privileged period as an obligatory end.

If the *sovereign* individual benefits from privileges, this happiness is granted to him because he is society incarnate.

But in a world in which no period or individual is privileged, extreme happiness no longer has a recognized value. It is found guilty, at least in general, as soon as it is held up as a principle.

This condemnation of happiness, which Christianity only partially[8] claimed as its own, but which the reigning morality ratifies without reservations, must not be envisioned imprecisely. It is founded on legal accounts and maintained between the individual and the society, but it is still necessary to ask if these accounts are just.

I do not contest the necessity of accounts. The individual does not really have the power to deny contracted debt. He can, if necessary, through crime: but again, through crime he draws a supreme happiness from the fact of having *violated* the contract that bound him, positively violated it, not simply denied it.[9] But we can less reclaim personal accounts than global ones, because it is possible that morality deceives us and itself.

Specifically, we must find out if the complete suppression of the rights of moments and of privileged individuals has not generally falsified the balance of accounts. It is finally a question of knowing if the condemnation of violent happiness—of happiness at the height of death—has not been pronounced on counterfeit coins.

This is the decisive question of morality.

On the whole, the accounts are not just. Society taken as a whole always disposes—more than ever disposes—of goods dedicated to the consumption of the festival and the sovereigns.

They are no longer individually just.

But only in average cases.

Possibility of illustrating pure happiness

a) Torture victim[10]

b) *Das ewige Antlitz*[11]
   Nietzsche (97)?
   Jonathan Swift (17–18)
   Frederick the Great (25–26)
   Marat (28)

Possibly André's hanging (no, impossible)

Possibly Pierre's Judith?

Possibility for an album [. . .]

It always seems derisive to address myself to readers: if I don't have the feeling of betraying them, at least I don't doubt betraying myself. I don't have the courage to keep quiet, but I have hardly any hesitation. I prefer a rigorous life, because nonchalance never dismisses the final silence. I also make myself laugh, but not contemptuously. Although I sometimes feel a great contempt for myself, I am conscious of my "glory" and of the "friendship" without which I would not write.

[. . .] I faithfully remember the end of a psalm: "Domine ut priusquam abem, et amplius non ero."[12] No words seem to me to express the taste of life more perfectly—this mixture of horror and seduction, both immoderate, but such that were one not, the other would not be. In the end, I have great contempt for those who respond to horror with a solemn *no*. Certain men, who live primitively, eat neither hare or deer, not wanting the timidity of these animals to overtake them through contagion. This no has the solemnity of flight or of the trembling that follows flight when flight is impossible. I do not want to become stronger than I am. I am on the side of the victims and I know fear personally. But to engulf life in a heinous stammering against life! I only want what the psalmist wanted.

• • •

Execration

It is necessary to maintain the perspective of the nothing into which everything is resolved, everything that is in the end on the level of being, the nothing with which continuity aligns itself. It is not a question of the negation of the possibilities of being, it is a question of the essential agreement between these possibilities, and their glorious forms, and the nothing that is the meaning of the continuity of being. Against Buddhism and in the Nietzschean sense.

What the affirmation of continuity was for me last year (that is, at the end of my nervous depression), I would like this page on which I am elaborating the slipping movement of my thought—or rather, its slipping—on which I determine its perspectives, to be in relation to the anguish that invades me so easily today. Not that I necessarily want to lift this anguish, but I escape from *every* closed perspective.

In sum, this nothing is not a defined goal, as in Buddhism, but a movement in which the goal is, without doubt, nothing, which, envisioned in its totality, differs from the nothing toward which it tends. [. . .]

Not only is it morally necessary for me to doubt the value of the search for knowledge (at the summit, not in practice, but this execration at the summit is fundamental for me, this execration is the purpose of my attitude, by the very fact that in the midst of others I write), but from the very beginning placing morality—all in all, this is traditional—at thought's point of departure, I subordinate thought to history because in my eyes morality identifies itself with the history of prohibition

> beyond the first demand that condemns the search for personal interest
>
> stopped by the necessity to no longer condemn what the interdiction condemns, essentially I must condemn the transgression accomplished toward an interested goal, for example, the nonplayful war
>
> transgression for transgression's sake is the moral principle that I swear by
>
> this does not proceed without a search for what transgression independent of interest means
>
> evidently, there is a given to this principle: the refusal to know, atheology, the death of God
>
> this search is the same thing as religion, not as philosophy, but it is the ambition of this search to simultaneously suppress religion and philosophy
>
> there is no pure and simple suppression of philosophy as there is a pure and simple suppression of religion
>
> philosophy is a study and as such it continues, but its final value is denied
>
> in effect, philosophy results in its execration
>
> religion, on the contrary, is suppressed by the fact that it disappears with the devalorization of established personal interest
>
> there might even be a systematic "experience," but this experience has only one end, the liquidation of experience, of all systematic experience. From this a taciturn valorization—without literature—of nonsystematic experience. Without any other literature than the construction in the human mind of atheological renunciation.

Without literature does not signify any change in the meaning of poetic activity (except, perhaps, in fact, the change resulting from and following the general renunciation, the change that one must refrain from regarding otherwise than during the day of nonsystematized changes, following life in a world without aleatory possibility).

The mystical experience and the transgression of the interdiction that demands the conformity of thought to the possible
  from the opposition of thought to violence

Discourse endures, whereas transgression is in the instant
The idea of incompletion: that is transgression.

• • •

The Tragic Die

Two possibilities appear within the limits in which we *actually* live, one, eternal, proceeds from reason. The other is tragedy: the world is entirely what we are, it is at risk, there is nothing in it that is not at risk. The idea of God would reconcile reason and tragedy, reason and gambling. Divine creation would open up gambling, but it would open it up rationally. This aspect, in (Catholic) orthodoxy, is given without reserve. Jansenism is the lament responding to the vision of reason's Almighty. But in Jansenism the Almighty is given to I don't know what entity that, being outside reason, does not gamble. The God of the Jansenists does not gamble. He would no longer be the almighty if he gambled. The death of God begins when a man glimpses the scandal of scandals, which is expressed idiotically: *If I were God, I would possess the Almighty and I would gamble it. Without the power of gambling it, would I possess the Almighty? I would not be God without being a man if I were not at every moment, painfully, if I were not at every moment gaily, laughably at risk!* Man is a tragic die. If he were not, would he have conceived God? But inasmuch as the thought of God invaded man, the movement without which man could not have conceived God was paralyzed. The world envisioned from God's perspective in a static form, the world without play reduced to reason, rapidly distances itself from violence and from the terror of gambling; it rapidly distances itself from the subversive apparition of God. [. . .]

The love of God is the amazed recognition of whatever discovers itself in proportion to everything that is terrifying in the world. But the revelation is not bearable for long. In truth, God is the means of perceiving whatever is the most terrible and therefore of enduring it. Before God, the devout person remains amazed, delighting in an infinite violence that he imagines contained in the limits of goodness. [. . .]

• • •

Gambling

"Life has but one true charm: the charm of gambling" (Baudelaire).[13]

Gambling, through the course of history, is led by the masters. Gambling is the privilege of the masters: to be a slave is not having the good fortune with which to gamble.

The inferior rebellious class abolishes privileges, thus gambling itself is abolished, humanity diminished.

Those who command—the masters—look on death with indifference.

Fear of death obligates the slave to work. Taking death seriously tends one toward servitude.

Work is accomplished while waiting for a result; and while waiting, humans sense something that eludes animals: the inescapable approach of death.

Those who work, for this reason, feel death approach: death does not gnaw at those who gamble, but its shadow extends over the work. The accomplishment of work announces the seriousness of death under the threat of which work is completed: the indignant person who does not work does not eat and, for lack of eating, is promised death.

Part VIII

Outside *The Tears of Eros*

Elements of a new book of aphorisms

The Catastrophe

After Two Wars, Peroration

The Catastrophe

Research principle, groping:

Exclusion of all nonscientific research, evidence at the same time of the limits of scientific research . . . Beyond these limits, nothing more . . .

Asking the unlimited question, the essential question is impossible. The impossibility of moving from an analytic interrogation to this essential question. Might responses to the analytic interrogation be given, and if so, what essential truth do these responses reveal? What do these responses lead to? And why am I before this paper, writing, *in search of the key*? I imagine: *there is no key*, these innumerable truths, with which science populated the universe, mean nothing to me, if not as a measure of my desire to solve a particular problem. The key would give me the meaning of *my* truth, of a dominant truth, in the crowd where it is lost. Who am I? If not this terminal question (the terminal question) sinking with me into the night. Now I obliterate in myself every nascent response and, through my effort, from which there is no imaginable result, I see only the point where, the broken bridge and the rails of intelligence giving way in the void, I am no more than the hurtling train, the catastrophe . . . Flash of lightning in the night, unintelligible truth, conditioned by the oblivion of the truth, conditioned by the same oblivion of the question.

December 17, 1959

Groping in obscurity . . .
Would this suppose the possibility of turning on the lamp?
Inevitably . . .
But not the certainty of this possibility.
If there is no God?
The lamp is turned on in God?
But, in place of God, a *regularity* alone would rule, neither God nor man would know what it [is]?
Finally, there would be *God's place* in man. And, whether God exists or doesn't exist, God himself would be absent from this place. Gasps, ecstasies, we actually attain them, but [God?]
We know how God constituted himself before those who adored him.
This place, we know it, is that of the divine—the sovereign opposite of work, which wouldn't know how to be subordinate. But man subordinated the divine to work: he replaced the divine *obscurity* with the postulation of a divine light equivalent to our only certain light, that of work.
But in God's direction the point of connection with the perspective of work does not abolish a more necessary movement, determining the supreme dissociation of these subordinate perspectives and not their supreme association; only the memory of a necessity to which no graspable possibility responds subsists in the final moment of this supreme association.
If we want to grasp something that escapes us and, furthermore, if it ceases to escape itself, it is certain that we destroy our sovereignty, that we subordinate it and that we destroy what we glimpsed of the sovereign.

The question of finality

language implies the idea of finality
the collapse of language
   the dissociation of language
implying Surrealism
   the monism of which is destruction
though dualism is stupid
there is only opposition, not two
philosophical principles but of the banal duality
of work and of play
   work that *in the construction* of language
is linked to play, to language, makes of the world
a reality living in conformity with the principle of
work, of finality,
   but the reciprocal is true
what the scholars haven't understood, if
finality dissolves what becomes of language
   what reassures us
we can meditate—in disorder—on
   the inaccessible meaning of everything that is

The principle of erotic crisis

discussion of the meaning of the word *pleasure*

the fact that in pleasure there is not only collapse, that possible pleasure appears suddenly as salvation. It isn't salvation that occurs but a
dissolution, but death

the fundamental questions to envision in the
peroration after two wars

At this point, *[illegible]* truths are on the same plain. Men are free, insofar as their necessity asserts itself, by imposing this necessity on everyone: the truth is public salvation (often public salvation is the cry of the panic-stricken—then what? Maybe it's best to play with them? . . . but here I'm talking about something else; besides, what I say hardly *matters*: by definition, by vocation!).

Impossibility from Alpha Centaurus to the Earth as from the Earth to Alpha Centaurus. The possibility of a marvelous realization of thought from generalized communication. In fact, it suffices to have defined the impossibility that would result from exhaustion and from choice. An impossibility on the same order as that of reading everything. Necessity of abandoning the project while en route.

From whence the imagination of a divine thought.

Of a thought, an objective thought, that would drift toward the negation of sacred thought

In passing, the impetus is cut

discursive thought and sacred representation remain radically separated, the impossibility of going further

God is in sum the indifference toward the false possibility of going further. Or despair? Equality of indifference and of despair

Despair and indifference appear equally unacceptable. But the middle solution is in the squirrel's game, a moment in its course

The standard is inscribed in the reconciliation of the irreconcilable: this one maintained as such . . .

Neither the fact that I don't believe in God (on the contrary, there is something of an impiety in this belief), nor the fact that the prohibitions on sexuality, if we must maintain them, must nevertheless be veiled, oppose me to the essence of the reigning morality. Furthermore, basing freedom on communication between men (the form of immanence from the universality of consciousness), and not on the transcendence of a principle (there is immanence at the base of work—foundation of prohibitions—as at the base of our consciousness of the sacred—founding the violation; confusion alone ordains transcendence), I believe in making a dynamic, growing freedom possible, without any increased threat.

The sacred insofar as response to the concept at the basis of finality
the sacred place, from destined to predestined place
nevertheless the contrary has meaning

Divine ignorance

the kind of beatitude that we attain surreptitiously, involuntarily, in a fit of sobs

at the threshold of sobs, without having expected it, we perceive a world that doesn't leave us any other possibility of rest than unhappiness, or the absence of any conceivable rest

[Appendix]

multiplicity of beings and vanity
from the unique end
    this isn't what interested me the most

    result = specifying which way
[neglecting?] . . . from the fact that a kind of indistinct
opening is maintained in the wave
this is in principle what we should have suppressed
at all costs: I have the audacity to say no

    ending in disorder in recognizing that at all costs, one should
have . . .

    chance introduced before the work
    later, I should specify, but
on one hand I know my inferiority I
    recognize it, but I confess—I am not
    saying this is negligible. No!

    I confess my powerlessness
    appendix = no longer any interest for me

that the appendix is much less the expression of my thought than the affirmation of Hegel's value

I am well aware that the effort necessary for difficult comprehension is no longer possible for me to the same degree

the principle that the last interrogation begins only at the furthest point from comprehension

a philosophy of work is possible

less rigor in the 1942 text

the appendix proves the necessity I found myself maintaining but this renunciation: others proceed better on this point

Man—sliced and radically castrated in appearance—is what he is only by the suppression of the *obscoena*

Nature is what it is only in the resurrection of the brandished *obscoena* like a scandalous torch but these—*resurgent*—*human ob-scoena* have nothing to do with the *obscœna* of animals. It is a question of nature in the latter and in the former of scandal

the essential, work and play

insubordination—in sum, Christianity—is worthy insofar as it is an insubordination

the same in politics

the trick played on Christianity
who is the most submissive slave
obviously, the Christian bishop

what is true in
Christianity: rebellion

the writings of a wounded man, of a sick man, not a conquered man my essential ambiguity

affirmation-theft

What is the most agonizing form
of the affirmation; the best
constructed

anyhow, it seems to me, I should have started again

on the one hand, I know more about it
but on the other hand, I am finished being tired
and I won't have the patience, in the instant I forgot how to fail
so I couldn't do better

I don't have the necessary strength
in my mind Hegel is not
in question

the essential, play against work

I sink into the possible
that a humble renunciation represents
its paradoxical pride
enchants me—in the fullest sense.

Feeling of an audacity followed by failure. But this failure was not inevitable. Not that I attribute my failure only to my growing old. No doubt something else is more essential. In one sense, I wouldn't be in proportion to an extreme ambition. This can be interpreted in three ways. Either I don't have the fiber, me, or no one has it, or again, aged, I no longer have the fiber, that I would have had—that I would have had at least if I had worked . . . But I love death: in the idea of death, what I imagine isn't failure

Failure presupposes the possibility of success

Is there—or not—a relation between the accursed share and gambling

Would I be . . . this tenacious theoretician if nothing of the *guilty* attitude subsisted in me?

there is no failure, there is death
which isn't failure
a fiery death but not
ill-tempered happy even, the opposite of failure
would have the savor of a mute triumph.
 Why say that it would have . . .

the slowness of the pages [of?] the appendix
throws me into a kind of despair

ready to pray

Notes

Editor's Introduction

1. For the purposes of this introduction, *Le Pur Bonheur* refers to an anticipated volume in *La Somme athéologique*, while "Pure Happiness" refers to the article Bataille published under that title (see Part VII of this volume). Similarly, *Le Système inachevé du non-savoir* refers to the volume Bataille planned under that title, while *The Unfinished System of Nonknowledge* refers to the present collection.

2. These addenda were silently omitted from the English edition of *Inner Experience*, trans. Leslie Anne Boldt (Albany: State University of New York Press, 1988). Hereafter, this edition will be cited parenthetically in the text.

3. Included in Part VII of this volume, originally, *Botteghe oscure* 21 (1958):20–30.

4. For inclusion in *La Somme athéologique*, *Guilty* was appended with *Alleluia/ Catechism of Dianus*, a short text originally published as a separate book, with lithographs by Jean Fautrier (Paris: Auguste Blaizot, 1947).

5. This reedition would almost certainly have included Bataille's selection and arrangement of Nietzsche's writings, *Mémorandum* (Paris: Gallimard, 1945).

6. See *Œuvres complètes*, 6:360–74; 7:599–600; 8:561, 628, 631ff.; 12:642–43, 646–48.

7. There are a number of noted absences: *Theory of Religion* (trans. Robert Hurley [New York: Zone Books, 1992]) is more or less widely available, as is Bataille's essay "Hegel, Death, and Sacrifice" (trans. Jonathan Strauss, *Yale French Studies* 78 [1990]:9–28). Other essays, such as "Sommes-nous là pour jouer ou pour être sérieux?" that Bataille anticipated including in *Le Pur Bonheur* in 1958 (see *Œuvres complètes*, 12:100–125), are reviews, and are stylistically separate from the writings collected here. *Mémorandum*, although a significant absence here, is long and consists primarily of quotations from Nietzsche. Finally, Bataille pseudonymously published a selection from the notebooks that would become *Guilty* under the title "L'Amitié" (Friendship) in 1940. Its absence here is explained by the near replication of these materials in *Guilty*.

8. Denis Hollier, *Against Architecture: The Writings of Georges Bataille*, trans. Betsy Wing (Cambridge: MIT Press, 1992), 162.

9. See Michel Surya, *Georges Bataille, la mort à l'œuvre* (Paris: Gallimard, 1992), 12ff.

10. Georges Bataille, "Autobiographical Note" (1958), trans. Annette Michelson in Georges Bataille, *My Mother, Madame Edwarda, The Dead Man* (London: Marion Boyars, 1989), 218.

11. See, in particular, Marcel Mauss, *Sacrifice: Its Nature and Function* (1899) (Chicago: University of Chicago Press, 1969) and *The Gift: Forms and Functions of Exchange in Archaic Societies* (1925) (Glencoe, Ill.: Free Press, 1954).

12. Léon Chestov, *L'Idée de bien chez Tolstoï et Nietzsche (Philosophie et prédication)*, trans. Georges Bataille and T. Beresovski-Chestov (Paris: Éditions du Siècle, 1925). For an English version, see Lev Shestov, *Dostoevsky, Tolstoy, Nietzsche*, trans. Bernard Martin (No Place: Ohio University Press, 1969).

13. André Breton, *Manifestoes of Surrealism* (1929), trans. Richard Seaver and Helen L. Lane (Ann Arbor: University of Michigan Press, 1969) 184.

14. See Georges Bataille, *Visions of Excess: Selected Writings, 1927–1939*, ed. Allan Stoekl, trans. Allan Stoekl, Carl R. Lovitt, and Donald M. Leslie (Minneapolis: University of Minnesota Press, 1985); Denis Hollier, ed., *The College of Sociology (1937–39)*, trans. Betsy Wing (Minneapolis: University of Minnesota Press, 1988); Georges Bataille, *L'Apprenti Sorcier*, ed. Marina Galletti (Paris: Éditions de la Différence, 1999).

15. See Georges Bataille, *Blue of Noon*, trans. Harry Matthews (London: Marion Boyars, 1986).

16. See Bataille, *Visions of Excess*.

17. See Georges Bataille, "The Psychological Structure of Fascism" in ibid.

18. See *Acéphale: Religion-Sociologie-Philosophie, 1936–1939*, Précédé de *L'Acéphalité ou la religion de la mort* de Michel Camus. Reedition (Paris: Jean-Michel Place, 1980).

19. Hollier, ed., *The College of Sociology*, 11.

20. See *Method of Meditation*, in this volume.

21. Georges Bataille, *Guilty*, trans. Bruce Boone (Venice: Lapis Press, 1988), 11. Hereafter, references will be given parenthetically in the text.

22. See *Œuvres complètes*, 2:266–70.

23. Bataille, *Visions of Excess*, 239.

24. This draft appears in *Œuvres complètes*, 7:181–280 under the title *La Limite de l'utile*.

25. Georges Bataille, *The Accursed Share: An Essay on General Economy*, vol. 1, *Consumption*, trans. Robert Hurley (New York: Zone Books, 1991), 10. Hereafter, this edition will be cited parenthetically in the text.

26. Georges Bataille, *On Nietzsche*, trans. Bruce Boone (New York: Paragon House, 1992), 184. Hereafter, references to *On Nietzsche* will be cited parenthetically the text.

27. Maurice Blanchot, *Thomas the Obscure* (1941), trans. Robert Lamberton (Barrytown, N.Y.: Station Hill Press, 1988); *Aminadab* (Paris: Gallimard, 1942).

28. Dianus, "L'Amitié," *Mesures* 6:2 (1940).

29. See Surya, *Georges Bataille*, 385–87; Pierre Prévost, *Rencontre Georges Bataille* (Paris: Jean-Michel Place, 1987), 87–96; Michel Fardoulis-Lagrange, *G.B. ou un ami présomptueux* (Paris: Le Soleil Noir, 1969).

30. As Surya suggests (*Georges Bataille*, 386), 1943, the date assigned to this lecture by the Gallimard editors (*Œuvres complètes*, 6:476) is most likely inaccurate.

31. Maurice Blanchot, *The Unavowable Community,* trans. Pierre Joris (Barry-town, NY.: Station Hill Press, 1988), 18; translation modified.

32. Strictly speaking, Acéphale, the secret society, did not produce the journal *Acéphale: Religion-Sociologie-Philosophie.*

33. Friedrich Nietzsche, *The Birth of Tragedy,* trans. Walter Kaufmann (New York: Random House, 1967), §13.

34. Bataille had published a number of Nietzschean "Propositions" in *Acéphale* 2 (January 1937): 3–13. Cf. *Œuvres complètes,* 1:447–65, and Bataille, *Visions of Excess,* 197–201.

35. See *Inner Experience,* 102.

36. Friedrich Nietzsche, *Thus Spoke Zarathustra: A Book for Everyone and No One,* (1883–85), in Walter Kaufmann, ed. and trans., *The Portable Nietzsche* (New York: Penguin, 1959), 152.

37. Friedrich Nietzsche, *Beyond Good and Evil,* trans. Walter Kaufmann (New York: Vintage, 1966), §268.

38. Significantly, the third panel in each of Bataille's major trilogies deploys a reading of Nietzsche against one or the other of these totalitarianisms: *The Accursed Share,* vol. 3, *Sovereignty* against Stalinist communism, *On Nietzsche* against Nazi fascism.

39. Bataille is quoting Friedrich Nietzsche, *La Volonté de puissance,* vol. 2, ed. Friedrich Würzbach, trans. Geneviève Bianquis (Paris: Gallimard, 1948), §585.

40. Georges Bataille, *Choix de Lettres,* ed. Michel Surya (Paris: Gallimard, 1997), 183. Hereafter, cited parenthetically in the text.

41. See Surya, *Georges Bataille,* 403.

42. Written in December of 1943 and first published in *Revue de la Table Ronde* 3 (March 1944). See Gabriel Marcel, "The Refusal of Salvation and the Exhaltation of the Man of Absurdity," in *Homo Viator: Introduction to a Metaphysics of Hope,* trans. Emma Craufurd (New York: Harper and Row, 1962), 185–212. Hereafter, this edition is cited parenthetically in the text.

43. Elements of Bataille's "Post-Scriptum 1953" can be read in response to Marcel's attack, in particular Bataille's derision toward "mystical humanism" and insistence that "nonchalance is the naked aspect, the obscene aspect of rigor."

44. Marcel, "The Refusal of Thought," 185. Leslie Anne Boldt translates *supplice* as "torment" throughout *Inner Experience,* obliterating the connection between Bataille's experience of personal torture and his meditation on images of torture, specifically that of the *100 Pieces.*

45. Jean-Paul Sartre, "Un Nouveau Mystique," *Cahiers du Sud* 260, 261, 262 (October, November, December 1943). Reprinted in Jean-Paul Sartre, *Situations I, Essais critiques* (Paris: Gallimard, 1947), 133–74.

46. See Jean-Paul Sartre, *Being and Nothingness: A Phenomenological Essay on Ontology,* trans. Hazel Barnes (New York: Washington Square Press, 1966), 796.

47. See Sartre, "Un Nouveau Mystique," 166.

48. See Georges Bataille, *Literature and Evil,* trans. Alastair Hamilton (London: Marion Boyars, 1973).

49. Bataille, *Choix de Lettres,* 174. See also Marcel Moré, " 'Georges Bataille' et la mort de Laure," in Laure, *Écrits de Laure,* ed. J. Peignot et le Collectif Change (Paris: Pauvert, 1977), 283–87. Cf. also Fabre-Luce in *Journal de la France* 1944, 586–87.

50. See Georges Bataille, "Discussion of War" (with Koyré, Landsberg, Moré, and Wahl), *Digraphe* 17 (December 1978).

51. Prévost, *Rencontre Georges Bataille*, 112.

52. See *Guilty*, 41; *Inner Experience*, xxxiii.

53. See Alexandre Kojève, *Introduction to the Reading of Hegel*, ed. Raymond Queneau (1947), English translation ed. Allan Bloom, trans. James H. Nichols Jr. (New York: Basic Books, 1969). See Alexandre Kojève, "The Idea of Death in the Philosophy of Hegel," trans. Joseph Carpino *Interpretation* 3 (winter 1973): 114–56.

54. Raymond Queneau, "Premières Confrontations avec Hegel," *Critique* "Hommage à Georges Bataille" 195–96 (August–September 1963): 699.

55. See Friedrich Nietzsche, *The Will to Power*, trans. Walter Kaufmann and R. J. Hollingdale (New York: Vintage, 1968); §656: "The will to power can manifest itself only against resistances; therefore it seeks that which resists it."

56. For an elaboration of this confrontation, see Denis Hollier, "De l'au-delà de Hegel à l'absence de Nietzsche," in Philippe Sollers, ed., *Bataille* (Paris: U.G.E. 10/18, 1973), 75–105.

57. See Bataille, *Choix de Lettres*, 352. *Méthode de Méditation* first appeared as a separate book in 1947 (Paris: Éditions Fontaine).

58. *La Haine de la poésie* (Paris: Minuit, 1947) was reedited by Bataille in 1962 as *L'Impossible* (Paris: Minuit, 1962) (trans. Robert Hurley [San Francisco: City Lights Books, 1991]). *La Haine de la poésie* included "L'Orestie" (written between fall 1942 and fall 1944, published in 1945), "Histoire de Rats" (written after 1944, published in 1947), and "Dianus" (written after 1944, previous unpublished). *L'Impossible* would change the order of these texts, placing "Histoire de Rats" at the head of the volume and "L'Orestie" at the back, and add a new introduction.

59. See Bataille's letter to Georges Ambrosino of April 23, 1947, in which Bataille discusses cowriting *The Accursed Share* with Ambrosino, finally arguing that he, Bataille, will write the first volume, that Ambrosino should write a second volume on energy, and that they should collaborate on both of these and on future volumes, perhaps even collaborate with other "experts" in various fields as necessary for the future volumes. See Bataille, *Choix de Lettres*, 369–73.

60. The following year, Bataille would anticipate a volume of *La Somme athéologique* under the title *Le Monde nietzschéen d'Hiroshima* (see later in this note). The atomic bombings of Hiroshima and Nagasaki in August 1945, more so even than the Nazi death camps, represented the twentieth-century world of mass death to Bataille. Within *The Accursed Share*, this conception of death as mass death falls under the dark shadow of the Marquis de Sade, while in his early anticipation of *La Somme* Bataille attempts to affirm the necessity even of mass death with a difficult Nietzschean hypermorality. For an anticipation of both *De l'Angoisse sexuelle au malheur d'Hiroshima* and *Le Monde nietzschéen d'Hiroshima*, see "Concerning the Accounts Given by the Residents of Hiroshima," *Critique* 8–9 (January–February 1947) (trans. Alan Keenan, in Cathy Caruth, ed. *Trauma: Explorations in Memory* [Baltimore: Johns Hopkins University Press, 1995] 221–35).

61. These titles include *Sade et l'essence de l'érotisme* (Sade and the essence of eroticism) (announced as forthcoming in *La Haine de la poésie*), *La Part maudite*,

II: De L'Angoisse sexuelle au malheur d'Hiroshima (The accursed share, II: From sexual anguish to the misfortune of Hiroshima), *L'Angoisse sexuelle—art et cruauté* (Sexual anguish—art and cruelty), *The History of Eroticism,* and *Erotism* (1957) trans. Mary Dalwood (San Francisco: City Lights Books, 1986). *The Accursed Share: An Essay on General Economy; vol. 2, The History of Eroticism* (trans. Robert Hurley [New York: Zone Books, 1993]) was written during the winter of 1950 and spring of 1951, from articles published in *Critique* (cf. *Œuvres complètes,* 8:524), but remained unpublished during Bataille's lifetime. It was redrafted alongside *Sovereignty* in 1953–54 and again in 1957 for publication as *Erotism*. In a 1957 interview with Marguerite Duras, Bataille explicitly acknowledged *Erotism* as volume 2 of *The Accursed Share*. (see Marguerite Duras, *Outside: Selected Writings,* trans. Arthur Goldhammer [Boston: Beacon Press, 1986], 11).

62. In addition to the notes for this volume collected in *Œuvres complètes,* 8:631–48, see Georges Bataille, "The Age of Revolt," in Michael Richardson, ed. and trans., *The Absence of Myth* (London: Verso, 1994), 158–76; "L'Affaire de L'Homme révolté" (*The Rebel* affair) (*Critique* 67 [December 1952]: 1077–82; *Œuvres complètes,* 12:230–37). Bataille's development of the idea of rebellion in his "Lectures on Nonknowledge" should also be read against his reading of Camus's *The Rebel* (1951).

63. "La Sainteté du mal: Sade et Camus, Le Divin et le mal," *Critique* 10 (March 1947), "La chevalerie," *Critique* 38 (July 1949), "Le Maléfice," *L'Âge d'Or* 4 (4th trimester 1946; préface à *La Sorcière* de Michelet), "Baudelaire," *Critique* 8–9 (January–February 1947), "Simone Weil," *Critique* 40 (September 1949). For this outline, see *Œuvres complètes,* 6:361.

64. *Literature and Evil* seems to have taken the place of this volume without taking the place of the volume on Nietzsche and communism, though these themes are present in the subtext of *Literature and Evil*. In the interview with Duras cited in note 61, Bataille claims to be working on the volume on Nietzsche and communism while *Literature and Evil,* for its part, had just been published.

65. The place of Sade in Bataille's thought during this era should be noted—Sade had only recently emerged from the hell of libraries, to follow Blanchot's phrase, with the publication of several new editions of his work in the years immediately following World War II. Klossowski's *Sade, My Neighbor,* though it collected previously published articles and lectures, first appeared in 1947, and Blanchot's most important essay on Sade, published in his *Sade et Lautréamont,* appeared in 1949. Bataille's borrowings from Sade include not only certain elements of his notion of sovereignty (in opposition to Hegelian Mastery), but also, and perhaps more important, his understandings of animality and immanence follow directly from his reading of Sade. Bataille's use of literary repetition owes something to Sade. And although their positions are opposed on this point, Sade's black recognition of the necessity of death, even mass death, casts its dark shadow across Bataille's troubled acceptance of mass death in the age of Hiroshima and Auschwitz. Sade functions for Bataille as a dark Hegel, a rationalist of the night. For this reason, André Breton's comment to André Masson to the effect that Bataille "is the closest to Sade of all of us" might be recognized for all of its tragic implications.

66. *Œuvres complètes,* 6:360; *Choix de Lettres,* 408; *Œuvres complètes,* 5:483 for a list of these "Études d'athéologie."

67. Bataille, *Mémorandum*, in Bataille, *Œuvres complètes*, 6:209–72.

68. Presumably concerning the "secret society" Acéphale, whose members included Pierre Klossowski, Patrick Waldberg, and Georges Ambrosino, among others.

69. In addition to "Pure Happiness," Bataille's contributions to *Botteghe oscure* include: "Letter to René Char on the Incompatibilities of the Writer," *Botteghe oscure* 6 (1950): 172–87 (trans. Christopher Carsten, *Yale French Studies* 78 [1990]: 29–43); "L'Amour d'un être mortel," *Botteghe oscure* 8 (1951): 105–15; "The Sovereign," *Botteghe oscure* 9 (1952): 23–38 (in this volume); "Nonknowledge," *Botteghe oscure* 11 (1953): 18–30; "L'Être indifférencié n'est rien," *Botteghe oscure* 13 (1954): 14–16; "Les Larmes et les rois," *Botteghe oscure* 17 (1956): 35–55. Two of these essays, "L'Amour d'un être mortel" and "Les Larmes et les rois," were rewritten from drafts for *The Accursed Share* for publication in *Botteghe oscure*. For "L'Amour d'un être mortel," see *Œuvres complètes*, 8:496–503 and 135–48; and, for English, Bataille, *The Accursed Share*, vols. 2 and 3, trans. Hurley, 157–71. For "Les Larmes et les rois," see *Œuvres complètes*, 8:247–61, 272–82; and, for English, Bataille, *The Accursed Share*, vols 2 and 3, trans. Hurley, 197–211, 225–35.

Bataille's contributions to *Troisième convoi* include: "On the Subject of Slumbers," *Troisième convoi* 2 (January 1946): 3–4 (in Richardson, *The Absence of Myth*, 49–51); "Take It or Leave It," *Troisième convoi* 3 (November 1946): 24–25 (in Richardson, *The Absence of Myth*, 96–97); and "The Absence of God," *Troisième convoi* 4 (May 1947): 3–5 (in this volume).

Bataille's contributions to *Deucalion*, Cahiers de philosophie, include: "Initial Postulate," 2 (June 1947): 151–58 (in this volume); "Hegel, Death, and Sacrifice," *Deucalion* 5 (1955): 21–43 (in *Yale French Studies*); and "Critique of the Foundations of the Hegelian Dialectic," *Deucalion* 5 (1955): 45–61 (in Bataille, *Visions of Excess*).

Bataille's contributions to *La Nouvelle N.R.F.* include: "Beyond Seriousness," *La Nouvelle N.R.F.* 26 (February 1955): 239–48 (in this volume); "Le Paradoxe de l'érotisme," *La Nouvelle N.R.F.* 29 (May 1955): 834–39; "La Peur," *La Nouvelle N.R.F.* 95 (November 1960) (reprinted as "Introduction" in *Guilty*, 5–8).

70. "Aphorisms for the 'System,'" "Notebook for *Pure Happiness*," and "Outside *The Tears of Eros*" (all in this volume) offer a glimpse into the workshop of this destruction.

71. There has been no shortage of books and articles presenting Bataille's "system" in global terms. Denis Hollier's *Against Architecture: The Writings of Georges Bataille*, remains a standard reference. Robert Sasso's *Georges Bataille: le système du non-savior* (Paris: Minuit, 1978) might be read as a theoretical companion to the present collection. Peter Connor's *Georges Bataille and the Mysticism of Sin* (Baltimore: Johns Hopkins University Press, 2000) promises to be relevant, though it was not available for consultation at the time of this writing. Several contributions to Carolyn Bailey Gill, ed., *Bataille: Writing the Sacred* (London: Routledge, 1995), are particularly relevant to the themes developed in this volume, notably those by Geoffrey Bennington, Leslie Anne Boldt-Irons, and Marie-Christine Lala. Mark Taylor's *Erring: A Postmodern A/Theology* (Chicago: University of Chicago Press, 1984) uses Bataille, among others, in developing its author's own arguments for an atheology.

72. See Georges Bataille, "Hegel, l'homme et l'histoire," *Monde-nouveau Paru* 96 (January 1956): 21–33 and 97 (February 1956): 1–14; *Œuvres complètes,* 12:349–69.

73. See Georges Bataille, "Sommes-nous là pour jouer ou pour être sérieux?" *Critique* 49 (June 1951): 512–22 and 51–52 (August–September 1951): 734–48; *Œuvres complètes,* 12:100–25.

74. *Botteghe oscure* 21 (1958): 20–30; *Œuvres complètes,* 12:478–90.

75. "The Congested Planet" appeared in *La Ciguë* 1 "Hommage à Georges Bataille" (January 1958). This issue also included writings by Michel Leiris, René Char, Jean Fautrier, André Masson, Jean Wahl, Marguerite Duras, Louis-René des Forêts, and André Malraux.

76. See *Œuvres complètes,* 6:363.

77. Georges Bataille, *The Impossible,* trans. Robert Hurley (San Francisco: City Lights, 1991), 9.

78. See also Georges Bataille, "Qu'est-ce que l'histoire universelle?" *Critique* 111–12 (August–September 1956): 748–68; *Œuvres complètes,* 12:414–36 and 642–45.

79. See *Œuvres complètes,* 6:365.

80. This is not to say that this book is randomly organized nor that it merely follows a compositional chronology in its presentation. Editorial informality—or even that editorial formality which prioritizes theoretical concerns over the necessities of consequential writing—is a betrayal of Bataille's oeuvre.

Socratic College

[Bataille most likely delivered this lecture at his Paris apartment, at 259, rue Saint-Honoré, sometime during the spring of 1942. The title was added by the Gallimard editors. The date given in the *Œuvres complètes,* for this text, spring 1943, is most likely incorrect. The text appears in Georges Bataille, *Œuvres complètes,* 6:279–91.—*Trans.*]

1. [*Inner Experience* (1943), trans. Leslie Anne Boldt (Albany: State University of New York Press, 1988).—*Gallimard note.*]

2. [See ibid., 102.—*Trans.*]

Nietzsche's Laughter

["Nietzsche's Laughter" was originally published in *Exercice du silence,* Brussels, 1942. Our text is from Georges Bataille, *Œuvres complètes,* 6:307–14.—*Trans.*]

1. [Friedrich Nietzsche, *La Volonté de puissance,* vol. 2, ed. Friedrich Würzbach, trans. Geneviève Bianquis (Paris: Gallimard, 1948), §585.—*Trans.*]

2. [Friedrich Nietzsche, *Beyond Good and Evil: Prelude to a Philosophy of the Future,* trans. Walter Kaufmann (New York: Random House, 1966), §55.—*Trans.*]

Discussion on Sin

["Discussion on Sin" consists of three texts: first, Pierre Klossowski's notes from a lecture given by Bataille at Marcel Moré's home, on March 5, 1944; second, Father Jean Daniélou's prepared response to Bataille's lecture; and, third, a transcript of the discussion that followed these presentations. The lecture itself represents an early version of the "Summit and Decline" section of *On Nietzsche* (see Georges Bataille, *On Nietzsche,* trans. Bruce Boone [New York: Paragon House, 1992], 13–49). See the Editor's Introduction for additional information on the context of and participants in this discussion. "Discussion on Sin" was originally published in *Dieu Vivant* 4 (1945). Our text can be found in Georges Bataille, *Œuvres complètes,* 6:315–58.—*Trans.*]

  1. [It is unclear as to which member of the *Dieu Vivant* editorial staff this letter was addressed.—*Gallimard note.*]

  2. [Bataille's primary change to "Summit and Decline" consists in the addition of an appendix to *On Nietzsche* treating the words "Nothingness, Transcendence, Immanence" in light of the "Discussion on Sin." See Bataille, *On Nietzsche,* 188–89.—*Trans.*]

  3. [Friedrich Nietzsche, *La Volonté de puissance,* ed. Friedrich Würzbach, trans. Geneviève Bianquis (Paris: Gallimard, 1948), §552.—*Trans.*]

  4. [Friedrich Nietzsche, *The Will to Power,* ed. Walter Kaufmann, trans. Walter Kaufmann and Roger Hollingdale (New York: Vintage, 1967), §1051; translation modified in conformity with Bataille's French. See Nietzsche, *La Volonté de puissance,* §557—*Trans.*]

  5. [The passages between brackets were omitted by Bataille on the *Dieu Vivant* page proofs of this text but were restored by the Gallimard editors.—*Trans.*]

  6. [πλημμέλημα, Greek, meaning trespass, fault, error, or sin.—*Trans.*]

  7. [*peccatum,* Latin, meaning error or mistake.—*Trans.*]

  8. [François Mauriac, *Life of Jesus,* trans. Julie Kernan (New York: David McKay Company, 1937), 54.—*Trans.*]

  9. ["Boredom." See Martin Heidegger, "What Is Metaphysics?" in *Martin Heidegger: Basic Writings,* ed. David Farrell Krell (San Francisco: HarperCollins, 1993). For example, page 99: "Boredom is still distant when it is only this book or that play, that business or this idleness, that drags on. It irrupts when 'one is bored.' Profound boredom, drifting here and there in the abysses of our existence like a muffling fog, removes all things and human beings and oneself along with them into a remarkable indifference. This boredom reveals beings as a whole."—*Trans.*]

  10. [See Søren Kierkegaard, *The Journals,* quoted in Robert Bretall, ed., *A Kierkegaard Anthology* (Princeton, N.J.: Princeton University Press, 1946). See, for example, page 134: "The first form of 'the interesting' is to love change; the other is to desire repetition, but in self-contentment and with no pain attached to it." —*Trans.*]

  11. [*Œuvres complètes,* 6:332 has *exstare* for what should be *exstase* (ecstasy). The etymology of *ecstasy* traces the word back to a Greek stem meaning "to put out of place." Classically, ecstasy refers to "insanity" and "bewilderment." A later Greek shift in meaning references the "withdrawal of the soul from the body, in a mystic or prophetic trance." Still, later classical medical writers use the word to mean "trance" generally. See *O.E.D.*—*Trans.*]

  12. [Abbé H. Godin and Abbé Y. Daniel, *France, pays de mission* (Lyons: Éditions de L'Abeille, 1943).—*Trans.*]

  13. [*Dolorism* refers to a doctrine that valorizes pain as useful. A literary trend based on this notion is discussed in Julien Teppe's *Apologie pour l'anormal; ou Manifeste du dolorisme* (Paris: Éditions de "La Caravelle," 1935).—*Trans.*]

14. [Charles de Brosses, or the Président de Brosses, (1709–77) was a parliamentarian and libertine from Dijon. He wrote widely on historical, legal, and literary matters of the day, but remains best remembered for his *Lettres familières sur l'Italie* (1799), which offer a learned tour of famous sites and works of art. —*Trans.*]

Method of Meditation

[Extracts of this text originally appeared in the journal *Fontaine* 48–49 (January–February 1946) under the title "Devant un ciel vide"(Before an empty sky). Éditions Fontaine published the complete text separately as a small book in 1947. In a note from 1945 (see *Œuvres complètes,* 5:459), Bataille associated "Method of Meditation" with the poetic texts that he would collect as *La Haine de la poésie* (Minuit) in 1947 and republish with modifications as *The Impossible* (trans. Robert Hurley. [San Francisco: City Lights Books, 1991]) in 1962. This project was, however, dropped. In 1954, Bataille included *Method of Meditation,* along with "Post-Scriptum 1953" as appendixes to the Gallimard reedition of *Inner Experience.* Both texts were silently omitted from the English version of *Inner Experience.* Our text appears in *Œuvres complètes,* 5:191–228.—*Trans.*]

1. I was unable to avoid expressing my thought in a philosophical mode. But I do not address myself to philosophers. What I persist in saying, however, is hardly difficult to grasp. Even leaving out the obscure passages because of their intensity of feeling would entail smaller misunderstandings than a professor could read into them.

2. The separation of beings, the abyss separating *you* from *me,* usually has a primary meaning. In our sphere of life, however, the difference between one and another is only a deepening of precarious possibilities. If it is true that in one case, that in a given time the passage from *you* to *me* has a continuous character, the apparent discontinuity of beings is no longer a fundamental quality.

This is the case with twins born from the same egg. Mark Twain used to say that one of the twins having drowned, we'd never known which one. The egg, that I was, was able to divide itself into two different individuals one from the other in that one saying "me" would have in this way radically excluded the other, but I don't know *how* each of them differed from this me who is neither one nor the other. In fact, this difference that we enter profoundly as a wound is only a lost *continuum.*

3. [Claude Bernard (1813–78) was a celebrated nineteenth-century physician who wrote a widely influential textbook on experimental medicine in 1865. His thought was of particular importance to Émile Zola's literary Naturalism—*Trans.*]

4. Few propositions are more agreeable to me than that of *Zarathustra* (Part III, "Of Old and New Law-Tables," §23): "And we should call every truth false which was not accompanied by at least one laugh!" [Friedrich Nietzsche, *Thus Spoke Zarathustra: A Book for Everyone and No One,* in Walter Kaufmann, ed. and trans., *The Portable Nietzsche* (New York: Penguin, 1959), 322.—*Trans.*]

5. If we had knowledge worthy of the name, which didn't limit itself to fragmentary perceptions, we could relate each object to any other object, indifferently. But this operation has value only if one of the terms of this relation occupies one or

the other of the two positions in the series of appearances, *solidity* or *sovereignty*. The first in that it withdraws at most an object depended on by others, assuring its autonomous substance. The second in that it challenges the possibility of other objects in relation to which the sovereign moment would have a meaning. Solidity still maintains its autonomy by remaining apart, through a principle of conservation. And this conservation of solidity has its meaning in definitive ends: this is the condition of activity. In sovereignty, autonomy proceeds contrary to a refusal of preservation, to a prodigality without limit. In a sovereign moment, the object is not a substance *losing itself*. Sovereignty differs in no way from a limitless dissipation of "wealth," of substance; if we limited this dissipation, there would be a reserve for other moments, which would limit—*abolish*—the sovereignty of an immediate moment. Science relating objects of thought to sovereign moments is in fact only a *general economy*, considering the meaning of these objects in relation to others, finally in relation to the loss of meaning. The question of this *general economy* is situated on the plain of the *political economy*, but the science designated by this name is only a *restricted economy* (restricted to market values). This is a question of the problem essential to the science treating the use of wealth. The *general economy* makes evident in the first place that a surplus of energy is produced that, by definition, cannot be used. Excess energy can only be lost without the slightest goal, in consequence without any meaning. It is this useless, senseless loss that *is* sovereignty. (In this the *sovereign* like the *solid* is an inevitable and continuous experience.) The science that considers it, far from being in the domain of dreams, is the only entirely rational *economy*, changing Keynes's "bottle" paradox into a fundamental principle.

I have no intention of adding to this short explanation more than an allusion to the "work" that it *introduces* (*The Accursed Share*, vol. 1, 1949 [trans. Robert Hurley (New York: Zone Books, 1988)]; vols. 2 and 3 projected [see Georges Bataille, *The Accursed Share*, vols. 2 and 3, trans. Robert Hurley (New York: Zone Books, 1991)]).

6. The parallel between Heidegger's descriptions and this position are incontestable.

This is understood:

—in spite of the caution that Heidegger inspires in me;

—in spite of the difference between the paths followed.

Even more, however, than the text of volume 1 of *Being and Time* (in appearance at least), his inability to write volume 2 reconciles me with Heidegger.

On the other hand, I want to indicate notable differences:

—I set out from laughter and not, as Heidegger does in *What Is Metaphysics?* [in Martin Heidegger, *Basic Writings*, ed. David Farrell Krell (San Francisco: HarperSanFrancisco, 1993), 89–110], from anxiety: some consequences result from this perhaps, justifiably, on the level of sovereignty (anxiety is a sovereign moment, but in escaping itself, negative);

—Heidegger's published oeuvre, or so it seems to me, is more a fabric than a glass of alcohol (it is really only a treatise on fabrication); it is a professorial work, in which the subordinate method remains *glued* to its results: what matters to me, on the contrary, is the moment of *detachment*, what I teach (if it is true that . . .) is a drunkenness, this is not a philosophy: I am not a philosopher but a *saint,* maybe a madman.

7. Here, by *sacrifice* I mean not only the rite but every representation or account in which the destruction (or the threat of destruction) of a hero or more generally of a being plays an essential role; and, by extension, the representations and accounts wherein the hero (or the being) is put at risk in the erotic mode (by *sacrificial effusion* I equally designate the effusions that the processes of film and the novel strive to obtain, however poorly).

8. This statement is not complete: heroic behavior, anger among others, and finally absurdity are also sovereign moments.

9. Sacrifice, which formerly had a major position, has a minor position in modern societies in the form of art.

10. But not, however, what we can call *archaic sovereignty,* which seems to have implied a sort of powerlessness.

11. In this conclusion I purposely return to the terms of a passage from *Inner Experience,* borrowed from Maurice Blanchot. [See *Inner Experience,* trans. Leslie Anne Boldt (Albany: State University of New York Press, 1988), 102.—*Trans.*]

12. Evidently, I was unable *in the night* to define what I call the *sovereign operation.* I described the play of complex elements, of still ambiguous movements, and *the sovereign moments* are outside my efforts. These moments are of a relative banality: a little ardor and surrender suffices (a little cowardice, however, strays from it the instant after we babble). To laugh to tears, sensually come to screaming, evidently nothing is more common (strangest is our servility when speaking of serious events after the fact, *as if they were nothing*). Ecstasy is close by: one imagines the provoking enchantment of poetry, the intensity of mad laughter, a vertiginous feeling of *absence,* but these simplified elements, reduced to the geometrical point, in indistinction. Again I will show the apparition of a beloved face, in the night, at the window of an isolated home, but it's frightful, a dead woman's face: all of the sudden, beneath this blow, night changed into day, the trembling from cold into a mad smile, *as if it was nothing*—because this sharp ravishing hardly differs from any mediocre state (only the painful, tedious moments offer an exchange, betraying the richness of their means).

The Absence of God

["The Absence of God" appeared in *Troisième convoi* 4 (May 1947): 3–5. Our text appears in *Œuvres complètes,* 11:229–30.—*Trans.*]

Initial Postulate

["Initial Postulate" was originally published in *Deucalion,* Cahiers de philosophie, Éditions de la revue *Fontaine* 2 (June 1947): 151–58. Our text comes from *Œuvres complètes,* 11:231–35.—*Trans.*]

1. The usual feelings of beauty, pleasure, ugliness, pain, tragedy, comedy, anguish . . . also respond to moments of greater importance within the given instant, but anxiety about the future maintains the primary place there.

2. It is pleasant that a writer as outside reflective thought as Henry Miller

would have given this proposition an at once decisive and concise form: "I am a man without a past and without a future. I *am*—that is all" (*Black Spring* [New York: Grove Press, 1963], 21); an aesthetic form: "One must act *as if* the past were dead and the future unrealizable. One must act *as if* the next step were the last, which it is" (ibid., 23); a lyrical form: "murder is in the air, chance rules (*Tropic of Capricorn* [New York: Grove Press, 1961], 214); this last phrase positively related to the feeling of the present instant. We know that Miller made ecstasy the principle of value.

3. No doubt one might propose immediacy as the end without any contradiction, but the fact of introducing the moment into the categories of language always involves difficulties. It is not that, on the subject of the instant, one might be wrong to oppose it to ends pursued up to this point; it is in speaking, anyway, that one puts a system entirely contradictory to one's nature in play.

4. In the sense that it is: "more than intolerable."

5. The immediacy about which I am speaking, it's true, like Kierkegaard's "religious," is attained only through the negation of the ethical. But whereas K.'s negations and affirmations might be inserted into the closed circle of Hegel's system (which is a dialectic of action and of history), because they are engulfed in history and in action, the negation that I am introducing takes place only once the circle is closed, beyond the sphere of history and of action. In fact, the instant can only be "major" so long as man no longer has anything *to do*, when he discovered Hegelian satisfaction and when his dissatisfaction is no longer connected to the active negation of such and such a determined form, but to the negation, which no activity can assimilate, of the human situation. In this way, one sees that this doctrine has an anticipatory character. Insofar as social relations will be what they are, according to André Breton's expression, "the artificial precariousness of man's social condition . . . will hide the real precariousness of his human condition from him."

6. [On the amok, cf., for example, Georges Bataille, "The Surrealist Religion," in Michael Richardson, ed. and trans., *The Absence of Myth* (London: Verso, 1994), 74.—*Trans.*]

7. [André Breton, *Manifestes du surréalisme* (1929) (Paris: Gallimard, Collection "Folio," 1995), 74; *Manifestoes of Surrealism,* trans. Richard Seaver and Helen R. Lane (Ann Arbor: University of Michigan Press, 1969), 125.—*Trans.*]

The Consequences of Nonknowledge

[This and the following three lectures constitute Bataille's "Lectures on Nonknowledge." Bataille viewed these four lectures as a coherent series. See the editor's introduction for additional information about them. Our text for this lecture comes from *Œuvres complètes,* 8:190–99.—*Trans.*]

1. [A. J. Ayer, "The Idea of Truth and Contemporary Logic."—*Gallimard note.*] [For a treatment of similar themes contemporary with this presentation, see A. J. Ayer, "Truth," in *Revue Internationale de Philosophie* 25; fasc. 3 (1953), and, for a longer version, in *The Concept of a Person and Other Essays* (London: Macmillan, 1963), 162–87.—*Trans.*]

The Teaching of Death

["The Teaching of Death" appears in *Œuvres complètes*, 8:199–210.—*Trans.*]

1. [A "Gribouille" is someone who is naive or stupid and who often gets into trouble.—*Trans.*]

2. [On the amok, see above, "Initial Postulate," n. 6.—*Trans.*]

3. [Pierre Janet, *De L'Angoisse à l'extase: Études sur les croyances et les sentiments*, 2 vols. (Paris: F. Alcan, 1926–28).—*Trans.*]

Nonknowledge and Rebellion

["Nonknowledge and Rebellion" appears in *Œuvres complètes*, 8:210–13. —*Trans.*]

1. [*Le jeu:* This French term offers a greater variety of meanings than are suggested by the English word *play*. This lecture exploits a great many of these meanings and associations from the closely related notions of games and playing to notions of gambling and risk taking more generally. *Le jeu* will be found behind most of these English words *(gamble, games, play, risk)* in this translation.—*Trans.*]

Nonknowledge, Laughter, and Tears

["Nonknowledge, Laughter, and Tears" appears in *Œuvres complètes*, 8:214–33. —*Trans.*]

1. [Francis Jeanson, *Signification humaine du rire* (Paris: Seuil, 1950).—*Gallimard note.*]

2. [Marcel Pagnol, *Notes sur le Rire* (Paris: Éditions Nagel, 1947).—*Trans.*]

3. [Alfred Stern, *La Philosophie du Rire et des Pleurs* (Paris: Presses Universitaires de France, 1949).—*Trans.*]

4. [See *Inner Experience,* trans. Leslie Anne Boldt (Albany: State University of New York Press, 1988), 66.—*Gallimard note.*]

5. [Henri Bergson, *Laughter: An Essay on the Meaning of the Comic* (1900) (Copenhagen; Los Angeles, and Saint Paul, Minn.: Green Integer, 1999).—*Trans.*]

6. [Friedrich Nietzsche, *La Volonté de puissance*, vol. 2, ed. Friedrich Würzbach, trans. Geneviève Bianquis (Paris: Gallimard, 1948), §585.—*Trans.*]

7. [Charles Eubé, "Le Fond tragique du rire," *Critique* 68 (January 1953): 33–47.—*Gallimard note.*]

8. Ibid., 46.

9. [Ernest Hemingway, *The Old Man and the Sea* (New York: Scribner's, 1952). —*Trans.*]

Aphorisms for the "System"

[Bataille gathered the texts in this section in file folders under the title "Aphorismes réunis fin 1952 pour le Système." The Gallimard editors present this material in *Œuvres complètes*, 8:561–92 as notes to the "Lectures on Nonknowledge." —*Trans.*]

1. [Section titles in brackets follow the Gallimard editorial divisions of the text as described in *Œuvres complètes*, 8:561–62.—*Trans.*]

2. [Remember that in 1924 Bataille translated, with T. Beresovski-Chestov, a book by Lev Shestov, *L'Idée de bien chez Tolstoï et Nietzsche* (Éditions du Siècle, 1925); in English: as *The Good in the Teaching of Tolstoy and Nietzsche: Philosophy and Preaching*, trans. Bernard Martin, in Lev Shestov, *Dostoevsky, Tolstoy, Nietzsche* (No Place: Ohio University Press, 1969) (cf. *Œuvres complètes*, 1:7, editor's note, and *Œuvres complètes*, 8:459, autobiographical note (see Georges Bataille, *My Mother; Madame Edwarda; and The Dead Man*, trans. Austryn Wainhouse [London and New York: Marion Boyars, 1989] 218.)—*Gallimard note.*]

3. I should find names for the two parts of the atheology. On the one hand, the negative atheology, on the other, one can call it neither positive nor scientific. [*Gallimard note*: The main text can be found in Box 18, A: 138–48 while the text of the note comes from Box 20, A 220.]

4. At any rate, in the limits of consciousness. In fact, it is certain that my research from the very beginning was spontaneously brought to bear on the entirety of the domains envisioned later, without having *understood* that the unity was given within the effect in question.

5. [See Georges Bataille, "De l'Existentialisme au primat de l'économie," *Œuvres complètes*, 9:279–306.—*Trans.*]

6. [*Anerkennen* means recognition. See G. W. F. Hegel, *Phenomenology of Spirit*, trans. A. V. Miller (New York: Oxford University Press, 1977), 111ff. —*Trans.*]

7. [Here the translators have omitted text from *Œuvres complètes*, 13:579–81 as it can be found reproduced in *Œuvres complètes*, 12:536–38 in the "Notebook for *Pure Happiness.*" The version of this text in this volume collates the slight variation found in the two Gallimard versions.—*Trans.*]

8. [Jean-Paul Sartre, "Un Nouveau Mystique," *Cahiers du Sud* 260, 261, 262 (October, November, December 1943). Reprinted in Jean-Paul Sartre, *Situations I, Essais critiques* (Paris: Gallimard, 1947), 133–74.—*Trans.*]

9. [See Jean-Paul Sartre, *Being and Nothingness: A Phenomenological Essay on Ontology*; trans. Hazel E. Barnes (New York: Washington Square Press, 1966), 438.—*Trans.*]

10. [Here the translators have omitted text from *Œuvres complètes*, 13:585 as it can be found reproduced in *Œuvres complètes*, 12:529–30 in the "Notebook for *Pure Happiness*"(in this volume).—*Trans.*]

11. [Second part of *Le Système inachevé du non-savoir?*—*Gallimard note.*]

12. [As noted earlier (see note 44 to the Editor's Introduction), Leslie Anne Boldt translates *supplice* as "torment" rather than as "torture" throughout *Inner Experience*. It is significant that Bataille and his early commentators were sensitive to the ramifications of this particular word choice while Anglophone readers of Bataille have not always been.—*Trans.*]

13. [Here the translators have omitted text from *Œuvres complètes*, 13:588–90 as it can be found reproduced in *Œuvres complètes*, 12:539–40 in the "Notebook for *Pure Happiness.*" The version of this text in this volume collates the slight variation found in the two Gallimard versions.—*Trans.*]

The Sovereign

[A letter Bataille wrote to Jean Bruno on January 23, 1952, indicates that "The Sovereign," published in *Botteghe oscure 9* (1952): 23–38, constitutes an introduction to the problem of atheology and to *La Somme athéologique* as a whole. "The Sovereign" was not, however, included in the 1954 reedition of *Inner Experience*. Our text appeared in *Œuvres complètes*, 12:195–208.—*Trans.*]

1. In this discussion, I wasn't able to specify the essence of this deception, which I describe as putting me at risk, not only in an unexpected way, but resolved in such a way that the being for which the instant hangs in the balance is in some way at risk, as if it were a question of a sleight of hand. And this sleight of hand is so well played that the public (*the being* is the public just as much as he is the obfuscator or the victim) is uplifted by the immense applause, like the sea is by a wave: I dream of a kind of applause wherein exaltation is immeasurable, the beauty of the trick being so great that it sets a restrained sob free. (No one admits it, but it's hardly disputable that we weep over things that would move an entire crowd to jubilation.) In the brief offering of the instant, one must say that ego consciousness is refined, because a consciousness that grasps nothing beyond the present itself, forgetting everything else, cannot be conscious of an ego that could not distinguish itself from other egos without recourse to duration. Even in death (and even in the imagination of death), the instant still isn't this brief offering in an isolated way, in a way already identical to death; at the extreme, there is a fulguration that is lost. But knowing that it loses itself and wants to lose itself, I obtain the agreement of this excessive jubilation which, swelling in the sudden upheaval, irresistible but happy, springs from the final abandonment of being.

2. A long essay is missing at this point, and it seems to me that even if it were not missing, something else would be missing, which I must pass over in silence. And no doubt I should have, someone will say, kept quiet thus far . . . Did I have to give myself vertigo to be engaged in the labyrinth without narrative escape endlessly taken up by history—and renewed—from one night to the next, or from this tomb to this cradle? But if we cease to link the objective forms that history composes and recomposes (as mastery and servitude are . . .) to the *inner experiences* (both real and those that imagination readily reveals to me) that respond to them, we would renounce what we really are, the being given to each of us, where each objective form only takes its place when linked to the meaning it has on the level of a subjective given. It's there to do, really tabula rasa, as they say, but from somewhere where we have placed the authentic, fundamental given, we've only locked ourselves into a pedantic attitude, where only our stupidity, whether timid or solemn, prevents us from clearly confessing that nothing is given as simply as we might claim: I touch the ground, *separately,* from everything else . . . Anyway, this *ground* on which we found the *clearly* known isn't so clear for the consciousness to which it gives the opposed feeling of the *night,* of what is as simple as the world would be to those who, seeing nothing and discerning nothing, don't know how to say *I think,* lacking distinct objects of thought likely to give rise to a distinct "I," the precise meaning of which not only distinguishes this "I" from other objects but from this thought—which manifests itself in it . . . But outside of these brief representations, which are

only articulated for a moment and which free us at the turning point where we thought that we would finally *see,* that only know in effect that it is the world (or is in it) that this complete night, without any conceivable name, infinitely escapes itself.

3. In fact, how can we count on attention to grasp in ourselves a present outside of which nothing divine, sovereign, or uncalculated is offered to us? Attention that takes the present for its object would necessarily entice us: toward this end, attention should first reduce the present to a future. Because attention is an *effort* with a result in view, it has the form of *work,* and it is simply nothing more than a moment of work. We can work without attention, but the most inattentive work was first a consequence of attention brought to bear on a difficult operation. It is the effort applied to the discernment of a given aspect of an object. But if we want to discern this aspect, it is in order to change this object. We might not want to change anything in the *reality* of the object thus proposed to our attention, but at least we are then changing (at least losing) the consciousness we have of it: we are changing the insufficiently known object into one that is better known. In this way, attention paid to the instant cannot *in truth* have the instant itself as its object, because the assigned object is the instant in an operation before we make it better known, and consciousness, an end in itself, cannot *in truth* be consciousness insofar as it is precisely only an operation with an intended result, or as such it ceases to count as soon as it is acquired—unless we will one day have the opportunity to make the result known to others. This amounts to saying that in principle attentive consciousness is never contemplation in the strict sense: it engages in the unlimited development (endless servitude) of discourse. In this way, attention, if it envisions the instant, changes it, in fact, from what unconsciously escaped us, into what escapes us consciously, despite the attention we bring to it.

4. How can we imagine the *ruined authority* that can exist in this world, outside of the instant, a worthy truth for everyone interested in something greater than "this table is green," "this man is older than that one"—who responds to questions other than those of practical interest? But the instant is silence.

Nonknowledge

[*"Nonknowledge" appeared in Botteghe oscure 9 (1953): 18–30. Our text appears in Œuvres complètes, 12:278–88.—Trans.*]

1. [*"Deus sum, nil a me divini alienum puto."* Latin: "I am a god. I think that nothing divine is alien to me." Here Bataille is paraphrasing Terence (Publius Terentius Afer, cia. 185–159 B.C.), the Roman inventor of the comedy of manners, who wrote: "Homo sum, humani nihil a me alienum puto" or "I am a man: I think that nothing of the human is alien to me."—*Trans.*]

2. [Adelgundis Jaegarschmid was a former student of Husserl's who became a nun. This quotation does not appear in Husserl's collected letters, Edmund Husserl, *Briefwechsel,* ed. Elisabeth Schuhmann (Dordrecht: Kluwer Academic Publishers, 1994).—*Trans.*]

Post-Scriptum 1953

[*"Post-Scriptum 1953" appeared in the 1954 reedition of Inner Experience* following "Method of Meditation." It was silently omitted from the English translation of

Inner Experience, trans. Leslie Anne Boldt (Albany: State University of New York Press, 1988). Our text appears in *Œuvres complètes*, 5:231–34.—*Trans.*]

1. In my eyes, *Method of Meditation* was situated as an extension of *Inner Experience*.

2. Here I cannot specify a proposition that necessarily, or by its nature, can be expressed only in a limping manner.

3. Must the zoophilic be cited on this occasion? More important, naive men attribute to animals ways of being and reacting analogous to those of men. The beliefs of Hindus and Buddhists grant animals souls . . . It is a question of, if I am not mistaken, the inconsequence of the illogisms of childish thought and dreams. Ways of seeing such as these initially suppose the affirmation according to which it is evil and atrocious to treat that which we are as a thing. In this or that measure, then, an animal fictively receives the prerogatives of the human being, it is assimilated from the outside to that which the human being has determined separates itself from the animal.

Aphorisms

["Aphorisms" appeared in *Arts* 424: 14–20 (August 1953): 5. Our text appears in *Œuvres complètes*, 12:293–94.—*Trans.*]

Beyond Seriousness

["Beyond Seriousness" appeared in *La Nouvelle N.R.F.* 26 (February 1955): 239–48. Our text appears in *Œuvres complètes*, 12:313–20.—*Trans.*]

1. Kojève was no less correct for this. Impossible not to see a resolution, a change into other things, a negation of God in Hegel.

2. [See Friedrich Nietzsche, *The Will to Power*, ed. Walter Kaufmann, trans. Walter Kaufmann and Roger Hollingdale (New York: Vintage, 1967), §1051. —*Trans.*]

The Congested Planet

["The Congested Planet" appeared in *La Ciguë* 1, "Hommage à Georges Bataille" (January 1958): 47–49. Our text appears in *Œuvres complètes*, 12:475–77. —*Trans.*]

Pure Happiness

["Pure Happiness" appeared in *Botteghe oscure* 21 (1958): 20–30. Our text appears in *Œuvres complètes*, 12:478–90. Passages between brackets were excised from the text for its publication in *Botteghe oscure* by Bataille, but restored in a later publication in *Gamma* 1 (1974) and are maintained in the *Œuvres complètes*, by the Gallimard editors.—*Trans.*]

1. The violence I am dreaming of, having no meaning but itself, independent of its effects (of its utility), is not forcibly limited to the "spiritual" domain, but it can be. If it is not, this can have consequences, if not immediately. The only immediate consequence of unlimited violence is death. Violence reduced to a means is an end

in the service of a means—it is a god become a servant, deprived of divine truth: a means has no meaning but the desired goal, that which serves the means should be an end: in the inverted world, servitude is infinite.

Notebook for "Pure Happiness"

["Notebook for *Pure Happiness*" appears in *Œuvres complètes*, 12:525–47 and collects various manuscript materials related to Bataille's project for a book-length manuscript under the title *Le Pur Bonheur*. See the editor's introduction for a description of this project.—*Trans.*]

 1. [Brackets indicate Gallimard editorial omissions [. . .] and uncertainties *[word?].—Trans.*]

 2. [These two paragraphs are reproduced in both *Œuvres complètes*, 8: 585 and *Œuvres complètes*, 12:529–30.—*Trans.*]

 3. [Our text here is a collation of *Œuvres complètes*, 8:579–81 and *Œuvres complètes*, 12:536–38 which both reproduce notes from box 18, A: 115–23. —*Trans.*]

 4. [See "The Congested Planet" (beginning of Part VII of this volume) for a different version of these opening paragraphs.—*Trans.*]

 5. [Beginning with this sentence and continuing through the next page or so, through the paragraph ending with "filthy suffocation," our text collates *Œuvres complètes*, 8:588–90 and *Œuvres complètes*, 12:539–42, which both reproduce notes from box 18 A: 231–40.—*Trans.*]

 6. [*Œuvres complètes*, 8:588 gives this word as "unintelligible."—*Trans.*]

 7. [*Œuvres complètes*, 12:541 finds these last two words illegible.—*Trans.*]

 8. Martha and Marie, the mystics, religious luxury.

 9. Genet. (In this book, one must see that the suppression of the criminals that kings were gave a *royal*, sacred character to the criminal. Cite Rimbaud.) [On the criminal in Rimbaud, see his famous letter to Paul Demeny dated May 15, 1871. Therein he writes of the poet as a *seer* who undergoes an "Unspeakable torture, where [the poet] needs all his faith, all his superhuman strength, where he becomes among all men the great sufferer *[malade]*, the great criminal, the most accursed— and the supreme Sage! Because he reaches the *unknown*!"—*Trans.*]

 10. [This image is most likely the same image Bataille reproduced in *The Tears of Eros*, trans. Peter Connor (San Francisco: City Lights Books, 1988), 204].—*Trans.*]

 11. [Ernst Benkard, *Das Ewige Antlitz: Eine Sammlung von Totenmasken* (Berlin: Frankfurter Verlags-Anstalt, 1926). Translated by Margaret Green as *Undying Faces: A Collection of Death Masks* (London: Hogarth Press, 1929). The title of this work is misspelled in *Œuvres complètes*, 12:543. We have standardized the page references for the images in keeping with the English translation.—*Trans.*]

 12. ["Domine et priusquam abe[a]m et amplius non ero." Latin: "Oh Lord, that I may go away before and will not be anymore." This phrase is a misquotation of Psalm 38:14: "remitte mihi ut refrigerer priusquam abeam et amplius non ero". *The Jerusalem Bible* (ed. Alexander Jones [Garden City: Doubleday and Company, 1968]) translates the last stanza of this psalm (renumbered as 39:12–14) as: "Lord, hear my prayer, listen to my cry for help, do not stay deaf to my crying. I am your

guest, and only for a time, a nomad like all my ancestors. Look away, let me draw
breath, before I go away and am no more."—*Trans.*]

13. [Charles Baudelaire, "Squibs," in *Intimate Journals,* trans. Christopher Isher-
wood (San Francisco: City Lights Books, 1983), 29.—*Trans.*]

Outside *The Tears of Eros*

["Outside *The Tears of Eros*" represents the contents of a notebook for a new book
of aphorisms kept by Bataille from 1959 to 1961 while he was writing *The Tears of
Eros.* It is included here in keeping with Bataille's notion that *Le Système inachevé
du non-savoir* would collect "the rest of my aphorisms" (*Œuvres complètes,* 6:364).
Our text appears in *Œuvres complètes,* 10:665–86.—*Trans.*]

Index

Abel, Lionel, 118
Absolute knowledge, xxxii, 84, 112, 178, 203, 243, 247
Absurdity, 61
Acéphale (group), xv, xvi, xx, 277 n. 32, 280 n. 68
Acéphale (journal), xv, xvii, xxii, 277 n. 32
Acephallus, xv
Activity (acts, action), xvi, xxviii, 10, 16, 21, 22, 33, 36, 54–56, 62, 68, 85, 86, 90, 91, 94–97, 107, 108, 131, 168, 171, 178, 189, 202, 224, 225, 238, 248, 284 n. 5, 286 n. 5
Adam, 28, 54
Adamov, Arthur, xxvi, 27, 44, 46, 58, 62, 70
Aesthetics, 105–7, 171, 172
Alcohol, 19, 20, 45, 284 n. 6. See also Intoxication
Alcoholism, 18
Alienation, 149, 187, 194
Ambiguity, 9, 21
Ambrosino, Georges, xv, xxxii, 111, 112, 278 n. 59, 280 n. 68
Amok, the, 108, 119–23, 127, 128, 286 n. 6
Amor fati, 23
Angela of Foligno, 19
Anguish, 14, 29, 64, 123, 124, 127, 137, 138, 146, 156, 162, 168, 191, 200, 204, 208, 210, 212, 244, 251, 285 n. 1

Animality, xxxviii, xxxix, 6, 20, 117, 126, 127, 189, 194, 207, 215, 216, 221, 222, 228, 233, 239–42, 245, 247, 254, 268, 279 n. 65, 291 n. 3
Annihilation, 31
Anthropology, xv
Anthropomorphism, xxiii, xxvi
Anxiety, 14, 21, 25, 130, 162, 169, 178, 202, 224, 238, 284 n. 6, 285 n. 1
Apathy, 202, 249
Aphorisms, xxiv, xl, xliii, 171, 210, 257, 293
Aquinas, Thomas, xxxiv
Aréthuse, xiv
Aristotle, 23
Aron, Raymond, xxxi
Art, xlii, 106, 210, 285 n. 9
Asceticism, 32, 95, 97
Assemblage, 12
Atheism, 237
Atheology, xxxviii–xli, xliv, 41, 146, 155, 159, 160, 166, 252, 280 n. 71, 288 n. 3, 289
Auschwitz, 279 n. 65. See also Death camps
Authenticity, 5
Authority, xxi, 12, 15, 91, 98, 162, 186, 195, 290 n. 4
Automatic writing, 105
Autonomy, 33, 168–70, 185, 228, 241, 284 n. 5
Ayer, A. J., 111, 112, 115, 286 n. 1

295

Georges Bataille (1897–1962) has increasingly been recognized as one of the foremost French thinkers of the twentieth century. A librarian by profession, he was also founder of the French review *Critique*. He was the author of numerous books, including *Visions of Excess: Selected Writings, 1927–1939*, also published by the University of Minnesota Press.

Michelle Kendall is a freelance translator and painter. **Stuart Kendall** is a freelance translator, editor, and writer. Their forthcoming publications include translations of Paul Éluard's *Love, Poetry* and a volume of poetry and fiction by Georges Bataille titled *The Hatred of Poetry*.